T0337936

# Behavioral Finance for Private Banking

Founded in 1807, John Wiley & Sons is the oldest independent publishing company in the United States. With offices in North America, Europe, Australia, and Asia, Wiley is globally committed to developing and marketing print and electronic products and services for our customers' professional and personal knowledge and understanding.

The Wiley Finance series contains books written specifically for finance and investment professionals as well as sophisticated individual investors and their financial advisors. Book topics range from portfolio management to e-commerce, risk management, financial engineering, valuation and financial instrument analysis, as well as much more.

For a list of available titles, visit our website at www.WileyFinance.com.

# Behavioral Finance for Private Banking

*From the Art of Advice to the
Science of Advice*

Second Edition

KREMENA BACHMANN
ENRICO G. DE GIORGI
THORSTEN HENS

WILEY

For general information on our other products and services or for technical support, please contact our Customer Care Department within the United States at (800) 762-2974; outside the United States at (317) 572-3993, or fax (317) 572-4002.

Wiley publishes in a variety of print and electronic formats and by print-on-demand. Some material included with standard print versions of this book may not be included in e-books or in print-on-demand. If this book refers to media such as a CD or DVD that is not included in the version you purchased, you may download this material at http://booksupport.wiley.com. For more information about Wiley products, visit www.wiley.com.

*Library of Congress Cataloging-in-Publication Data is Available*

ISBN 9781119453703 (cloth)
ISBN 9781119453734 (ePDF)
ISBN 9781119453710 (ePub)

Cover Design: Wiley
Cover Image: © Nomad_Soul/Shutterstock; © Menna/Shutterstock;
© crystal51/Shutterstock; © Peshkova/Shutterstock

Printed in the United States of America

10 9 8 7 6 5 4 3 2 1

# Contents

# Behavioral Finance for Private Banking

# CHAPTER 1

# Introduction

*Behavioral finance* is an interdisciplinary research area that combines insights from psychology with finance to better understand investors' behavior and asset prices. It has managed to bridge the gap between theory and practice. Moreover, the psychological research that behavioral finance is based on recently got a foundation in biological differences found in the brain.

*Traditional finance* has focused on the ideal scenario of thoroughly rational investors in efficient markets. According to this standard paradigm in finance, individuals rationally search for information and know all available actions that serve their preferences. The latter are stable over time and robust to the occurrence of unanticipated events. As a result, rational investors searching for superior returns detect and eliminate any predictability in the asset prices—the market is efficient. According to traditional finance, the market remains efficient even if some investors behave irrationally. Indeed, rational investors will detect any mispricing generated by irrational investors and exploit it with the use of arbitrage strategies, which are assumed to be unlimited.[1] Consequently, any mispricing will very quickly be corrected, irrational investors will be driven out of the market, and the market will again quickly become efficient. A statistical consequence of prices being unpredictable is that returns are (log)-normally distributed—which is the content of the central limit theorem—a cornerstone of statistics. Consequently, optimal decisions can be taken based on the two parameters of a normal distribution: the mean and the variance. Thus, the *mean-variance optimization* and the efficient markets hypothesis are logical consequences of the rationality assumption.

In practice, however, we observe that even professional investors behave irrationally. Moreover, there is empirical evidence that the use of arbitrage strategies to exploit observed mispricing is limited (e.g., implementing an arbitrage strategy could be expensive and typically not at zero risk).

---

[1] An arbitrage strategy is a strategy that generates positive returns at no risk. The assumption that arbitrage is unlimited means that arbitrage strategies can be implemented in the real-world and their costs is low.

The consequence of irrational investors and limited arbitrage is *inefficient markets*. As we will discuss in detail, investors are not always able to make rational decisions so that market prices show anomalies. For example, investors tend to adopt the behavior of other investors, and this herding behavior causes short-term predictability that leads ultimately to market crashes. Consequently, asset returns are no longer normally distributed. For example, they have *fat tails* (i.e., too many very bad returns)—which Taleb (2007) called *black swans*. Moreover, in inefficient markets, the mean-variance optimization is no longer rational. Thus, ignoring the insights from behavioral finance can be costly for investors adhering to traditional finance.

Behavioral finance emerged when Nobel laureate Daniel Kahneman and his colleague Amos Tversky conducted psychological research to question the assumptions of rationality—a cornerstone of the classical decision theory. Kahneman & Tversky (1979) developed a new theory, which they called *prospect theory*. Prospect theory has two phases: an editing phase and an evaluation phase. In the first phase, Kahneman and Tversky show how choice alternatives are mentally coded and transformed to be evaluated in the second phase. The editing phase has developed into a rich knowledge of behavioral biases—the topic of the next section. In the evaluation phase, Kahneman and Tversky develop a new decision model, which is the main content of our section on decision theory. The knowledge of behavioral biases is very valuable for a better understanding of clients in wealth management. Prospect theory also offers a risk measure that is consistent with the client's experience. With this measure one can construct asset allocations that better suit the clients than the asset allocations based on the volatility used in traditional finance. Prospect theory states that investors dislike losses more than volatility. In fact, investors react more to losses than they react to gains. Unlike volatility, the psychological risk measure is not the same for all investors, but is a characteristic of the individual. For this reason and others, the advantages of having a quality risk profiling procedure are numerous.

In this book, we apply these insights from behavioral finance to truly identify the client's situation from a holistic standpoint. With discoveries in the way people deal with information and respond to it in investment risk taking, it is reasonable to say that behavioral finance gives more attention to the investor's behavior. A more realistic investor, as described in behavioral finance, has a different perception and a different understanding of risk than the theoretical investor in the traditional decision theory. Consequently, this investor will need to invest differently than the theoretical investor in the traditional decision theory.

The book combines new research results with practical applications. It draws on the rich research body of behavioral finance and on profound experience in the practice of wealth management. The book starts with the behavioral biases—the mistakes that people make when dealing with information and making financial decisions. The chapter describes the biases, discusses their implications for financial decisions, and suggests strategies with a proven success in moderating the biases. The following four chapters discuss the cultural dimensions of the biases and their biological foundation as well as their moderation and suggest how advisors could proceed in assessing the biases of their clients.

Thereafter, we explain decision theory (rational and behavioral) as a foundation of finance and show how it can be used in the construction of clients' portfolios and for the design of structured products. The question of how optimal portfolios should be adjusted over time is discussed in the following two chapters. The last chapters show how the new insights that behavioral finance has generated can be applied to client advisory, to designing behaviorally founded risk profiles, and to structuring the wealth management process. Thus, our books give a scientific foundation to financial advice given in private banking, which in practice is seen more as an art than a science. We believe that practitioners find some useful foundation for their work and that the transition from the art of advice to the science of advice is not disruptive but smooth.

This book is the second edition of the book *Behavioral Finance for Private Banking* that was published in the middle of the financial crisis. Many banks and financial advisors used the existing body of knowledge to improve their products and advisory services. A tool that we have developed demonstrates how this can be done.[2] In addition, this book benefits from insights of new areas of research such as cultural finance, neurofinance, and fintech. Finally, it compares the insights behavioral finance has gained with the new regulatory requirements in Europe (MiFID II) and in Switzerland (FIDLEG).

We are grateful to Mei Wang and Marc Oliver Rieger for their collaboration in the assessment of the cultural dimensions of investors' behavior. Moreover, this work greatly benefited from BhFS Behavioral Finance Solutions, a spinoff firm of the University of Zurich and the University of St. Gallen, which allowed us to present their tools. Last but not least we are grateful to the Wiley team and to Marie Hardelauf for their patience and help in editing our book.

---

[2] Access to a demo version of the tool can be requested from info@bhfs.ch.

# CHAPTER 2

# Behavioral Biases

**B**ehavioral finance research is driven by observations suggesting that individuals' decisions can be irrational and different from what previous theories assume. In this chapter, we will see that individuals' decisions can be systematically wrong because people's decisions are driven by emotions or misunderstandings or because people use inappropriate rules of thumb, also called *heuristics*, to handle information and make decisions. Certainly, financial markets are very complex so that optimization can lead to fragile results and good heuristics are preferable.[1] But what is typically observed is that people apply successful heuristics from other domains without properly assessing their effect in the investment domain. One example for the latter is *adaptive learning,* which is very successful in many day-to-day situations like choosing food: One tries out a new wine. If one likes it, one buys it again. However, in finance it leads to buying assets when they are expensive and selling them when they are cheap, as the *roller coaster* in Figure 2.01 illustrates.

To more deeply understand why we may observe such behavior, we consider a typical decision-making process and discuss how each stage of the process can be biased. First, decision makers select the information that appears to be relevant for their decisions. Then, they process the selected information to form beliefs and to compare alternatives. After deciding, individuals receive new information as a feedback. This feedback influences, in return, the way the decision makers search for more data, that is, the loop is closed.

The chapter provides evidence that certain mistakes can occur in each of these steps. It discusses the relevance of these mistakes for investors and suggests strategies to avoid the mistakes.

---

[1]A good example is the superiority of the equal weights asset allocation (1/N) over mean-variance optimization, as DeMiguel, Garlappi, & Uppal (2009) have shown.

**FIGURE 2.01**  Market dynamics and decision behavior of a typical investor

## 2.1  INFORMATION SELECTION BIASES

When confronted with information, individuals need to judge how relevant it is for the task they need to handle. Thereby individuals seem to consider only particular information while disregarding other that might be relevant as well. For investment decisions, such information filtering can be dangerous since there is uncertainty about the relative importance of economic factors for the future—investment rules that have worked in the past do not always work in the future. So, are there any patterns in the way people select relevant information, and why should we expect that their impact is systematic?

### 2.1.1  Attention Bias

The first observation on individuals' selection of information is that it can be biased due to a specific task. People gather information that they think is relevant for dealing with the problem and disregard others, which they would otherwise notice. This is demonstrated in an experiment, where participants have been asked to watch a video with two basketball teams: one team wearing black shirts and another one wearing white shirts (Simons & Chabris, 1999). The task was to count the passes of the white team. Afterward, participants have been asked whether they have observed something unusual. Some participants spotted that there was a second ball. But only a few noticed a big black gorilla walking slowly through the picture, stopping in the middle, winking, and passing slowly away. The reason for not seeing the gorilla is the *attention bias*. Due to the limited attention that people have, they can get only the information they consider important for solving a specific task. All other information remains disregarded, independent of how extreme it is. Hence, when people focus too much on one task, something unexpected can happen that they might not notice. Moreover, related experiments show that even when people know that something unexpected might happen (e.g., that a gorilla would appear), this doesn't help them notice other unexpected things.

**Relevance for Investors and Moderation** The attention bias is relevant for investors because all investors use media to inform themselves. But the media process follows certain patterns. Some media set the agenda, other media follow, and for some time all media report the same story. In these times, other investment relevant information is not seen—like the gorilla in the experiment just mentioned. For example, in summer 2011 we observed a global stock market downturn: From the end of July to the end of August, the DJIA fell from 12,700 to 10,700, the Euro Stoxxs 50 fell from 2,800 to 2,200, and the Nikkei from 10,000 to 8,750 (i.e., stock markets plunged by 16%, 21% and 12.5%, respectively). Looking at the words Internet users searched in Google[2] during summer 2011, we see that the public attention mainly focused on the US debt ceiling debate that was positively resolved by August 1st. So why did stocks decline after the showdown in the US Congress was resolved? One explanation is that the gorilla "US recession" was not seen in July, so the attention for a possible recession in the United States was hidden behind the budget ceiling debate while after that debate was over the recession attracted the attention of the public. Indeed, the search for the words "US debt" peaked in July 2011 while the words "US recession" peaked in August 2011. And indeed, the US business cycle slowed down considerably during the summer of 2011.

The best moderation of the attention bias is to agree on certain key information (e.g., macroeconomics, politics, valuation levels, sentiment of the market) that one always discusses with the investors irrespectively of whether it is topical or not.

### 2.1.2 Selective Perception Based on Experience

Perception of information is, by its nature, always selective. But in many situations people might not be able to see things just because they do not

---

[2]See www.google.com/insights.

expect them to occur given their experience. This has been demonstrated in an experiment with playing cards (Bruner & Postman, 1949). Participants were shown five playing cards and asked what they have seen. What researchers were testing is whether the participants would recognize doctored cards (e.g., a *black* three of a heart). They found out that, on average, participants needed four times longer to recognize a doctored card than a normal card. Most of the people were very sure that the doctored card was a normal card. Even when participants recognized that something was wrong, they sometimes misperceived the *incongruity* (e.g., people who were shown a black four of hearts declared that the spades were "turned the wrong way"). This experiment shows that experience can influence the way people look at new evidence. When people have enough experience with a specific situation, they often see what they expect to see based on their experience. Hence, in some cases, experience may lower performance.

**Relevance for Investors and Moderation** To give an example of how selective perception can affect investments, recall the stock market crash in the years 2007–2008. From the summer of 2007 to the beginning of 2009, the DJIA fell from 14,100 to 6,525, the Euro Stoxxs 50 from 4,500 to 1,800 and the Nikkei from 18,250 to 7,125—that is, stock markets plunged between 50% and 60% around the world. Unfortunately, none of the standard indicators could predict this decline. The P/E ratios and the Fed measure that could predict for example the crash of the dot-com bubble signaled no risk during the summer of 2007. Investors who used those risk measures because of the positive experience with them were caught by surprise during the stock market crash of 2007–2008. Indeed, that stock market crash did not come from overvaluation of stocks but from a bubble in the housing market in the United States, the United Kingdom, and Spain. This housing bubble resulted in a financial crisis, which then slowed down the global economy. Thus, experience with some indicators might seduce investors to stop thinking transversally.

The best way to deal with the selective perception bias is to ask yourself: What is my motivation to see things in a certain way? What expectations did I bring into the situation? Why do others not share my view?

### 2.1.3 Confirmation Bias

Previous experience influences the way we perceive information that we face, but it also affects the way we search for information. People tend to search for information that confirms one's beliefs or hypotheses, while they give disproportionately less consideration to alternative possibilities. This bias in information selection is known as the *confirmation bias*. It has been first discovered by Wason (1960). In his experiment, participants were asked to identify a rule applied to triples of numbers (e.g., 2, 4, and 6). To discover the rule, participants could decide on their own triples and receive a feedback on whether their numbers conform to the rule or not. While the true rule was "three numbers of increasing order of magnitude," most participants tested a specific hypothesis as for example "increasing by 2." However, those who test their rule can never discover that their rule is wrong because all examples that fit their rule fit also the true rule. Thus, to test the rule "increasing by 2," it is critical to try, for example, 2, 4, and 7.

Although there are circumstances where searching for confirmatory evidence can be useful in testing a particular hypothesis (Klayman & Ha, 1987), it is unlikely that people are aware of them and adjust their test strategy. It is more likely that people use the same test strategy that can be useful in certain circumstances, but which, like any all-purpose heuristic, can lead to serious mistakes.

In another experiment, individuals were asked to decide whether the costs of alternative treatment methods should be covered by the mandatory insurance or not (Jonas, Schulz-Hardt, Frey, & Thelen, 2001). They have been offered different expert reports, each of them providing arguments why these costs should be covered by the mandatory insurance and why not as a preparation for a final decision. The participants showed a clear preference for reports that supported their initial opinion. Such biased information search can lead to the maintenance of the initial opinion, even if this position is not justified based on all available information.

**Relevance for Investors and Moderation**  Like the experimental evidence already presented, different investors reading the same article discussing the future development of an asset may come to different conclusions regarding the prospects of the asset, depending on whether they hold the asset. As experiments suggest, it is more difficult to recognize news about a company as negative when holding shares of that company than when holding cash (Kuhnen & Knutson, 2011). Again, confirmation is sought but not information.

As a possible moderation, it is important to seek discussion with people who hold the opposite position. Thereby, one should try to avoid the natural impulse to seek for reasons why the opponent's opinion is wrong. Instead, one should listen to the arguments and evaluate them as rationally as possible. To avoid the tendency to see evidence in support of previous investment decisions, one could ask: How would I decide in the face of the new evidence if I must decide again today?

## 2.1.4 Availability Bias

Finally, the perception of information is influenced by its properties. Concrete, imaginable, and exciting information is more easily perceived and stored than abstract or statistical data. Such kind of information is also more "available" and easy to retrieve when one tries to think of an instance. This is the reason, why there is a discrepancy between people's judgment on the likelihood of an event and the statistical data. For example, most Americans think that homicide or car accidents kill more people than diabetes and stomach cancer and that tornados claim more lives than lightning, while the statistical evidence show that it is exactly other way around (Combs & Slovic, 1979). This bias in the perception is called *availability bias*. Because car accidents, tornadoes and murderers are on the headlines, they are more easily perceived and stored in memory than other information so that when people try to think of an instance this information influences the probability judgments because of its high availability. A close cousin to availability is *vividness*. It usually refers to how concrete and imaginable or how exciting some information is. Experiments show that decision makers are affected more strongly by vivid information than by abstract information.

**Relevance for Investors and Moderation**  A famous study by Barber & Odean (2008) shows that individual investors are net buyers of attention-grabbing stocks. For example, they buy into stocks in the news, stocks experiencing high abnormal trading volume, and stocks with extreme one-day returns. Attention-driven buying results from the difficulty that investors have searching the thousands of stocks they can potentially buy. Individual investors do not face the same search problem when selling because they tend to sell only stocks they already own. Barber and Odean find that many investors consider purchasing only stocks that have first caught their attention. Thus, preferences determine choices after attention has determined the choice set. However, attention-driven investments do not generate superior returns.

Overall, the information selection biases make investors use either a subset of evidence or evidence that is inappropriate for the decision problem. This motivates the development of erroneous beliefs and hinders learning. One approach to correct these developments is to compare explicitly over- and underestimated dangers with evidence for the opposite view. Advisors should, however, be cautious not to induce the opposite effect—that is, motivate clients who previously overestimated some risks to underestimate them. It is best is to show long-term empirical evidence for similar cases.

## 2.2 INFORMATION PROCESSING BIASES

Selected information needs to be evaluated. What does the evidence say about the likelihood of events? Which alternative is now more attractive? Some rules of thumb cause systematic misperceptions.

### 2.2.1 Representativeness Bias

When making judgments, people often rely on the degree to which their observations represent known characteristics. This rule of thumb is called *representativeness bias.*

To give an example of tasks where the representativeness bias can affect decisions, suppose that one observes A and needs to judge whether it comes from B or from C, where B and C are samples of observations with different characteristics. For example, A might be a person (e.g., a fund manager) and B might be a group (e.g., fund managers with skills) and C might be another group (e.g., fund managers without any skills). The judgment task is to estimate the probability that the person is a member of the group B (e.g., that the fund manager is skilled). Similarly, A could be an event and B might be a process. For example, B might be the process of flipping a fair coin and A might be the event of getting six tails in a row. The judgment task could then concern the estimation of the likelihood for observing the event with an unbiased coin.

Let us now consider some examples of how the representativeness bias can affect decisions. Suppose that a fund manager is known to beat the market in two of three years. Let B mean that the manager beats the market and F mean that the manager fails to beat the market. Now consider the following protocols of the success of the manager: (a) BFBBB; (b) FBFBBB; and (c) FBBBBB. Which of the three protocols is most likely?

Most of the people answering this question consider protocol (b) as most likely. The reason for their judgment is that if the manager beats the market in two of three years, the probability for success is two-thirds. Hence, a protocol is considered as most likely if the protocol's realizations match this probability. In protocol (a) the manager beats the market in four of five years, but in protocol (b) the manager beats the market in four of six years. Comparing the success rate in the protocols with the expected probability for success given in the description of the problem, people looking for a closer match judge protocol (b) as more likely. However, protocol (b) is in fact equivalent to protocol (a) but it has the additional condition that in the first year the manager fails to beat the market. By the properties of conjunct probabilities, it is less likely to observe protocol (b) than protocol (a).[3]

The observation that people fail to apply the conjunction rule correctly is known as the *conjunction fallacy*. It describes the tendency to overestimate the probability of conjunctive events. For example, suppose that you can build a complex machine consisting of 500 independent parts. Suppose also that each part were 99% reliable when used the very first time. What are the chances that the system would work on its first attempt? The answer is less than 1%, which surprises many people. In the example with the fund managers, the fallacy emerges due to the representativeness bias.

The representativeness bias emerges very often when people deal with *small samples*. People start to believe that a sample randomly drawn from a population should resemble other samples drawn randomly from the same population more closely than statistical sampling theory would predict. However, randomly drawn small samples may look quite different than larger samples drawn from the same population.

To demonstrate this, one could draw random numbers from 0 to 100 and order them in 10 equally large bins. The relative frequency of the numbers in each bin should be 10% as each number is equally likely to be drawn. This is true for a sample with 10,000 observations. However, a smaller sample with 10 observations, for example, may look quite different—that is, some bins may contain more than 10% of the observations; other bins may be empty. The smaller sample should, however, be considered as random as the sample with 10,000 observations, although each distribution looks different.

In some instances, the reliance on stereotypes leads people to ignore the relative frequency with which events occur (base rates). This has been demonstrated in an experiment where participants were told that psychologists have been interviewed and administered personality tests of engineers and lawyers (Kahneman & Tversky, 1973). Based on this information, the psychologists have written thumbnail descriptions. For example, a description of an engineer was:

> *Jack is a 45-year-old man. He is married and has four children. He is generally conservative, careful, and ambitious. He shows no interest in political and social issues and spends most of his free time on his many hobbies, which include home carpentry, sailing, and mathematical puzzles.*

---

[3]To see that this is true, assume that realizations are independent from each other and compute the probabilities of the three protocols. Rounding to full percentages for a) we get $\left(\frac{2}{3}\right)^4 \frac{1}{3} = 7\%$, for b) we get $\left(\frac{2}{3}\right)^4 \left(\frac{1}{3}\right)^2 = 2\%$, for c) we get $\left(\frac{2}{3}\right)^5 \frac{1}{3} = 4\%$.

One group of participants was told that there were 30 engineers and 70 lawyers. Another group was told that there were 70 engineers and 30 lawyers. When asked to estimate the probability that someone randomly selected from the pool of 100 descriptions would be an engineer, the average estimate in the first group was 30% and in the second group 70%. In other words, participants in both groups used the base rates given in the problem. However, when participants were provided with descriptive information as shown about Jack, they tended to ignore the base rates. The average estimate in both groups was the same. Thereby, it did not matter whether the information was informative or not. Even provided with information that is equally descriptive for an engineer or a lawyer, participants ignored on average the base rates and gave a median probability estimate of 50%. Hence, participants ignored the base rate information and simply judged the description as equally representative of an engineer and a lawyer. This observation remained in the literature as the *base rate fallacy*.

When do people tend to neglect base rates? People appear to use base rates when they are consistent with their intuitive theories on cause and effect. In one experiment, participants were asked to predict the average grade points of a student based on either causal factors (such as the number of hours in a week spent for preparation) or noncausal information (such as student's income). Participants were told that noncausal factors have the same predictive power as causal factors but on average participants used base rates more often when the information was causal.

**Relevance for Investors and Moderation**   The representativeness bias has important implications for investors looking for price patterns that they could exploit. After a short sequence of positive returns, they might develop the belief that the economics producing them has turned in favor of good returns, even though this might not be true. Indeed, De Bondt & Thaler (1985) showed that portfolios of prior losers (stocks with recent negative performance) outperformed portfolios of past winners (stocks with recent positive performance). That is, representativeness bias led investors to overreact to positive (negative) information relative to prior winners, as these appeared more representative for the recently observed good (bad) returns. The best moderation to address this fallacy is to reveal it by statistical evidence.

### 2.2.2   Conservatism

There are also circumstances where people overweight the base rates and ignore new information. This is called *conservatism*.

The famous Monty Hall problem (derived from the TV show *Let's Make a Deal*) is one example. In this problem, there are three doors; two have a goat and one a car behind it. You are asked to choose one of the doors—not knowing which door hides which object. Then, before you can open it someone who knows what is behind the doors opens one of the doors you have not chosen that hides a goat. The question is whether observing this action you need to swap away from your door to the other door that is still closed. Many people answer "no," because at that point there are two doors and one car and one goat left. So, they assume that the chance of getting the car when sticking to the originally chosen door is 50%. However, this is wrong, since the action of opening a door that you have not chosen and behind which there is a goat reveals important information. Indeed, comparing the two strategies "sticking to your door" and "swapping with the other door" shows that following the latter you win in two out of three cases, while the former is only successful half that often.

Another example that shows the effect of conservatism has been proposed by Edwards (1968):

> *There are two urns; each one contains 10 balls. Urn A contains 7 red and 3 blue balls, while urn B contains 3 red and 7 blue balls. One urn is randomly chosen by flipping a fair coin. 12 balls are now drawn from this urn with replacement. The result is the following: 8 red and 4 blue balls were drawn. What is the probability that the randomly drawn urn is urn A when observing this result (8 red and 4 blue balls)?*

People answered the question with probabilities very close to the base rate of 50%. However, in this example the information that 8 of the 12 balls drawn from the urn are red and only 4 are blue is very important, because statistical rules would imply a probability of urn A of 97% (i.e., close to 100%).

Representativeness bias (see Subsection 2.2.1) and conservatism seem to generate opposite effects of information processing on beliefs. Griffin & Tversky (1992) suggest that people update beliefs based on the strength and weight of new evidence. Strength refers to how salient and extreme new information is, while weight is its statistical content (i.e., its relevance from a statistical point of view). Griffin &Tversky (1992) argue that people tend to focus too much on strength and too less on weight, that is, when information seems salient and extreme, people tend to focus on it and update beliefs accordantly, while if information does not appear relevant and important, people tend to ignore it. Therefore, when strength is high but weight is low, new information is overweighed and the representativeness bias arises. By contrast, when strength is low but weight is high, new information is underweighted and conservatism arises.

**Relevance for Investors and Moderation** The conservatism bias makes investors react to slowly to new information. Even professionals cannot avoid the bias. Their earnings estimates adjust too slowly to new information so that the market price of companies reporting positive (negative) earnings surprises tend to drift up (down) for a while. In the empirical literature, this observation is known as the *post-earnings-announcement-drift* (Bernard & Thomas, 1989).

The best strategy to avoid the conservatism bias is to use statistical rules when updating beliefs.

## 2.2.3 Gambler's Fallacy

When you go to the roulette table you might wonder why the casino records the numbers that have previously been drawn. This information is clearly irrelevant but customers demand it as input for their strategies. Under the assumption that both colors are equally likely to be drawn, a common strategy is to bet on the color that was underrepresented in the previous draws. This strategy, however, is not more successful than any other. The reason is that the proportion of red and black numbers remains the same after each drawing—that is, each color remains equally likely to be chosen. The probability for drawing a color would change only if the numbers were removed each time after they have been drawn. This misperception of randomness is called the *gambler's fallacy*.

Even well-trained students in statistics fall prey of the gambler's fallacy when it is hidden more subtly than in roulette. When people are asked to write down a random sequence of coin tosses without flipping a coin, they tend to avoid long runs and include more alternations between heads and tails than one would normally find in a random sequence. In a random sequence, the probability that the coin changes from heads to tails or from tails to heads is 0.5. The probability that the coin changes its side after two identical outcomes is $0.5 \times 0.5 = 0.25$ and the probability for three identical outcomes is $0.5 \times 0.5 \times 0.5 = 0.125$. In the sequences written by individuals, however, the coin changes its side more often (see Figure 2.02). Moreover, there are almost no series with five and more identical outcomes while in a random sequence the probability for observing five identical outcomes is 6.25%.

The tendency to expect more alternations to occur than would occur in a random sequence is even more pronounced when people are asked to alternate randomly between more than two choices. For example, when people are presented with panels of six or eight push buttons and asked to generate a random pattern of button pressing, the excessive alternation is even stronger than in the case with two buttons.

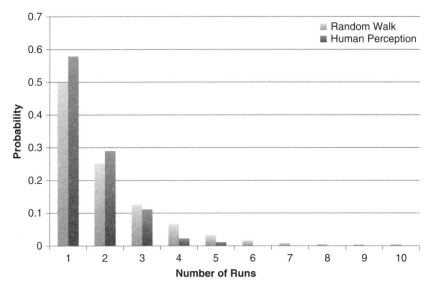

**FIGURE 2.02** Predicted and true probabilities for runs with the same outcomes

**Relevance for Investors and Moderation** Under the gambler's fallacy, people underestimate the probability of long sequences with the same outcome. In finance, the gambler's fallacy might lead people to bet prematurely on trend reversals. One signal for a trend reversal is a new all-time high (or all-time low), after which many investors sell (buy) because they belief that it is time for prices to fall (raise). Consequently, they might sell winning assets too early and hold losing assets too long—a trading behavior known also as the *disposition effect* (see Section 2.2.14).

As in the case of the representativeness bias, to overcome the gambler's fallacy, it is best to use proper statistics.

### 2.2.4 Hot-Hand Bias

The representativeness bias may also introduce a belief in a *hot hand*. This was first demonstrated for basketball players. A player with a hot hand was one who had a better chance of making a basket after more successful shots than after the player had missed a shot. Statistical analysis shows however that streak shooting did not exist—the successes and failures of the same player were statistically unrelated so that streak shooting was only an illusion. To test whether people see patterns in random sequences, participants have been asked to look at six different series with "successes" (X) and "failures" (O) (Gilovich, Vallone, & Tversky, 1985). Each series contained 11 Xs and 10 Os, and the probability for alternating was set to 0.4, 0.5, 0.6, 0.7, 0.8 and 0.9. More than half of the people classified the sequence that alternates on half of all possible occasions (e.g., XOXXXOOOOXOXXOOOXXXOX) as *streak shooting*—they saw patterns in random series. Moreover, like the gambler's fallacy, they judged a series as most random when its probability of alternation was about 0.7 and the probability of repetition was 0.3. Hence, people saw randomness when there was a pattern and saw patterns when the sequence was random.

The misperception of randomness is observed in the assessment of one's own skills. In an experiment by Ayton & Fischer (2004), participants have been asked to predict the next outcome of a binary sequence with red and blue balls. Consistent with the gambler's fallacy, the longer the run of a color, the less likely participants were to predict that color the next time. Moreover, there was a significant linear trend in confidence as a function of run length of successes. Participants seem to believe that they got "hot," although there were no serial dependencies in the outcomes that they were predicting. More generally, people seem to expect to see streaks in contexts involving intentional agents such as humans. If there is no such agent, people behave according to the gambler's fallacy.

The belief in the existence of managers with a hot hand is so dominant that people forget to consider the sample size in their judgments. To demonstrate how this can happen, suppose that there are 1,000 managers without any skills trying to beat the market. Odds are that after one year, 500 managers will beat the market. After the second year, 250 managers will report to have beaten the market for two subsequent years. And after a decade, there will be one manager who beats the market for 10 subsequent years—purely by chance alone. Suppose, now, that there are 10,000 managers without any skills trying to beat the market. There will be 10 managers who will report to have been beating the market for 10 subsequent years without any skills. Hence, the more managers try to beat the market, the higher will be the number of managers who manage to report an impressive performance without any skills.

**Relevance for Investors and Moderation** For investors, this misperception of randomness can be dangerous, as they might engage in active trading even though any success can be considered as a pure chance. Similarly, they might be willing to pay management fees to managers reporting exceptional returns, while the probability that the performance is mainly chance-driven is quite high. A recent study by Heuer, Merkle, & Weber (2017) shows that private investors (readers of a large German newspaper) estimating the probability that top-performing funds are managed by skillful managers ignore the population size and other cross-sectional information. They seem not to realize that in a large sample, there will be a few strong performers by pure chance. Investors do not recognize that in a large fund population, a rare outperformer is less likely to have a skilled manager than in a small fund population. Instead, they mostly rely on the return of the fund to judge the skill of the manager and neglect the number of competitors.

Proper statistical testing of the hypotheses one believes to find in data can help to moderate this bias.

### 2.2.5 Anchoring

When making assessments, individuals appear overly influenced by *arbitrary* values mentioned in the description of the problem, even if they are aware that these values are not informative, and even if the values are absurdly high or low. The impact of these values on individuals' decisions is known as *anchoring*. The following examples illustrate the anchoring effect.

In an experiment by Kahneman, Slovic, & Tversky (1974), participants were asked to answer questions stated in two ways. In the first step, participants were asked to estimate whether the true value is above or below a certain level, which was determined by spinning a wheel of fortune that the participants could observe. In a second step, participants were asked to give an exact estimate.

For example, in the first step the participants in one group were asked to answer the question, "Is the percentage of African countries in the United Nations greater or less than 65?" The participants in another group were asked, "Is the percentage of African countries in the United Nations greater or less than 25?" After answering these questions, all participants were asked to provide an exact estimate.

Participants who were randomly assigned to the group in which the needle of the wheel of fortune landed on 65 gave subsequently a median estimate of 45%, and the participants for whom the needle landed on 10 gave a median estimate of 25%.

Experts are not immune to the effect of anchoring, as demonstrated by studies with real estate agents and professional traders. In a study by Northcraft & Neale (1987), real estate agents were given the opportunity to value a house for sale—one appraised at $74,900 or another appraised at $135,000. All agents received the same information on the properties with one exception: For some agents, the price was listed at 11% to 12% below the true appraisal value, for others it was 4% below value, and for others it was 11% to 12% above the value. The agents could visit the property; afterward, they were asked to provide their best estimate on the value of the property.

The agents gave estimates that were clearly anchored to the apparent listing price for both properties: agents with a low listing price gave on average a lower appraisal value than agents with a higher listing price. Interestingly, when asked what their top three considerations were in making these judgments, only 1 agent of 10 mentioned the listing price. So, it is likely that agents were simply unaware that they have been anchored by the listing price.

**Relevance for Investors and Moderation**  The effect of anchoring is robust and pervasive. People adjust their estimates insufficiently from anchor values regardless of the judgment topic. The present is a particularly strong anchor. People may fail to anticipate the possibility of dramatic changes and remain unprepared for such scenarios. Consensus estimates and estimates by the companies are anchors that people have difficulties to ignore when making own predictions. When receiving information about the possible earnings of a company under the best economic conditions, people have difficulties to estimate earnings correctly under real conditions.

As anchoring often goes unnoticed, one effective approach to avoid the anchoring bias is to generate reasons that are inconsistent with the anchor. In one study by Chapman & Johnson (1999), participants were asked to estimate the winning chance of the Republicans by indicating whether this chance is higher or lower than the last two digits of their social security number. Before giving their final estimate, some of the participants were asked to list one reason why the Republicans would win, some why a Republican would not win, and some were not instructed to list any reasons. A significant anchoring bias was observed only for the participants who did not provide any reasons and who listed reasons that were consistent with the anchor (e.g., supporting arguments in the case that they expected that the Republicans would win). Hence, considering reasons that were inconsistent with the anchor, e.g. arguments against the outcome expected by the participants, can help to eliminate the bias. This consider-the-opposite strategy proves effective also in real settings, such as when purchasing a used car (Mussweiler & Pfeif, 1991).

## 2.2.6  Framing

Anchors influence individuals' decisions, because people fail to see through the way in which information is provided. This failure is the reason why alternative descriptions of a decision problem may give rise to different preferences contrary to the principle of invariance underlying a rational choice. The intuition behind the normative concept is that variations of the form that do not affect the actual outcomes should not be relevant to the choice.

Although this rule appears to be simple, there are many cases where it is violated. For example, people are influenced by whether payoffs are framed as gains or as losses, as the following example by Tversky & Kahneman (1981) demonstrates. People must choose two lotteries—one from each pair of lotteries. The first choice was between (A) a sure gain of $2,400 and (B) a 25% chance of a $10,000 gain and a 75% chance of winning nothing at all. The second choice was between (C) a sure loss of $7,500 and (D) a 75% chance of a $10,000 loss and a 25% chance of losing nothing at all. The payoff was the combination of the two lotteries that have been chosen. Note that the choice between (A) and (B) is a lottery among gains while the choice between (C) and (D) is a lottery among losses. However, since both can be combined with a payoff from the other pair, losses and gains in each choice do not matter. Yet, people perceive the choices differently and seem to evaluate the two lottery pairs in isolation so that the gain or the loss frame dominates. As is known from prospect theory, people are risk averse in gains but risk seeking in the domain of losses; thus, the following typical choice follows: Lottery A is usually chosen because the expected payoff of B is $2,500 and the extra $100 is not enough to tempt people into taking a chance. Lottery D is typically preferred to C because it offers a chance to avoid a loss.

The interesting thing about the problem is that choosing B and C turns out to be better than choosing A and D. The combined payoff from choosing A and D is a 75% chance of losing $7,600 and a 25% chance of gaining $2,400 and that from B and C is a 75% chance of losing $7,500 and a 25% chance of winning $2,500. Thus, if one chooses A and D, one has $100 less than when choosing B and C, whatever happens.

**Relevance for Investors and Moderation**   The optimistic or pessimistic way an investment or a recommendation is framed can affect investor's willingness or lack of willingness to invest. Even long-term investors may change their risk-taking behavior when they are confronted with short-time price fluctuations, an effect call myopic loss aversion and discussed in Subsection 2.2.12. Therefore, the best approach to avoid being biased by a frame is to search for alternative representations of the problem and check whether the decision will change. In general, it is always advantageous to adopt as broad a frame as possible. For example, when reviewing performance, it is advantageous to avoid statements that pay attention to what happened in the last month, quarter, or year but more to what happened over the lifetime of the investment. The frame for the presentation should be chosen in dependence of client's goal. For example, for clients with a retirement goal, the level of wealth generated by the investment should be presented as income per month or year that the client can expect to be able to spend after retirement.

A second example concerns the choice of pension plans by employees. Researchers found out that savings are often split equally over the available alternatives, which has consequences for the overall risk exposure. This choice heuristics is called *naïve diversification heuristics* or 1/*n* diversification heuristic (for the most recent evidence on this topic see De Giorgi & Mahmoud, 2016 and De Giorgi & Mahmoud, 2017). People choosing 401(k) plans aiming to hold on average 60% in stocks and 40% in bonds by investing in mutual funds turn out to hold more stocks than bonds if they may choose among more stock or bond funds (Benartzi & Thaler, 2001). So, depending on the array of equity and bond funds offered, pension funds decide differently on the weights of their equity and bond exposure. More generally, if an attribute receives more weight in the decision problem simply because it is presented in more detail, then the final decision would be biased. The phenomenon is known as the *splitting bias*.

The best way to avoid the framing bias is to use different frames when making decisions. Warnings are also effective in avoiding the framing bias, in particular if the people are actively involved in the evaluation process (Cheng & Wu, 2010).

### 2.2.7 Overconfidence

If individuals express confidence in their judgments that exceeds the accuracy of those judgments, they are *overconfident*. To get an understanding of the origins of this bias, consider the following examples.

The first one illustrates the *better than average bias*. It is well known that more than 50% of car drivers think that they are a better driver than the average driver. If the population of drivers is symmetrically distributed, only half of them can be above the average. Hence, the *group* of car drivers must be assessed as overconfident.

A subtler aspect of the overconfidence bias is the *miscalibration bias*. It is usually demonstrated in experiments asking individuals to state confidence intervals for numerical answers to several knowledge questions. For example, individuals are asked: "What is the average diameter of the moon (in km)?" As an answer, individuals must state a lower and an upper bound so that they are 90% sure that the correct answer lies within the stated interval. Miscalibration bias is indicated by intervals that are too narrow, meaning that the correct answer lies outside the subjective confidence interval for more than 1 out of 10 questions.

Because asking for the 90% confidence interval could be too difficult, Huisman, van der Sar, & Zwinkels (2012) suggest asking for the maximum and minimum bounds. They ask actively trading private investors three questions:

1. On what level will the AEX Index end in two weeks?
2. On what level will the AEX Index end maximally in two weeks?
3. On what level will the AEX Index end minimally in two weeks?

The answers to these questions allow an evaluation of the investors' expected volatility. To assess the investors' overconfidence, the latter is compared with the implied volatility, that is, the market's expectation of future volatility. Over the total of 2405 responses obtained from all 21 surveys between 2009 and 2010, 72% of the individual investor's volatility forecasts were lower than the implied volatility, a result suggesting a significant underestimation of the risk among private investors.

Overconfidence is observed also in the interaction with other investors. In an experiment by Huber (2007), students were invited to trade a dividend-paying asset on a double auction for 10 periods. The students have different information levels. Some are told in advance the dividends of the next nine periods, some get to know the dividends of the next 8, 7, ... etc. periods, and some only know the next period's dividends. The interesting finding in this experiment is a J-curve effect when displaying the returns the students make as of their information level (see Figure 2.03). The best-informed students clearly make the highest returns but the medium well-informed students do worst. When asked why, the students with medium information level said that they tried to exploit the least informed students. But asking the least-informed students, they say that they knew they were worse off from the outset and thus they did not engage in active trading. As an effect, the best-informed students could exploit the medium-informed ones.

The moral of this example is that it is fine to have no clue if one is aware of this and invests accordingly, such as buying ETFs (exchange-traded funds) of a well-diversified index. The worst is to be overconfident. That is, to believe that "The best plan is ... to profit by the folly of others,"[4] because then it might happen that you are the fool exploited by the others.

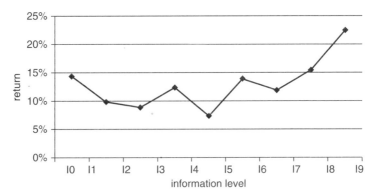

**FIGURE 2.03** Average return per information level

---

[4]Pliny the Elder, from John Barlett, comp. 'Familiar Quotations', 9th ed. 1901.

**Relevance for Investors and Moderation**  Overconfident investors overestimate the precision of information signals. This is particularly relevant for individuals who are incompletely informed; that is, they engage in active strategies in the mistaken belief that they can profit from noninformed market participants. Consequently, they take more risks that they can afford. Due to the belief that they possess special knowledge, overconfident investors trade too much. However, empirical evidence by Barber & Odean (2000) shows that those individuals who trade most make the lowest profits.

Finally, it is worth mentioning that overconfidence can result from an *illusion of control*. People suffer from an illusion of control if they believe to be able to control an exogenous random process. A typical everyday example is that people believe driving a car is a saver means of transportation than taking the plane. When one derives a car, one thinks to be able to control better the risks than being exposed to it in a plane. However, statistically the opposite is true. There are much fewer injuries and lives lost when people go by plane than by car. For example, after the terrorist attacks of September 11, 2001, many people switched from planes to cars and in the subsequent year 3,000 more lives were lost in traveling in the United States (Makridakis, Gaba, & Hogarth, 2010).

Before trying to de-bias overconfident clients, advisors might want to flag certain decisions. Overconfidence is greatest when judgments are difficult. In such cases, advisors should proceed cautiously.

First, advisors could try to explain overconfident investors that other investors also try to outsmart them. So, the best performing investors are those who find the right balance between their skills and investment style.

Second, the advisor could also keep a list with decisions that were not successful, as people are more likely to remember successful decisions and use them to form a judgment on their own skills. Alternatively, the advisors could ask overconfident clients to list reasons for and against a preferred decision. When people consider reasons why their preferred decision might be wrong, they might not change their mind but they are able to make more accurate decisions as demonstrated by Koriat, Lichtenstein, & Fischhoff (1980).

Finally, if overconfidence is difficult to be reduced, advisors could "recalibrate" it. For example, if the client is 90% sure but was only 70% accurate, then it is probably best to treat "90% confidence" as "70% confidence."

### 2.2.8  Present Bias

When asked whether one prefers $100 in two weeks from now or $102 in two weeks and a day, most people prefer the latter. However, when asked whether they prefer $100 now or $102 in two days, most people want the $100 now. Thus, most likely in two weeks from now they would be tempted to reverse their choice.

**Relevance for Investors and Moderation** A high present bias hinders people from making decisions that hurt today but pay off significantly later. Examples include stopping smoking, starting a diet, or beginning to save for retirement. These biases are also called self-control bias. A remedy against present bias is to have the investor agree and commit well before the actual decision needs to be taken. The Save More Tomorrow (SMarT) pension scheme (Thaler & Benartzi, 2004) is a good example. People using it agree to increase their savings whenever their salary increases in the future. This hinders them from spending the whole salary when it is increased.

### 2.2.9 Probability Weighting

Kahneman and Tversky (1979) discovered that the size of the probabilities is also an important determinant of people's decisions and apply probability weighting to describe this fact. Specifically, they find that investors react to probabilities in such a way that very rare events are overweighed and events with a higher probability are underweighted. Probability weighting is different than misestimation of probabilities. When people are asked to estimate how likely it is that they will die in an airplane accident, for example, they will probably overestimate this probability. By contrast, probability weighting allows us to represent that, for example, psychologically, the mathematical step from 0 to 1% probability is a huge step, since it is the step from an event being impossible to being possible. This is surely a larger step psychologically than a change from 49% probability to 50% probability, which might be described as the psychological step from "quite likely" to "a little more likely." People overweight probabilities in cases where they know the true probabilities but still behave as if these probabilities are higher.

**Relevance for Investors and Moderation** One result of the overweighting of small probabilities is that people pay for tickets in the national lottery even though the price is higher than the expected payoff from the ticket. The simple prospect of gaining a huge amount outweighs the high price. Similarly, investors might decide not to invest into risky assets, because of some rare negative events, which are overweighted into their decision. As we will discuss in Section 6.6, probability weighting could also lead to violations of the rationality principle, "more is better than less," and, therefore, we list it in this chapter.

## 2.2.10 Reference Point and Loss Aversion

Another important discovery of Kahneman and Tversky (1979) is that whatever the prospects, positive or negative, their value depends on an individual *reference point,* which determines whether a prospect is perceived as a gain or a loss. The reference point could correspond to a target return the investor intends to achieve, or a benchmark portfolio with respect to which a fund manager's performance is evaluated. Experimental studies also show that investors use a weighted sum of the price at which they bought a stock and the last price of the stock as a reference point to evaluate their current position (Baucells, Weber, & Welfens, 2011). The referent point is likely to change over time, as shown, for example, by Arkes, Hirshleifer, Jiang, & Lim (2008) that after gains people tend to increase the reference point, while after losses they are more reluctant to decrease it.[5]

The reference point is important because losses loom more than for gains—for example, after a loss of 100, investors require more than 100 to feel compensated for the previous losses. On average, they require even twice as much. This observation is called *loss aversion.*

**Relevance for Investors and Moderation** Investment decisions could differ substantially in dependence of the reference point as the same economic situation can be seen either as a gain or as a loss and loss aversion can dictate a different behavior. However, using a reference point to evaluate payoffs does not necessarily induce irrational decisions. The irrationally may come from updating the reference point over time, because payoffs we initially considered as gains could then be coded as losses, leading to time-inconsistent preferences. This issue will be discussed in Chapter 8.

## 2.2.11 Mental Accounting

Thaler (1985) defines *mental accounting* as the set of operations and strategies individuals use to organize, formulate, and evaluate decisions. For example, people group expenditures into categories (housing, food, etc.), and their spending is sometimes constrained by implicit or explicit budgets; they also categorize funds to spend as flows (regular income versus windfalls) or as stocks (cash on hand, home equity, pension wealth, etc.) (Thaler, 1999).

Such categorization would not matter if funds were fungible. But they are not, as the following example by Heath & Soll (1996) illustrates. Two

---

[5]The adaptation of the reference point also displays cross-cultural differences (Arkes, Hirshleifer, Jiang, & Lim, 2010).

groups of individuals were asked whether they would be willing to buy a ticket to a play. One group was told that they had spent $50 earlier in the week going to a basketball game; the other group was told that they had received a $50 parking ticket earlier in the week. Those who had already gone to the basketball game were significantly less likely to go to the play than those who had gotten the parking ticket because the money was booked in different accounts so that budget restrictions applied differently.

**Relevance for Investors and Moderation**  In the context of investments, people use mental accounting to sort assets to satisfy different goals such as security, potential, or aspiration. Financial advisors often recommend using certain securities for certain goals. The problem with this investment approach is that investors make decisions within each goal. Neglecting the correlations between the returns of assets belonging to different goals may, however, create inefficiencies in the portfolio construction. Hence, given that there are significant correlation effects that must be considered, advisors need either to take them into account when calculating an optimal portfolio or motivate the client to keep only one account by confronting him with the monetary costs from using several mental accounts. We will again address this issue in Section 11.5, where we consider goal-based investing.

### 2.2.12  Myopic Loss Aversion

An important example of mental accounting has been proposed by Benartzi & Thaler (1995) to study how investors aggregate subsequent returns to evaluate inter-temporal investment decisions. If an investor applies short evaluation periods (e.g., evaluate the portfolio performance on annual base), then the investment problem is narrowly or *myopically* framed (i.e., the inter-temporal investment decision is framed as a sequence of independent one-year investment problems). As we will discuss later, the evaluation period is irrelevant for investors modeled as in traditional finance (see Section 8.1). However, if the investor is loss averse, the myopic framing of the problem changes investors' risk perception and consequently their willingness to invest in risky assets. The combination of a myopic frame and loss aversion is called *myopic loss aversion*, which we now illustrate in the following example.

There are two investors: one who calculates the gains and losses in portfolio every day and another one who only looks at the portfolio once per decade. Since, daily, stocks go down in value almost as often as they go up, the investor's loss aversion will make stocks appear very unattractive. In contrast, loss aversion will not have much effect on perception of stocks of the other investor since at 10-year horizons stocks offer only a small risk of losing money.

For example, consider an investment with a 50% chance for a return of 20% and 50% chance for a loss of 10%. After one period, an investment with an initial value of 1,000 can be worth either 1,200 or 900. Hence, investors with a one-period-horizon face a loss in one of two cases—that is, with a 50% probability. After two periods, there are four possible states with the outcomes: 1,440, 1,080, 1,080, and 810, respectively. Hence, an investor with a two-period horizon would face a loss (810 < 1,000) only in one out of four cases (i.e., the probability for a loss is 25%).

**Relevance for Investors and Moderation** The more often investors check the value of their portfolios, the more likely it is that they are confronted with losses. This is dangerous for investors with a high loss aversion because they might lose confidence in their investment strategy for no good reason. This is because investment strategies are usually designed to serve medium- to long-term financial needs. Observing higher losses in the short term is seldom a good reason for abandoning a strategy.

As framing causes the problem, the best approach to avoid it is to adapt a broader frame. Advisors should avoid reviewing the performance in the last quarter, month, or year, but rather, discuss how the latest performance changed the chances of reaching the investment goal since the beginning of the investment. In the context of previously achieved gains, recent losses take on a different meaning.

### 2.2.13 Narrow Framing

Narrow framing is another example of mental accounting and refers to the observation in an experimental setting that people tend to evaluate risks in isolation, independently from other risks they face (see Tversky & Kahneman, 1981). In portfolio selection, narrow framing might imply that investors evaluate single stocks, ignoring the overall portfolio performance. Barberis & Huang (2009) and De Giorgi & Legg (2012) show that narrow framers tend to hold less risky assets, because the risk diversification potential is ignored when single positions are evaluated independently. Therefore, narrow framing has been successfully applied to solve the nonparticipation puzzle (Mankiw & Zeldes, 1991), that is, the empirical observation that households generally invest less into stock markets than traditional finance would suggest.

**Relevance for Investors and Moderation** Narrow framing is extremely relevant when reporting to clients. If the performance of single positions is emphasized instead of the overall portfolio performance, clients tend to overestimate or underestimate the portfolio risk. Narrow framing could also lead to underdiversification, because investors only select the few assets they like most and naively diversify among them. Therefore, it is important to also emphasize the importance of having a well-diversified portfolio.

### 2.2.14  The Disposition Effect and the House-Money Effect

Mental accounting may also explain the *disposition effect*. It describes the investors' tendency to hold losing assets too long and sell winning stocks too early, given that these assets belong to different accounts. Empirical evidence by Odean (1998) shows that individual investors are more likely to sell stocks that have gone up in value, rather than stocks that have lost.

One explanation for this observation is that investors make two mistakes at once: they build two mental accounts—one for the realized gains (or losses) and another one for "paper" gains (or losses)—and they take investment decisions that make their previous investment decision (to buy an asset) look better (Barberis & Xiong, 2012). If a loss occurs, investors would keep it as a paper loss (investors do not sell the asset) because this is associated with a lower utility loss than selling the asset and realizing the loss. If a gain occurs, the investor is better off if the gain is realized (the asset is sold) than if the gain as kept as a paper gain.

The mental accounting bias can be also used to explain the *house money effect*—a greater willingness to gamble with money that was recently won. The reason is that the utility loss associated with a loss is diluted if the loss is aggregated with an earlier gain and the investor is ready to take more risks.

**Relevance for Investors and Moderation** This sort of mental accounting is clearly irrational since it hinders clients in facing the real economic situation of their assets. Moreover, the disposition effect occurs because clients do not plan their investments ahead, but backward. Assets that made a loss with respect to the buying price are kept in the paper account, while gains with respect to the buying price are realized. This is like justifying the actions one has already taken and not like looking ahead for the best continuity of the investments.

One possibility to avoid holding losses too long is to use a stop-loss strategy. When applying this strategy, investors define at the beginning the maximum loss they are willing to accept. Whenever the losses reach this level, the investment is liquidated. However, stop-loss strategies do not cure the problem of backward looking, but only the symptoms (holding losses too long). A better approach when observing paper losses is to check whether the initial reasons for investing is still valid.

## 2.2.15 Affinity

The affinity bias occurs when people make investment choices based on their values and not on economic rational. People might buy the stocks of a green energy company because they agree with the company's philosophy. They buy companies that produce goods they like or they invest in a company if the CEO is familiar to them (Ackert, Church, Tompkins, & Zhang, 2005). Finally, they might predominantly buy stocks from their home country—which is the *home bias*. For example, Swiss investors might hold more than 4% Swiss stocks in the portfolio. Note that 4% is the share that Swiss stocks have in the global market capitalization of equities.

**Relevance for Investors and Moderation** While it is obvious that buying the shares of one's favorite wind farm is typically not a good investment and that the familiarity with the CEO is not a good criterion to invest in a company, it is not so clear that the home bias is a waste of money. The uncertainty is related to the definition of the home of a company. Usually, the home country is defined by the location of the companies' headquarters, although the company might generate most of its profits outside of this country.

If the home bias is driven by affinity bias, it needs a moderation. One possibility is to compare the returns of the stocks that the investor buys due to affinity with the returns of some benchmark.

## 2.2.16 Regret Aversion

Emotions such as worry, fear, or happiness influence decisions as much as heuristics do. Most of the emotions may occur in the absence of a decision since they are related to outcomes or uncertainty. Regret, however, is directly linked to the decision at hand. Regret is a negative emotion that we experience when realizing or imagining that our present situation would have been better, had we acted differently.

There is some indication that regret may be related to the distinction between acts and omissions. Some studies have found that at least in the short run,[6] people usually assigned a higher value to an inferior outcome when it resulted from an act rather than from an omission. Presumably, this is a way of counteracting the regret that could have resulted from the act.

---

[6]In the long run, this is typically reversed. One regrets more the foregone opportunities (Beike, Markman, & Karadogan, 2009).

The following example illustrates this.[7] George, John, and Paul[8] were considering changing their investment positions. George held many stocks and, based on his own analysis, decided to sell stocks and buy bonds instead. John was in the same situation as George, and like him, switched to bonds. However, John based his decision on his financial advisor's recommendation rather than on his own analysis. Paul has traditionally held bonds. Paul thought that the market would rebound, and he considered changing his usual practice by purchasing stocks but at the end did not do so. The market appreciated by 30%.

Whose self-image suffered the most? George, who traded out of stocks and into bonds based on his own analysis? John, who traded out of stocks and into bonds based on his advisor's recommendation? Paul, who continued to hold bonds, or nobody because self-image doesn't matter in such situations? In this scenario, 70% of the people answering this question say that George suffers most, but only 12% say that John feels most pain. Moreover, nobody says that Paul's self-image is affected. This is because Paul committed an error of omission by decided not to act. Such errors cause less regret than errors of commissions as done by George and John. So why would one feel less pain if deciding like John and not like George? The reason for feeling less badly is that John can blame his advisor for the bad outcome. We may say that John holds a *psychological call option* that protects him from regretting decisions.

A recent empirical study on the trading behavior of individual US investors show that investment decisions minimizing the emotional burden of regret potentially lowers individual investors' economic welfare by reducing their motivation to move to more suitable investments. For example, using detailed trade data for two brokers Strahilevitz, Odean, & Barber (2011) find that investors are reluctant to repurchase stocks previously sold for a loss and if the investors previously sold a stock for a gain, they are less likely to repurchase that stock if its price has gone up than if it has gone down since they sold it. The authors explain this behavior with the investors' aversion to regret. The first effect is observed because an investor selling a stock for a loss is likely to be disappointed and to regret having purchased the stock at the first place. Thus, the purchase of this stock will lead to a painful experience and people instinctively avoid repeating behavior that previously resulted in negative emotions. The second effect is observed for two reasons. First, if the price increases after the investors have

---

[7]This example is taken from Shefrin (2008): *Beyond Greed and Fear*, Harvard Business School Press.

[8]Question: Who is missing? Answer: Ringo! (The Beatles)

sold, they would regret their decisions to sell but if the price decreases after they have sold, they would feel wealthier by selling earlier and repurchasing at a lower price.

Note that the tendency to repurchase stocks that have dropped in price after being sold is not driven by a general belief that stocks mean-revert, as the investors who exhibit this behavior tend to choose recent winners when buying stocks that they have not owned previously.

The aversion to regret might change people's opinion after deciding. People change their mind to make the decision look more attractive and thereby reduce the potential dissonance regarding the possibility that the decision turns out to be wrong. For example, in a study with race-goers, researchers found that after placing a $2 bet, race-goers increased their estimation as to the likelihood of their horse winning the race (Knox & Inkster, 1968).

**Relevance for Investors and Moderation** As seen in the previous example, the emotion of regret is higher when errors arise from rejection rather than acceptance of a status quo option. Such asymmetry in the regret feeling might drive a status quo bias on subsequent decisions. Having lost money, the fear of regret often keeps investors out of the market for a considerable time, thus missing the investment opportunities of buying when the market is down.

The negative feeling of regretting past decisions influences repurchasing decisions. Hence, regret reduces investors' motivation to move to more suitable investments. In fact, the empirical evidence suggests that considering trading costs and commissions, the investors should better invest in an index rather than trading in and out of common stocks under the bias of regret.

To avoid trading decisions that serve emotions, investors should follow a strategy that is defined at the beginning of the investment. The strategy should define conditions under which the exposure should be increased but also conditions when the investment should be liquidated. Such conditions may be linked to previous performance but before implementing a strategy based on them, its performance should be tested empirically. By following a well-designed strategy defined in advance, one avoids emotional decisions by looking backward.

## 2.3 BIASES AFTER RECEIVING FEEDBACK

Each decision receives feedback, which reveals new information and determines whether the decision was successful or not. Thereby it gives rise to additional biases affecting the individual's decision-making behavior, which are summarized in the following. To avoid these biases, it is essential that one documents all decisions that were taken, including the information on which it was based and the reasoning behind it.

### 2.3.1 Hindsight Bias

When evaluating past decisions, people often believe that one should have been able to anticipate events much better than was the case. In hindsight, people consistently exaggerate what could have been anticipated in foresight. They even wrongly remember their own predictions to exaggerate in hindsight what they knew in foresight. It appears that when we receive knowledge about the outcome, we immediately make sense out of it by integrating it into what we already know.

**Relevance for Investors and Moderation**   The problem with hindsight bias is that even if one is aware of it, one may still be unaware of exactly what it is. Warnings about the danger have little effect. A more effective manipulation is forcing oneself to argue against the inevitability of the reported outcomes (i.e., trying to convince oneself that it might have turned out otherwise). One might further track down some of the uncertainty surrounding past events in their original form.

### 2.3.2 Self-Attribution Bias

People are not always rational in attributing success and failure. They tend to attribute success to their own efforts but failure to bad luck or to another person. For example, a father suffering from this bias might be proud of himself when his son gets a good grade at school but he may be angry with the teachers if the son gets a bad grade.

**Relevance for Investors and Moderation**   When discussing the investment results some clients attribute those decisions that worked out successfully to their own skills, while they blame their advisor for the loosing investments. This is particularly bad when the advisor had initially recommended not to do that investment, but the client insisted on it. For this purpose, it is essential that decisions are documented—especially those that resulted from an overruling.

### 2.3.3 Outcome Bias

Good decisions usually lead to good outcome and bad outcomes are usually a result of bad decisions. Therefore, in the absence of other information, it is reasonable to use outcome information to judge the quality of the underlying decisions. However, people use the outcome of decisions to evaluate the quality of others' decisions although they had perfect information about what the decision makers knew at the time of the decision (Baron & Hershey, 1988). Nevertheless, perfect information may not be sufficient to judge the quality of decisions if there is uncertainty regarding the optimal choice (Jones, Yurak, & Frisch, 1997). Ratner & Herbst (2005) address this uncertainty by introducing two brokers where the one had a greater chance of success than the other. This could not eliminate the outcome bias. While at the beginning participants chose the broker with the greater chance of success, after bad outcomes, they switched to the other broker, with a lower chance of success.

**Relevance for Investors and Moderation** The outcome bias leads people to invest with those asset managers that have recently been successful, as they mistakenly believe that good outcomes reflect high-quality decisions. This is well documented in the empirical literature on the flow of funds. Since performance persistence of mutual funds is not proven, investing in the last time winners is not a good rule. Moreover, after having lost with a mutual fund, people, based on this negative outcome, are likely to sell their position. Because of basing the investment and disinvestment decision in mutual funds on the recent outcome, investors waste 4% to 6% performance a year, as a study by Dalbar (2011)[9] shows.

To avoid outcome bias, one should analyze the long-term risk and returns of investment opportunities like mutual funds and use this information in subsequent decisions. Other interventions eliminating the uncertainty in the quality of decisions can be helpful as well (Bachmann, 2017).

## 2.4   ARE MORE HEADS SMARTER THAN ONE?

The previous sections show that individuals exhibit biases in the selection and processing of information. In many cases, however, decisions are made in groups, such as boards of directors deciding about company policy or managers of a fund making decisions about investing.

One possibility is that groups have more resources than individuals. In groups, the errors of individual members can be canceled. Groups can also serve as error-checking systems during interaction. Thus, groups should make fewer mistakes. On the other hand, people might be unknowingly

---

[9]Dalbar Inc. (2011): "Quantitative Analysis of Investor Behavior: Helping Investors change behavior to capture Alpha", Boston, USA.

influenced by the judgments of others so that mistakes are accumulated. Especially under uncertainty, people are more likely to use the judgments of others in forming their own opinion.

The following discussion addresses the question of whether groups are better in overcoming specific biases.

### 2.4.1 Confirmation Bias in Groups

The tendency to seek information that supports prior opinion is observed in groups as well. The more homogenous the members' preference, the stronger is the effect (Schulz-Hardt, Frey, Lüthgens, & Moscovici, 2000). The more group members had chosen the same alternative prior to the group discussion, the more strongly the group preferred supporting information. Only if the group is reasonably balanced on the issue of discussion does the confirmation bias diminish.

### 2.4.2 Representativeness Bias in Groups

When people are asked that an individual belong to a category, base rates are usually neglected. Group discussions do not always help. For descriptions that sound like members of categories, the probability judgments of groups were farther from the base rate than those of individuals (Argote, Devadas, & Melone, 1990). Thus, group discussion appears to amplify the tendency to judge primarily by representativeness when the individuating information is informative. Conversely, on the problem where the description did not sound like a member of a category, the estimates of groups were closer to the base rate than those of individuals. Thus, it seems that the probability estimates of groups will be more biased than individuals for cases where the individuating information is informative and less biased than individuals when the individuating information is uninformative.

### 2.4.3 Overconfidence in Groups

Although groups usually have more information than individuals, the process of group discussion does not always lead to an efficient use of information. Even if one of the individuals can play the "devil's advocate" and group members are asked to consider reasons why their estimates might be wrong, the interacting group does not show a lower overconfidence than individuals although participants had the impressions that group judgments were superior to individual judgment (Plous, 1995). One reason might be the *group polarization effect*. This is the tendency for group discussion to amplify the inclinations of group members. In most studies, participants are given a questionnaire in which they had to choose between a risky or conservative choice of action. Afterward, participants discuss the questions in groups and reach a consensus on what level of risk to take. The results are quite consistent—that is, group discussions usually lead people to take riskier actions than they would otherwise. When the initial inclination is toward caution, group discussions lead to a shift toward caution.

### 2.4.4 Gender Composition of Groups

Based on psychological research suggesting that, in finance, men are more overconfident than women, Barber & Odean (2001) find that male investors trade more than female investors but these trades do not pay out. So, what does this evidence mean for the performance of investment teams? Does the gender composition of the team matter for the performance? The empirical evidence suggest that it does but not in the way that one would expect. If female investors perform better because they are less overconfident, then one would expect to see a better performance of teams with mixed genders than in teams with only male investors. However, an empirical study analyzing the investment performance of management teams from the US mutual fund industry finds that gender diversity is negatively related to fund performance (Bär, Niessen, & Ruenzi, 2007). Similarly, another empirical study finds that mixed hedge fund teams underperform both female- and male-only managed hedge funds (Aggarwal & Boyson, 2016).

To explore the reasons for this counterintuitive result, Bogan, Just, & Dev (2013) designed an experiment where participants were asked to make investment decisions, which were very similar to the investment decisions that fund managers make. In their experiment, male participants took more risks than female participants, which is consistent with previous studies. However, all-male teams were not the most risk seeking: mixed teams with a majority male or a balanced gender composition were more willing to take risks than all-male teams. Hence, the underperformance of mixed teams could be linked to an excessive risk taking.

## 2.5 SUMMARY OF BIASES

This chapter outlines the main behavioral biases known so far, discusses implications for decision makers, and suggests strategies that can improve decisions. Table 1 provides a summary.

**TABLE 1**   Behavioral biases, consequences for investors, and suggested interventions

| Behavioral Bias | Consequences for Investors | Suggested Moderation |
|---|---|---|
| *Attention bias:* the involvement with a specific task determines which information is considered and which is not. | Information that turns out to be relevant is neglected. | Decide in advance which information must be considered. |
| *Experience-based perception:* information is not perceived because it is incongruent with previous experience. | Experience with certain decision models may hinder investors from thinking transversally. | Clarify why you see things this way; what expectations did you bring into the situation; why do the others do not share your view? |
| *Confirmation bias:* people search for information that confirms their beliefs or hypothesis. | Previous decisions influence which information is considered and how it is interpreted | Seek discussion with people holding the opposite opinion; think about how you would decide in the face of the new information if you need to decide again today. |
| *Availability bias:* information that is easily "available" in the memory is perceived as more common. | Investors buy attention-grabbing stocks but the latter do not perform better than similar investments. | Compare explicitly over- and underestimated dangers with evidence for the opposite view. |
| *Representativeness bias:* in judgments, people rely on the degree by which their observations represent known characteristics: (1) mistakenly expect that small samples "look" the same as large samples (2) rely on stereotypes in judgements and ignore base rates | Investors may become too optimistic after a short sequence of positive returns. | Employ statistical methods. |

**TABLE 1** (*Continued*)

| Behavioral Bias | Consequences for Investors | Suggested Moderation |
| --- | --- | --- |
| *Conservatism*: people overweight base rates and ignore new information. | Asset prices are positively correlated over time. | Employ statistical methods to update beliefs. |
| *Gambler's fallacy*: people believe that a random process is self-correcting. | Underestimation of long sequences with the same outcome. The premature belief in trend reversals motivates selling winners too soon. | Employ statistical methods. |
| *Hot-hand bias*: there is a misperception of randomness where people see patterns in random sequences. | Believe in the existence of skills even if the outcome can be only random. Engage in active trading even though any success can be considered as a pure chance. | Employ statistical tests. |
| *Anchoring*: arbitrary values influence judgments. | Estimates are biased toward the anchor. People fail to anticipate the possibility for dramatic changes. | Generate reasons that are inconsistent with the anchor, i.e., arguments against the expected outcome (consider-the-opposite strategy). |
| *Framing*: alternative descriptions of a problem give rise to different preferences. | Sensitivity to payoffs framed as gains and losses; sensitivity to the number of alternatives. | Adopt a broader frame. Consider using warnings. |
| *Overconfidence*: excessive confidence in the own skills leads to poor decisions. | Underestimate the risk of being wrong. Excessive trading, i.e., trading that do not generate additional returns | Think about reasons against a decision. Keep track on unsuccessful decisions. |
| *Present bias*: choice reversal takes place when payoff is now and not later. | Procrastination of planned actions | Commitment before the actual decision must be taken. |

(*continues*)

**TABLE 1**  (*Continued*)

| Behavioral Bias | Consequences for Investors | Suggested Moderation |
| --- | --- | --- |
| *Probability weighting:* rare events are overweighed and more common events are underweighted. | Pay for lottery tickets or insure rare risks. | Show the long-term consequences. |
| *Myopic loss aversion:* frame an inter-temporal investment decision as a sequence of independent one-period problems. | Abandon a strategy because of short-term losses. | Adopt a broader frame in line with the investment goal. |
| *Mental accounting:* analyze problems in isolated fashion. | Use mental accounts to sort assets while neglecting the correlation among them. | Use one account if the correlation among the assets needs to be considered. |
| *Disposition effect:* use mental accounts to separate paper gains and losses from realized gains and losses. | Hold losing assets too long and sell winning stocks too early. | Use stop-loss strategies. Check whether the initial reason for investing is still valid. |
| *Affinity:* make investment choices based on your values and not on economic rationale. | Home bias: invest in assets in the home country. | Compare the performance of portfolios influenced by affinity with the performance of neutral portfolios. |
| *Regret aversion:* negative emotion that we experience when realizing or imagining that our present situation would have been better, had we acted differently. | Investment decisions minimize the emotional burden of regret potentially lowers individual investors' economic welfare by reducing their motivation to move to more suitable investments. People make expectations that justify previous decisions. | Follow a strategy that is defined at the beginning of the investment. |

**TABLE 1** *(Continued)*

| Behavioral Bias | Consequences for Investors | Suggested Moderation |
| --- | --- | --- |
| *Hindsight bias:* people often believe that one should have been able to anticipate events much better than was the case. | People consistently exaggerate what could have been anticipated in foresight. | Argue against the inevitability of the reported outcomes, i.e., trying to convince oneself that it might have turned out otherwise. |
| *Self-attribution bias:* success is attributed to one's own efforts, failure to bad luck. | Attribute those decisions that worked out successfully to their own skills while they blame their advisor for the loosing investments. | Document decisions. |
| *Outcome bias:* use the outcome of decisions to evaluate the quality of decisions. | Switch to managers with the better recent performance. | Analyze long-term risks and returns and use them in subsequent decisions. Use interventions that eliminate the uncertainty in the quality of decisions. |

## 2.6   CONCLUSION

Investors face many pitfalls when they deal with information, and the resulting investment mistakes can be costly. Some of these mistakes are likely to last, as investors find it difficult to learn from them. Moreover, using the intelligence of other individuals and deciding in a team could even reinforce the mistakes that individuals do. On the other hand, there is evidence that certain measures could be helpful in reducing some biases. Hence, the way to good investment decision making goes through identifying the mistakes that one does and selecting measures that address them properly. Chapter 5 provides an example of how these tasks can be accomplished. The following two chapters show that the behavior observed in experiments has a cultural dimension and a biological foundation. This is important for understanding that the distribution of attitudes and mistakes is not uniform across different entities and some mistakes might be more difficult to moderate than others.

# CHAPTER 3

# Cultural Differences in Investors' Behavior

**O**ne branch of behavioral finance has developed in the realm of cultural research. It shows how behavior patterns differ in the cultures familiar to us. Cultural finance provides an essential foundation for globally active banks, and for a good reason. Despite advancing globalization, we can still identify some significant cultural differences around the world. Around 5,000 languages are spoken worldwide, eating habits vary from region to region, and there are some differences in our social conventions that we should know before crossing the globe. However, traditional finance barely acknowledges international cultural diversity. It is based on the premise that money is the great equalizer. Nowadays, investors can trade (nearly) any security they want just by pressing a few computer keys.

Traditional finance also dictates that in the end, we all want the same thing: to achieve high returns without taking on too much risk. For some 20 years, researchers in behavioral finance have been trying to determine whether finance is indeed subject to cultural differences. Even if we assume that investors around the globe are focused on the return/risk trade-off, researchers believe that culture can influence investors differently in terms of the type of investments, investment time horizons, and risk aversion. Ultimately, behavioral finance shows that while there is only one way to act rationally, there are many ways of acting irrationally. Thus, it would not be far-fetched to say that our culture helps determine which psychological pitfalls we are more likely to succumb to. In this chapter, we will show the fascinating cultural differences in investment behavior.

## 3.1   WHAT IS FINANCIAL CULTURE?

In the broadest sense, culture is everything that people create. Looking at the world's artistic treasures is an excellent way to identify the cultural differences that existed, and may continue to exist, in various regions of the globe.

The question is how to measure culture and make a numeric correlation to something as mundane as investment behavior and market returns. Because investment behavior is also part of our social behavior, we can take a cue from the cultural dimensions identified by Dutch sociologist Geert Hofstede. He found that our social behavior can best be described using the following five dimensions:

- The *Power Distance Index* (PDI) measures how hierarchical a society is.
- *Individualism* (IDV) measures whether a society rewards individualistic or collective behavior.
- *Masculinity* (MAS) measures the different roles women and men have in a society.
- *Uncertainty avoidance* (UAI) measures whether a society is adventures or avoids unknown situations.
- *Long-term orientation* (LTO) measures the importance of history and traditions in a society.

To give an example for the distribution of these dimensions, consider the countries in the two extremes of each dimension in Table 2.[1]

Subsequent studies find that individualism is positively related to the trading activities on the financial market—that is, individualism can be used as a proxy of overconfidence, which can explain differences in asset prices (Chui, Titman, & Wei, 2010). Using direct measures of the heuristics that investors use, other studies show there are significant cultural difference in the degree of overconfidence (Acker & Duck, 2008), in the tendency to rely on stereotypes in probability judgments (Spina et al., 2010), and also in the way people respond to different representation of information (Levinson & Peng, 2007).

**TABLE 2**   Countries with extreme values of Hofstede's cultural dimension scales

|       | Extremely Low Levels | Extremely High Levels |
|-------|----------------------|-----------------------|
| PDI   | Austria              | Malaysia              |
| IDV   | Colombia             | United States         |
| MAS   | Norway               | Japan                 |
| UAI   | Denmark              | Greece                |
| LTO   | Czech Rep.           | China                 |

*Source*: Hofstede (2001)

---

[1]Source: http://geert-hofstede.com/ shows an interactive map of cultural differences.

## 3.2  THE INTRA STUDY

A larger study (International Test of Risk Attitudes, INTRA) including 50 countries and nearly 7,000 respondents extends the previous analyses to a broader range of characteristics describing investors' behavior (Wang, Rieger, & Hens, 2016b, 2016a). These characteristics include loss aversion, patience, and probability weighting. The following questions from INTRA measure these characteristics[2]:

- *Loss aversion:* "Suppose there is a lottery with 50:50 chance to lose $100 or gain something. What is the minimum gain that you would require so that you would be willing to play this lottery?"
- *Patience:* "Which alternative would you choose: $3,000 today or $3,300 next month?"
- *Probability weighting with gains:* "What would you prefer: A sure payment of $2,000 or a lottery with a 1% chance of gaining 100,000?"
- *Probability weighting with losses:* "What would you prefer: A sure loss of $2,000 or a lottery with a 1% chance of losing 100,000?"

The results suggest the existence of interesting patterns. With respect to loss aversion, the results illustrated in Figure 3.04 show that people from

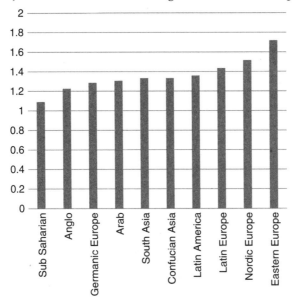

**FIGURE 3.04**  Loss aversion

---

[2]The numbers in these questions are those of the survey used in the US. For other countries they were adjusted to the local currency and the local level of income.

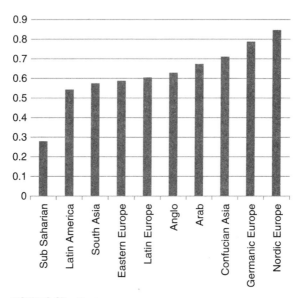

**FIGURE 3.05**   Patience

Eastern Europe require $170 to play a lottery in which they may lose $100, while people from the Anglo-Saxon countries, for example, would play this lottery even when they could win only $120.

With respect to the patience, the results suggest that investors in Nordic and German-speaking Europe are the most patient, while African investors (from the Sub Saharian countries Angola, Nigeria and Tanzania) are the least patient. This can be seen in Figure 3.05. The figure shows the percentage of people willing to wait for the 10% higher return next month. While almost all people from northern European countries would wait, only 28% of the African investors show the same degree of patience. The highest level of impatience is observed in Nigeria, where only 8% of the investors would wait for a 10% monthly return.

Regarding the country differences in probability weighting, the results suggest that in most countries there is a tendency to take unlikely events too seriously—whether they are largely positive or largely negative. In the first case, fantasies about what people could do with an extremely positive outcome are so tempting that these people fail to realize how unlikely they are to win. In the second case, anxiety about an event with a very negative outcome is so worrisome that people fail to realize how unlikely this is as well. The results are reported in Figures 3.06 and 3.07. The figures report proxies for the percentage of people in a country to accept lotteries with large but unlikely gains and losses, respectively.[3]

---

[3]Referring forward to prospect theory presented in Chapter 6 the numbers are 1 minus the parameters of probability weighting in gains and in losses, respectively, $\alpha^+$ and $\alpha^-$.

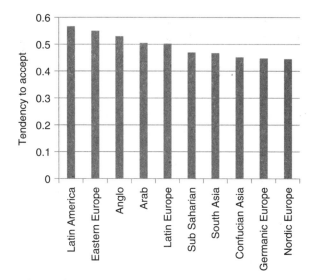

**FIGURE 3.06** Probability weighting with large unlikely gains

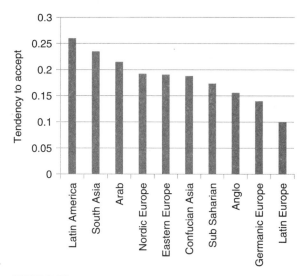

**FIGURE 3.07** Probability weighting with large unlikely losses

These interesting findings indicate that there are profound differences in investors' behavior across countries. Moreover, these differences can be better explained by Hofstede's cultural measures than by economic variables (Wang et al., 2016a). For example, people in collectivistic cultures show a greater ability to cope with losses because they receive more social support than people in individualistic societies. Countries with a higher PDI index are more unequal so that the average citizen is more pessimistic about the consequences of losses and consequently show a greater loss aversion. Countries with higher values of MAS tend to set the reference point high and consequently show a greater sensitivity to losses. It is an open question whether, as globalization continues, these differences would decline in the way that our differences in language, eating habits, and social customs have declined.

## 3.3  CONCLUSION

In traditional finance, behavioral biases have no meaning since there is only one way to invest. This narrow view got challenged by behavioral finance, which discovered a huge variety of deviations from rational behavior. This chapter shows that these deviations from rationality can be traced back to cultural differences. Even though we live in a global world and can access the Internet from all countries, we still have different cultures that determine the way we make financial decisions. Similarly, different cultures are prone to different biases. This is important knowledge for advisors of globally active banks.

CHAPTER **4**

# Neurological Foundations and Biases' Moderation

In Chapter 3, we saw that financial decision behavior has a cultural dimension. Now, we want to find out whether some drivers are easier to moderate than others. The insights from *neurofinance* could help us develop concepts for avoiding investment mistakes, as we will show in the next chapter.

Neurofinance is based on findings from brain research. In recent years, this knowledge has been available due to major technological advances, and is now ready to be applied in finance.

When the human brain began its complex development, simple neural networks were created. From there on, our brain continued to develop over millions of years. Our ancestors spent most of their time fighting for survival—foraging for food, reproducing, and avoiding natural enemies. Only about 3000 years ago we began using our brain for financial decisions as well. Therefore, it is not surprising that investors (professionals and amateur investors alike) systematically deviate from rational decision-making behavior.

## 4.1 THE HUMAN BRAIN

To understand neurofinance and its reasoning, we must first take a brief look at the neurosciences. The human brain consists of different parts, as illustrated in Figure 4.08. The oldest part, the inner core of the brain, is the stem. The brain stem controls key bodily functions such as circulation, respiration, and digestion. The next part that developed was the limbic system, responsible for our senses (in the thalamus) and also includes such instincts as survival and reproduction (in the hypothalamus), as well as emotions such as fears (in the anterior insula and the amygdala) (Kuhnen & Knutson, 2005). Not surprisingly, this part of our brain plays a large part in intuition. Three-quarters of the human brain consists of the cerebral cortex. What distinguishes humans from other species is the prefrontal cortex, its role in reasoning, short-term and long-term memory, as well as learning, planning, and self-control.

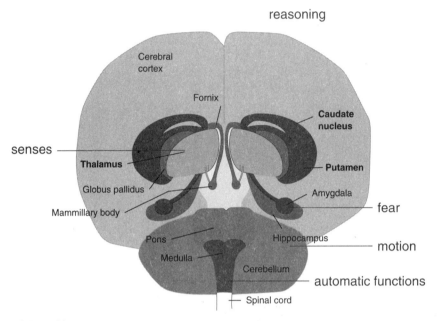

**FIGURE 4.08**　The human brain

Of critical importance is that the "older" parts of the brain have not changed much over the course of evolution. Instead, new parts have developed, such as the telencephalon, which oversees additional functions including planning and social conduct. When we must make decisions, our limbic system and telencephalon are activated. Intuition and emotions meet cognition. These systems do not always act in unison and emotions often get the upper hand, as best seen by measuring psychological and neuronal activity.

## 4.2　INSIGHTS FOR BEHAVIORAL FINANCE

To understand investment behavior, it is important to ask: How does our brain respond to gains and losses? How about risks? What about instant versus long-term gains, losses, and risks? Can our brain assess gains, losses, and risks correctly? Our neurons send signals to reveal an emotionally charged assessment of returns and risks. For instance, gains and losses sometimes affect different parts of the brain. Some of these parts, such as the striatum and the amygdala, clearly come from the limbic system and not from our rational prefrontal cortex. Thus, a clear separation of gains and losses is more natural than the concept of mean-variance analysis, which assumes that investors can find a balance on the expected return-variance trade-off.

When we talk about "a painful financial loss," we're not exaggerating. Financial losses are processed by parts of the brain responsible for the pain network. One of these areas is the amygdala. Patients with a damaged amygdala are not afraid of loss and often take high financial risks that they shouldn't. Neurofinance suggests that loss aversion is a hard-wired bias of investors (Tom, Fox, Trepel, & Poldrack, 2007) that should be taken more serious than, for example, framing effects. Similarly, the present bias has neurological reasons as well. The urge to get immediate gratification is caused by activation in the ventral striatum (Hariri et al., 2006), in particular in the nucleus accumbency—the pleasure center of the brain. On the other hand, biases related to probabilities have been related to activity in medial prefrontal cortex (Knutson, Taylor, Kaufman, Peterson, & Glover, 2005). This is a relatively new area of the brain, in which the reasoning is located. That distinguishes human beings from many animals.[1]

## 4.3 MODERATION OF BIASES

The observation that mistakes occur when different parts of the brain are more active than others is particularly helpful for designing measures that should help to overcome the mistakes. Since different parts of the brain control different processes, one could distinguish between mistakes that result under the influence of emotions and mistakes that occur due to a failure of cognitive processes. While both kinds of mistakes have biological origins, their moderation will probably require a different measure as their biological origins differ. Reasoning, for example, as one moderation technique, is more likely to be successful when moderating cognitive biases than in the moderation of emotionally driven mistakes.

To provide insights on the design of moderation techniques, Table 3 categorizes the biases discussed in Chapter 2 as cognitive or emotional. Cognitive biases could be moderated by educational measures (e.g., training). Emotional biases are more difficult to moderate. In some cases, the delegation of responsibility for the decisions can help to mitigate the mistakes. Another way to mitigate emotional biases is to separate decisions and outcomes—that is, by committing today to act in a certain way in the future.

---

[1] We have outlined the very basics of neurofinance. A good reference on neurofinance written for practitioners is the book of Peterson (2007): "Inside the Investor's Brain: The Power of Mind Over Money."

**TABLE 3** Cognitive and emotional biases

| Cognitive Biases | Emotional Biases |
|---|---|
| attention bias (see Section 2.1.1) | overconfidence (see Section 2.2.7) |
| selective perception bias (see Section 2.1.2) | present bias (see Section 2.2.8) |
| | loss aversion (see Section 2.2.10) |
| confirmation bias (see Section 2.1.3) | mental accounting (see Section 2.2.11) |
| availability bias (see Section 2.1.4) | myopic loss aversion (see Section 2.2.12) |
| representativeness bias, conjunction fallacy, | |
| | disposition effect (see Section 2.2.14) |
| base rate fallacy (see Section 2.2.1) | affinity (see Section 2.2.15) |
| conservatism bias (see Section 2.2.2) | regret aversion (see Section 2.2.16) |
| gambler's fallacy (see Section 2.2.3) | self-attribution bias (see Section 2.3.2) |
| hot-hand bias (see 2.2.4) | |
| anchoring (see Section 2.2.5) | |
| framing (see Section 2.2.6) | |
| probability weighting (see Section 2.2.9) | |
| hindsight bias (see Section 2.3.1) | |
| outcome bias (see Section 2.3.3) | |

## 4.4 CONCLUSION

Neurofinance gives important foundations for behavioral biases. Even though at this point, only a few biases can be traced back to the brain, we already know that reward and risk are experienced in different parts of the brain and that loss aversion and the present bias may have neurological reasons. This suggests that these properties of investors' behavior are unlikely to disappear and should be taken into consideration.

Therefore, it is essential to distinguish between characteristics that lead to irrational decisions and those that do not. While it is obvious that, for example, the present bias is a bias because it leads to a time-preference reversal, it is unclear whether loss aversion, for example, is irrational. In combination with the present bias, it leads to myopic loss aversion, which results in missing out long-term gains due to short-term pain. However, seen in isolation, loss aversion may be the right measure of an investor's aversion to risk—certainly measuring it better than an aversion to volatility.

After identifying characteristics that lead to irrational decisions, one can think about their moderation. The biological origins of the characteristics driving the irrational decisions provide insights on the question of which measures are more likely to work.

# CHAPTER 5

# Diagnostic Tests for Investment Personality

Systematically wrong decisions can result from the influence of at least four factors: limited financial knowledge, untypical investment experience, and psychological and emotional factors. In the following, we briefly discuss the importance of these factors and we show how advisors can elicit the factors' potential impact on the clients' investment mistakes. The latter can be used as a basis for the structure of the clients' portfolios and for the optimal degree of delegation of responsibilities along the investment process.

## 5.1   A CASE STUDY

Fritz Müller is desperate. Again, he lost more than half of his wealth with investments in stocks. During the summer 2009, he closely followed the media's sensational coverage of the dramatic rescue of UBS. He and his friends talked about it when they met up for coffee or an after-work drink. As a result, he bought shares of Credit Suisse and UBS at a price of 50 CHF, respectively, 20 CHF because he was convinced that after the financial crisis 2007–2008 they had reached the absolute bottom (Credit Suisse depreciated from 75 CHF to 25 CHF and UBS from 80 CHF to 20 CHF) and then he wanted to pick the nice rebound to come. But then came the summer 2011 in which the crisis of the euro turned into a tragedy. Even though Credit Suisse and UBS are Swiss banks their share prices were drawn into the dramatic sell-off of financial stocks in Europe: Credit Suisse shares fell to 20 CHF while UBS shares fell to 10 CHF.

Checking the behavioral biases from the previous chapter, we can see that many things have gone wrong for/with Fritz Müller. For example, his main sources of information were general media and discussions with friends. He invested with a strong home bias, he holds an underdiversified portfolio of stocks—and no bonds, commodities, or other assets. Fritz Müller tried to time the market since he was convinced that the rebound would continue, and finally, he underestimated the short-term risk in stocks.

The point of this chapter is to develop methods for detecting whether those biases are occasional mistakes or the results of general misperceptions of the investor. To do so, we show how a questionnaire can assess the financial knowledge and the psychological and emotional biases of an investor. At the end, the respondents receive a thoughtful diagnostic of their strengths and weaknesses as investors, which the client advisor could use as a starting point for potential investment improvements.

## 5.2  DESIGN OF DIAGNOSTIC QUESTIONNAIRES

Diagnosing the investors' behavioral biases is the first step in moderating them. Here we will suggest two methods: a commonly used method in psychology called *psychometrics* and a scoring method.

The psychometric methodology aims at measuring psychological aspects such as knowledge, abilities, attitudes, or personal traits. The information is normally collected with a questionnaire that asks similar questions multiple times. The difficulty of creating a questionnaire is in asking the right questions to gather necessary and useful information while fulfilling principles of reliability[1], validity[2], and standardization. The use of a psychometric questionnaire has the advantage that the questionnaire is standardized and therefore easy to administrate. The evaluation of the results is usually conducted with a scoring method. The answers to each question are given a certain score, and these scores are added for a total score. The total score can then be mapped to risk profiles, which can be linked to a general investment strategy. Of course, the scoring cannot account for nonlinear dependencies between different questions, which might well lead to considerable inaccuracies. If not combined with other methodologies, the psychometric approach does not provide sufficient information about the client. The questionnaire might also be perceived as too "psychological." A famous example for the psychometric method is the DOSPERT scale of Weber, Blais, & Betz (2002). DOSPERT (DOmain-SPEcific Risk-Taking) assesses risk taking in five content domains: financial (for investing and gambling separately), health/safety, recreational, ethical, and social domain. First, the authors tested many questions (101 items) on a large sample of people in the United States. After a careful calibration of questions, the final questionnaire consists of 40 questions while each dimension (domain) contains 4 to 8 questions. All questions are easy to understand and no specific knowledge is required. In 2006, a

---

[1]The reliability refers to the consistency of the suggested questions with the variable subject to a measurement.
[2]Validity refers to the quality of measuring what one aims to measure.

revised version with only 30 questions was published (Blais & Weber, 2006). Both versions can be downloaded from the website: www.dospert.org.

The diagnostic questionnaire that we suggest is defined along the dimensions *financial knowledge* and *emotionality*. The financial knowledge dimension aims to evaluate clients' familiarity with some basic empirical facts—that is, return characteristics of asset classes, diversification potential of portfolios, and the drivers of investment performance. The emotional dimension aims to evaluate clients' affinity to commit some common investment mistakes under the influence of psychological and emotional factors.

The questions can be answered on paper and the advisor can use the questions to address decision mistakes. Alternatively, advisors could make use of an interactive tool with the advantage that the consequences of biased investment decisions can be demonstrated in more detail and in different scenarios.

Overall, the questions aim to facilitate a dialog between the advisor and the client on some common investment mistakes. The results of the diagnostic test can be used in the discussion of the structure of the investor's portfolio and the degree of delegation that the client is willing to accept. This is particularly important for clients inclined to commit investment mistakes under the influence of psychological and emotional factors, as this influence often goes unnoticed by the client.

## 5.3 KNOWLEDGE AND INVESTMENT EXPERIENCE

### 5.3.1 Relative Returns of Assets Classes

In the past, some asset classes have proved to have a larger return potential than others. The following question helps to determine the client's perception of the returns and how it complies with the past.

Please sort the various asset classes by their historical long-run return potential:

- Commodities
- Hedge funds
- Real estate funds
- Bonds
- Stocks
- Saving account

The question can be illustrated graphically as in Figure 5.09. The client is asked to drag the names of asset classes and place them on curves with

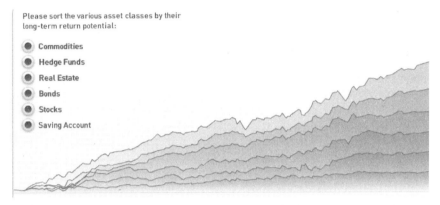

**FIGURE 5.09** Assessing the long-term returns potential of asset classes
*Source*: BhFS Behavioral Finance Solutions

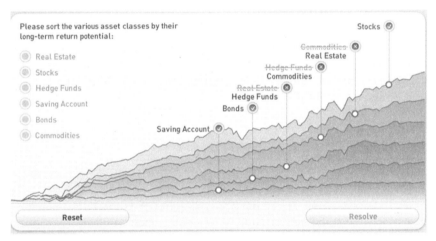

**FIGURE 5.10** The long-term return potential of asset classes as seen by Fritz Müller
*Source*: BhFS Behavioral Finance Solutions

different return potential. The curves go through different market phases and aim to help the client to gain a long-run perspective when answering the question. Figure 5.10 shows the answers of Fritz Müller.

Historically, the largest benefits have been derived from well-diversified stocks and real estate investments while bonds and the savings account did not fare as well. Fritz Müller has a slightly different perception of the historical return potential of the asset classes. He knows that in the long-run stocks do best and that bonds and the saving account have the smallest return; however, he thinks too highly of commodities. This may be, for example, because Fritz Müller remembered too much the recent past in which gold (one commodity) reached all-time highs during the financial crisis.

### 5.3.2 Short-Term Loss Potential of Asset Classes

Independent of client's understanding of risk, in the past some asset classes must be considered as riskier in the short-term than others. The following question helps to evaluate client's perception on the short-term risks and how it complies with the past.

Please sort the various asset classes by their historical short-run loss potential:

- Hedge funds
- Stocks
- Bonds
- Saving account
- Real estate funds
- Commodities

The graphical representation in Figure 5.11 is helpful to shape client's view on the meaning of short-term low and high losses.

Historically, the largest losses in the short-term could have been realized with stocks and commodities. If the client has a different perception of the short-term risk potential of the asset classes, it could be because of a lack of knowledge respectively investment experience, or because the risk

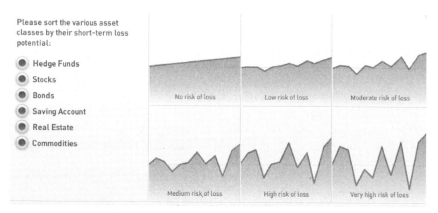

**FIGURE 5.11** Assessing the short-term risk potential of asset classes
*Source*: BhFS Behavioral Finance Solutions

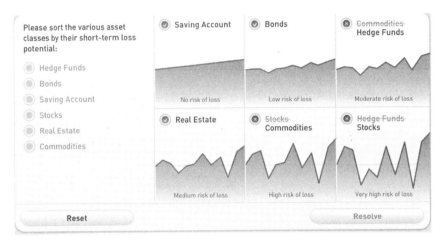

**FIGURE 5.12** The short-term risk potential as seen by Fritz Müller
*Source*: BhFS Behavioral Finance Solutions

perception is affected by the recent past. Wrong assessment of the risk potential in the short-run can be expected with inexperienced clients who did not yet go through different market cycles. Fritz Müller has answered as illustrated in Figure 5.12.

He got it right that the saving account and bonds are least risky, but he slightly underestimated the loss potential of stocks and was not totally right with respect to hedge funds and commodities.

### 5.3.3  Contribution to Investment Performance

The success factors of investment are best evaluated empirically. Ibbotson and Kaplan (2000), for example, show that up to 90% of the investment success can be tracked back to the long-run allocation of wealth in different asset classes. Stock-picking and tactical allocations play a less important role. The following question tests whether the client is aware of this fact.

Please put these factors in order according to their contribution to investment results:

- Product selection (the selection of products within each asset class)
- Market timing (the short-term overweighting and underweighting of asset classes)
- Investment strategy (the long-term assignment of wealth to asset classes)

Assigning numbers to the corresponding contributions as shown in Figure 5.13 makes the question more precise.

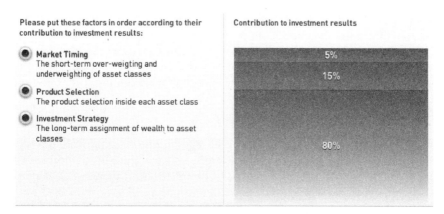

**FIGURE 5.13** Assessing the client's view on the performance contributors
*Source*: BhFS Behavioral Finance Solutions

If the client is not aware of the relevance of long-term diversification, it is likely that the judgment is affected by availability and representativeness biases. Market timing and product selection can be chosen because people easily keep in mind the success stories of portfolio managers beating the market (see availability bias, Section 2.1.4) and confuse it with long-term investment success (belief in hot hands; see Section 2.24).

Fritz Müller has answered the question on the performance contributors as in Figure 5.14.

**FIGURE 5.14** The performance contributors as seen by Fritz Müller
*Source*: BhFS Behavioral Finance Solutions

As can be seen, Fritz Müller is totally wrong in this respect. He really believes that market timing is more important than product selection and the investment strategy. Thus, his attempt to time the movements of Credit Suisse and UBS was the result of not being aware of the importance of a well-diversified investment strategy relative to market timing.

### 5.3.4 Diversification of Equity Portfolios

There's an old saying, "Don't put all your eggs in one basket." And indeed, the same holds true for stocks. The more stocks there are in the portfolio, the better is the diversification. However, after adding a certain number of stocks, the risk of the portfolio can no longer be significantly reduced but one has still to pay transactions and holding costs. Depending on the composition of the portfolio, a well-diversified portfolio should consist of at least 10 but not more than 20 titles.

With the following question, advisors can test whether the client tends to focus on some (probably well-known) titles or to overestimate the diversification potential and tend to pay too many fees.

How many securities do you think are needed to get a well-diversified equity portfolio?

- Less than 5
- 5–10
- 10–20
- More than 20

Alternatively, the client may decide by using a slider that adds curves into the picture according to the number of titles chosen (see Figure 5.15).

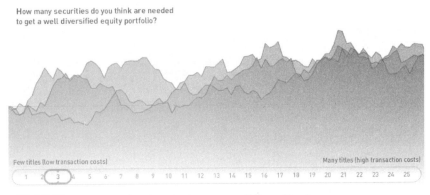

How many securities do you think are needed
to get a well diversified equity portfolio?

Few titles (low transaction costs)                    Many titles (high transaction costs)

1  2  3  4  5  6  7  8  9  10  11  12  13  14  15  16  17  18  19  20  21  22  23  24  25

**FIGURE 5.15**  Assessing the client's view on good diversification
*Source*: BhFS Behavioral Finance Solutions

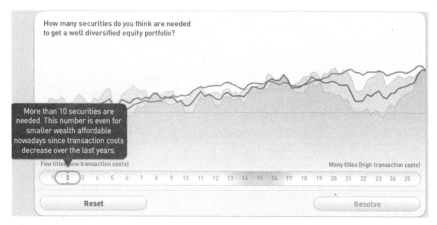

**FIGURE 5.16** Good diversification from Fritz Müller's point of view
*Source*: BhFS Behavioral Finance Solutions

Fritz Müller is convinced that two assets are enough to diversify. The tool gives him the following feedback (see Figure 5.16). It shows how volatile a portfolio with just two assets would be as compared to a well-diversified portfolio with 15 assets.

## 5.4 PSYCHOLOGY AND EMOTIONS

### 5.4.1 Attractiveness of High Returns

According to prospect theory, people tend to overweight unlikely events and underweight common events (see Section 6.2. in Chapter 6, "Decision Theory"). Since unlikely events are usually associated with extreme payoffs, we may conclude that people care more about the payment when it is high and more about the chances when the payment is average. For example, advisors may ask the following question.

Suppose you want to invest a substantial part of your wealth in one of the following short-term investments, A or B. Which one would you choose?

- Investment A returns 10% in 50 out of 100 cases.
- Investment B returns 50% in 10 out of 100 cases.
- Both investments are equally attractive to me.

The investment alternatives can be illustrated as in Figure 5.17.

As the risk preferences of the client are unknown, we assume that for positive payments they are not risk seeking. If the investor is indifferent between the investment alternatives, we may conclude that he is

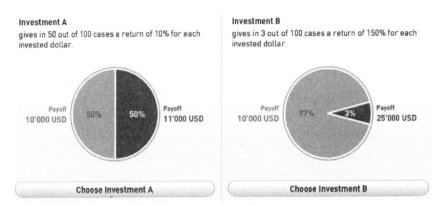

**FIGURE 5.17**   Assessment of client's focus on payoffs and probabilities
*Source*: BhFS Behavioral Finance Solutions

risk-neutral, as both alternatives have almost the same expected value. Risk-averse investors who choose investment B overweight the probability for gaining a return of 50%. Risk-averse investors, who pay equal attention to payoffs and chances, would choose Investment A.

Fritz Müller got this aspect of investing right and gets a positive feedback (see Figure 5.18).

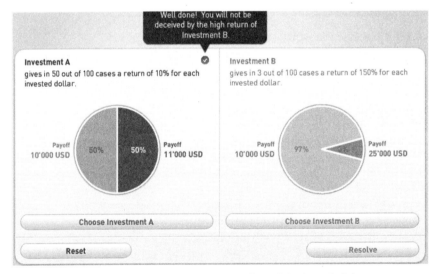

**FIGURE 5.18**   Fritz Müller's preference for payoffs with high probability
*Source*: BhFS Behavioral Finance Solutions

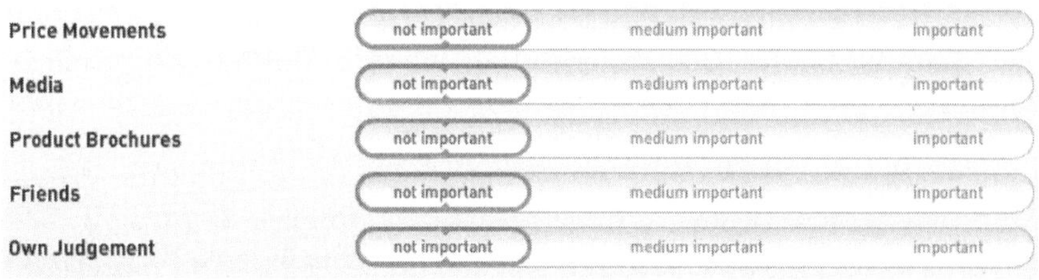

| Price Movements | not important | medium important | important |
| --- | --- | --- | --- |
| Media | not important | medium important | important |
| Product Brochures | not important | medium important | important |
| Friends | not important | medium important | important |
| Own Judgement | not important | medium important | important |

**FIGURE 5.19** Assessing client's view on the importance of different information sources
*Source*: BhFS Behavioral Finance Solutions

## 5.4.2 Relevance of Information Sources

To make an investment decision, investors must consider a lot of information at the same time. As humans have a limited capacity of absorbing and processing of information, they must weigh the relevance of the information sources. The more a specific source of information is appreciated, the higher the probability that certain heuristics will be used, which will favor misinterpretation.

How important are the following sources of information for your investment decisions on a scale of 1 (not important) to 3 (important)?

- Price movements
- Media
- Product brochures
- Friends
- Own judgment

An alternative illustration of the question is given in Figure 5.19.

If a client considers price movements as very important, the client must be warned for the following reasons. First, for nonexperts in statistics, analyzing price movements can be dangerous because it may cause an illusion of predictability (see representativeness bias, Section 2.2.1). Investors may build expectations on factors that have no predictive power. Additionally, investors may not be able to free their expectations from the recent price movement as an anchor (see anchoring bias, Section 2.2.5). If the prices were falling, the investors considering price movements as very important would adjust their expectations downward, but often insufficiently due to the anchoring effect. Consequently, they might not be prepared for extreme negative scenarios.

Media reports can be important sources of information, but investors should not overweight them since they are often lopsided (especially negative events) and do not adequately represent the facts.

Product brochures should be considered as marketing materials since their main goal is to attract an investor's interest. They are not meant to explain all the details, which is in many cases important for investors to judge the attractiveness of the products.

Trusting investment ideas and recommendations from friends can be dangerous because friends, as other people, tend to remember mainly their successful decisions. However, investment ideas usually hold for a certain period. Following the idea after it has proved successful is often a decision that comes too late.

Making one's own judgments is the best way to make decisions, given that one can make logical conclusions and avoid psychological traps. If this condition does not hold for clients, the advisor may conclude that the clients overestimate their own abilities (see overconfidence, in Section 2.2.7). Typically, overconfident investors underestimate the risks they take. Consequently, they may systematically fail their investment goals because they take more risks than they are psychologically able to bear in inferior scenarios.

Fritz Müller emphasizes too much media, friends, and price movements. So, he gets feedback as illustrated in Figure 5.20.

### 5.4.3  Emotional Trading

One of the biggest investment mistakes is that investors trade without a suitable strategy. A strategy is a plan that should guide investment decisions in the future. It must be defined at the beginning of each investment and should define conditions for increasing holding and liquidating the investments. Investors without a smart investment plan hold the risk to make decisions based on the past instead of being forward-looking. In cases where the future developments do not depend on the past, as in the

**FIGURE 5.20**  The importance of different information sources for Fritz Müller
*Source*: BhFS Behavioral Finance Solutions

case when the market is driven by random events, investing without a smart strategy may lead to emotional decisions that can be successful only by chance.

The following question helps advisors testing whether a client can define a smart strategy in the simplest case where market movements are random.

The market movement of a stock is completely random. You expect the stock price to go up in more than 50% of the cases. How do you decide?

- I buy and hold until I need the money
- I buy and wait until I realize a gain, then I sell and wait for the price to go down to buy again.

An alternative way testing client's behavior on random movements of the market is letting him play an investment game with $10,000 for 10 periods (see Figure 5.21). At the end of each period, the client is invited to hold or sell the asset, respectively, or to invest in the asset. After each decision, the clients see their gain or loss compared to their initial wealth and total return after transactions costs.

Afterward, the clients may compare the performance of their strategies with a buy-and-hold strategy, as illustrated in Figure 5.22.

Fritz Müller waits too long before he invests and gets out too quickly after a loss. If the price is driven by a random walk and on average one expects to make a gain as in our example, the better decision is to buy and hold the investment until the money is needed. Choosing to trade actively to time the market is inferior because the price movements are random. This means that after realizing a gain, there is no reason to sell

**FIGURE 5.21**   Assessing client's behavior on random movements of the market
*Source*: BhFS Behavioral Finance Solutions

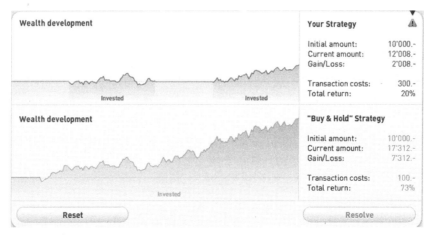

**FIGURE 5.22** The investment behavior of Fritz Müller on random market movements
*Source*: BhFS Behavioral Finance Solutions

and repurchase again, as the probability that the price is continuing to raise or fall is the same as before starting the investment. Price movements that are random are not self-correcting (see gambler's fallacy, Section 2.2.3). The chances for a gain remain the same all the time; they do not increase after the price falls. Hence, there is no reason to wait for falling prices if one wants to hold the asset. Investing actively on a random walk is not only costlier compared to a passive strategy, but also its relative performance is completely random.

### 5.4.4 Selling Decisions

The chosen investment strategy, which was established due to meticulous testing of all essential factors should not be relinquished if there is no danger to do so; and especially not because of random fluctuations or temporally limited developments. The following question helps advisors to test the client's awareness of this principle.

Which factors do you consider when you must decide to sell an investment?

- Suffered loss
- Downward trend
- Big price swings
- Investment reason changed

The options can be illustrated as in Figure 5.23.

Many investors commit the mistake of changing a chosen strategy during a crisis and thereby interfere with their long-term investment success. If the situation has not fundamentally changed, the investor should hold onto the original strategy even in times of a stock market crash.

Choosing to sell after a loss is inferior; the client should better look forward and check whether the investment is still priced fairly. Basing selling decisions on downward trends is not always advantageous, as trends can quickly change direction. If big price swings are considered as a reason to sell, then the advisor should prove whether the strategy matches the client's aversion to losses. Overestimating the loss tolerance of the client is dangerous because it frees emotions to dictate selling decisions.

Fritz Müller decides to sell after losses and gets the feedback as illustrated in Figure 5.24.

## 5.5   CLIENT'S DIAGNOSTIC PROFILE

The client's answers to the questions can be evaluated by using a simple scoring system in the two dimensions, financial knowledge and emotionality. Figure 5.25 gives the result for Fritz Müller: He indeed has a low financial knowledge and strong emotionality. Thus, his investment experience in the years 2009–2011 is not a single untypical event but the result of many systematic biases.

Other investor types can be seen in the background of Fritz Müller's result. For example, the opposite of the intuitive investor is an investor with high financial knowledge and few emotional and psychological biases is

**FIGURE 5.23**   Assessing the drivers of client's selling decisions
*Source*: BhFS Behavioral Finance Solutions

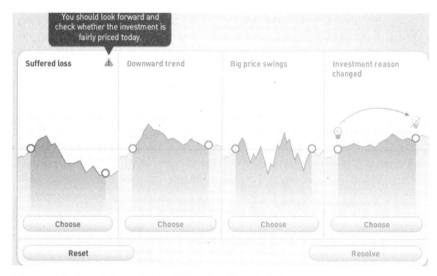

**FIGURE 5.24** The driver of Fritz Müller's selling decisions
*Source*: BhFS Behavioral Finance Solutions

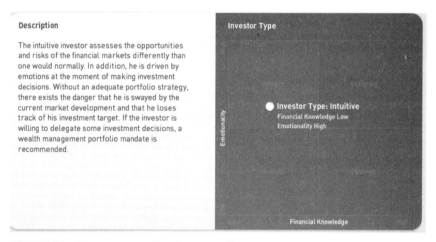

**FIGURE 5.25** Diagnostic profile of Fritz Müller
*Source*: BhFS Behavioral Finance Solutions

the ideal type (i.e., the strategic investor). The description of the strategic investor is given in Figure 5.26.

Moreover, there are the two types with high knowledge and low emotionality, which may be called realistic, and the opposite case with low knowledge and high emotionality may be called exploring. The

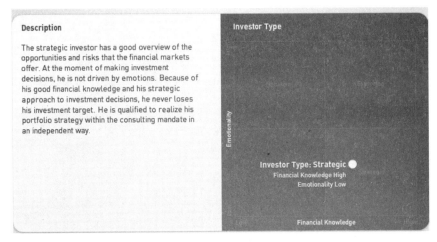

**FIGURE 5.26** Diagnostic profile of a strategic investor
*Source*: BhFS Behavioral Finance Solutions

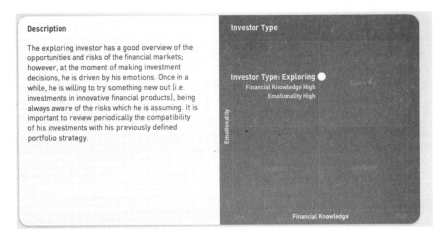

**FIGURE 5.27** Diagnostic profile of an exploring investor
*Source*: BhFS Behavioral Finance Solutions

descriptions of these investors are given in Figures 5.27 and 5.28, respectively.

The advisor may use the client's diagnostic profile to talk about the investment mistakes that the client might commit when making investment decisions. This could be also the basis for a discussion about the structure of the portfolio and the degree of delegation that the client is willing to

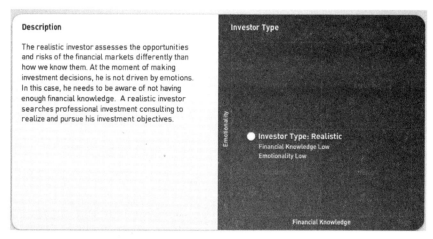

**FIGURE 5.28** Diagnostic profile of a realistic investor
*Source*: BhFS Behavioral Finance Solutions

accept. We suggest the following: An explorative investor should follow a core-satellite strategy, as the core assures that the important goals can be reached and the satellites satisfy the investor's appetite for exploring new ideas and experiences. Since the strategic investor has high financial knowledge and low emotionality, the investor wants sophisticated investment solutions like harvesting risk premium[3] with various investment strategies as well as a tactical overlay strategy and a good-tail risk hedge. The best choice for a realistic investor is a well-diversified EFT that implements the optimal strategic asset allocation at minimal costs. Finally, the advisor should convince intuitive investors to delegate their investment decisions.

---

[3]See Ilmanen (2011) for this approach.

# CHAPTER 6

# Decision Theory

## 6.1 INTRODUCTION

According to a famous study by Ibbotson & Kaplan (2000), the strategic asset allocation (SAA) determines more than 90% of the performance of an investor. This is true, however, only if the investors hold on their asset allocation over the stock market cycle. There is ample evidence that investors depart from the asset allocation recommended to them when they incur losses.[1] Thus, the question arises as to how to tailor an asset allocation that investors do really hold through.

This chapter lays the foundation for computing the SAA of private investors that best suits their investment psychology. It assumes that the returns of assets can be described by the probabilities with which they occur—that is, that we face a *decision under risk*. If this assumption cannot be made, we face a *decision under uncertainty* and it is better to evoke qualitative reasoning rather than doing sophisticated computations.[2]

The most famous psychologically founded decision theory is prospect theory of Kahneman and Tversky (1979). Before we dive into prospect theory, it is useful to recap the history of decision theory. In particular, expected utility theory, which goes back to Bernoulli (1738) and to von Neumann & Morgenstern (1944), is an important precedent of prospect theory. Moreover, most practitioners know the mean-variance analysis of Markowitz (1952) so that it is useful to also put this into perspective.

---

[1] See, for example, Dalbar Inc. (2016) reporting that average historical retention rates of equity mutual investors were below 4 years and systematically decreased after stock markets declined.

[2] One may argue that the returns of traditional asset classes like bonds and stocks have been observed long enough so that it makes sense to assign probabilities whereas the returns of alternative asset classes like hedge funds and private equity are too ambiguous for assigning probabilities.

## 6.2  A (VERY) SHORT HISTORY OF DECISION THEORY

The following timeline shows the history of decision theory from 1670 to now (Figure 6.29).

Humans have always been faced with taking risky decisions. Hunting a mammoth or a deer were quite different risk and reward combinations. Also, deciding whether to give in to the demands of an opposing tribe or fighting a war involve quite different risks. But in years past, no one would have thought that mathematical calculus was of any use in those determinations. Rather, sacrificing and praying to gods was the usual behavior before such decisions.

In 1670, Blaise Pascal suggested using a mathematical calculus instead: For any investment; write down all possible outcomes that you think are possible with that investment, determine their probability, and calculate the expected value. Then choose the investment with the highest expected value. Using this approach, it should be easy to decide between a coin toss in which one gets $6 when heads come and $2 when tails occur or a coin toss in which one gets $9 when heads come and $1 when tails occur. According to Pascal, the second coin toss is more attractive since its expected value is $5 while that of the first coin toss is only $4.

For 68 years, the expected value criterion was the dominant calculus applied to risky choices—at least among mathematicians. But in 1738, Daniel Bernoulli, a Swiss mathematician, had some doubt about whether it is always good to compare risky choices by their expected value. He gave the example of the St. Petersburg game, which has the following rules: A coin is tossed until it comes up heads for the first time. The payoff is $1 if heads comes in the very first toss, it is $2 when it comes up first in the

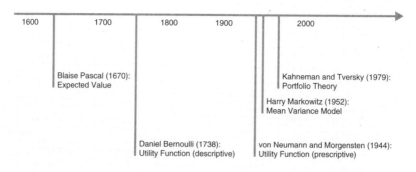

**FIGURE 6.29**  History of decision theory

second toss, and it is $4 when it comes up heads for the first time in the third toss. Thus, after each toss coming up tails, the payoff is doubled. Note that the expected value of this game is infinite[3]! Yet, it is not reasonable to pay an infinite amount for being allowed to play this game. Why not? Because, as Bernoulli wrote, you should also consider the *use* of the money that you gain. Certainly, this use depends on how rich you are. In the word of Bernoulli: "There is no doubt that a gain of one thousand ducats is more significant to the pauper than to a rich man though both gain the same amount." Bernoulli suggested extending the expected value criterion of Pascal by introducing a *utility function* that keeps track of the use from the money one gains. Bernoulli suggested that this function should be the natural logarithm—that is why the logarithmic utility function is still called the Bernoulli function.

To give an example, suppose you have a logarithmic utility function. Is it better to choose a coin toss in which you get $6 when heads and $2 when tails or to choose a coin toss in which you get $9 when heads and $1 when tails occurs? To answer this question, one computes the expected utility of both coins. For the first coin one gets $\frac{1}{2}\ln(6) + \frac{1}{2}\ln(2) = 1.24$. For the second coin, one gets $\frac{1}{2}\ln(9) + \frac{1}{2}\ln(1) = 1.09$. Thus, one would choose the first coin.

Bernoulli's suggestion was the birth of the expected utility criterion. Later, mathematicians suggested various mathematical functions to replace the logarithmic function. But most of these suggestions shared the important properties with the logarithmic utility, i.e., the utility function should be increasing at a decreasing rate. In Bernoulli words: the first thousand ducats increase the utility much more than a thousand ducats added on top of a million that one already owns. Today, this property is called "*decreasing marginal utility*".

In 1944, two mathematicians, John von Neumann and Oscar Morgenstern, wanted to clean up 300 years of decision theory during which a plethora of decision rules and utility functions had been suggested by asking which calculus is the most meaningful. They came up with a few basic axioms (i.e., basic principles) that each decision maker would agree to obey and proved that only the expected utility calculus is consistent with those axioms. Thus, they showed that after all, expected utility is the only way of making rational decisions (i.e., decisions consistent with basic principles). The result of von Neumann and Morgenstern, however, did not restrict the utility function—besides being increasing. Thus, in principle rational

---

[3]Drawing an event tree one sees that the expected value is $(\frac{1}{2})*1+(1/4)*2+(1/8)*4+(1/16)*8+\ldots=(1/2)+(1/2)+(1/2)+\ldots=\infty$.

decisions could involve a very complicated utility function, which made it practically impossible to apply.

In 1952, Harry Markowitz restarted the decision theory by suggesting building on the idea of reward and risk. The reward is what one aims for in taking the decision and the risk is what one wants to avoid. Markowitz suggested taking the expected value as the reward criterion and the variance as the risk measure—or the square root thereof, the standard deviation. In a first step, one could sort out all alternatives that are dominated by others having a higher reward for the same risk. Among the remaining alternatives one should then chose the one that suits best the trade-off between reward and risk that one finds most attractive.

So, how would one decide between the two coins if the mean-variance criterion of Markowitz is used? Recall that the mean payoff of the coin tosses is \$4 and \$5, respectively. The variances of the payoffs are \$4 and \$16, respectively.[4] Hence, the optimal choice depends on one's aversion to risk—that is, more risk-averse decision makers would prefer the first coin while less risk-averse decision makers would opt for the second coin.

While decision theory is one of the oldest areas of science in which many brilliant mathematicians made excellent normative contributions, in 1979, two psychologists Kahneman and Tversky published a new path-breaking decision theory, prospect theory. It is founded by observations on individuals' decision behavior in the experimental laboratory as well as in practice. This and their subsequent work got awarded the Nobel Prize in economics in 2002. Different from previous decision theories, prospect theory distinguishes two distinct phases in the decision process: an initial phase where choice alternatives are edited, the so-called *editing phase*, and a subsequent phase where edited choices are evaluated, the so-called *evaluation phase*. In the editing phase, people mentally organize and reformulate their choice alternatives to simplify their decision problem. Kahneman & Tversky (1979) define the editing phase as a "preliminary analysis of the ordered prospects, which often yields to a different representation of these prospects," while the evaluation phase is the successive phase where people evaluate edited prospects and choose the one with the highest value.

In the editing phase, some of the information selection biases or information processing biases discussed in Sections 2.1 and 2.2 could be observed. People also code payoffs in terms of gains and losses with respect to a reference point, as already described in Subsection 2.2.10. This can lead to inconsistent choices if the reference point is changed over time. As a matter

---

[4]Note that in a binary lottery with equal probabilities the standard deviation equals the distance of the payoffs to the mean.

of fact, the payoff distributions of edited prospects often differ from those of the original choice alternatives people faced.

The main ingredients of the evaluation phase of prospect theory are a *value function* and a *probability weighting function*. The value function describes that (1) people emphasize losses more than gains, both being calculated relative to some reference point and (2) that people prefer sure payoffs to risky payoffs when facing gains but they prefer risky payoffs to sure payoffs when facing losses. The main property of the probability weighting function is that people overweigh small probabilities relative to moderate probabilities.

Which coin would a prospect theory decision maker choose? Recall the first coin pays either $6 or $2 with equal probability while the second coin pays either $9 or $1 with equal probability. First, the choice will depend on the reference point. Supposing that the investor suffers from narrow framing and focuses solely on these two coins, the investor might argue that the highest payoff he can assure in the worst case is $2, which he obtains from choosing the first coin. Thus, the investor codes the payoffs of the two coins as: Coin 1 has a gain of $4 when heads and a gain/loss of $0 when tails. Coin 2 has a gain of $7 when heads and a loss of $1 when tails. If one assumes that the marginal utility remains constant, then the choice will depend on the loss aversion. Decision makers with a higher loss aversion will prefer the first coin while decision makers with a lower loss aversion would prefer the second coin.

Comparing the decision behavior of the three types of investors, we see that the three decision models, expected utility, mean-variance, and prospect, can change the preference of a risk-neutral agent for the second coin by introducing some notion of risk aversion. According to expected utility analysis, investors prefer moderate payoffs to extreme payoffs, according to mean-variance analysis investors avoid variance of payoffs, and according to prospect theory investors avoid losses. While these notions of risk sound similar and have little effect for simple cases like tossing a coin, they can lead to severe differences when applied to more realistic settings like computing asset allocations, as we will show in this chapter. Before proceeding to this application, the three decision theories will be presented more formally.

## 6.3  EXPECTED UTILITY

As we ultimately want to use our decision theories to form asset allocations, it is useful to find a framework that is suitable for this application. Note that each asset gives rise to a distribution of outcomes (e.g., buying a stock leads to returns that differ across various scenarios). We denote the probabilities with which the returns occur by $p_1, \ldots p_n$. The returns are called outcomes and are denoted by $x_1$ to $x_n$. In decision theory, one calls these objects lotteries.

Pascal's criterion of *expected value* can thus be written as:

$$E(x) = p_1 x_1 + p_2 x_2 + \cdots + p_n x_n = \sum_{i=1}^{n} p_i x_i$$

As already explained, the *expected utility* criterion is a generalization of the expected value criterion. Given some risk utility $u$ and returns occurring with probabilities $p_1 \ldots p_n$, the expected utility is defined as

$$EU(x) = p_1 u(x_1) + p_2 u(x_2) + \cdots + p_n u(x_n) = \sum_{i=1}^{n} p_i u(x_i)$$

Higher expected utility from a lottery means that the lottery payoffs are more useful for the decision makers (see Example 6.1). Their willingness to pay (WTP) for receiving the lottery payoffs is then determined by defining the sure payoff that the investor sees as equivalent to the lottery. We get it from the following equation:

$$u(\text{WTP}) = EU(x)$$

---

### EXAMPLE 6.1: Expected utility

As an example, consider a fair dice with six sides. If one is paid $1 for tossing $1, $2, for tossing 2 and so on, the expected utility of a person with $u(x) = \ln(x)$ from rolling the dice is:

$$U(x) = p_1 \ln(x_1) + p_2 \ln(x_2) + \ldots + p_6 \ln(x_6)$$
$$= \frac{1}{6}[\ln(1) + \ln(2) + \ln(3) + \ln(4) + \ln(5) + \ln(6)] = 1.1$$

To determine the willingness to pay (WTP) of this decision maker, we solve:
$$\ln(\text{WTP}) = EU(x)$$

Hence, $\text{WTP} = e^{1.1} = \$3$.

A standard utility function used in expected utility is $u(x) = \frac{x^\alpha}{\alpha}$. Note that for $\alpha = 1$, the expected utility reduces to the expected value. And when $\alpha < 1$, then the investors are risk averse in the sense that their willingness to pay for a lottery is less than the expected value of the lottery.[5] For example, if $\alpha = 1/2$, then the WTP for the second coin, which has an expected value of \$5, is determined by $\sqrt{WTP} = \frac{1}{2}\sqrt{9} + \frac{1}{2}\sqrt{1} = \$2$, which yields $WTP = \$4$.

Expected utility is the theory of rational choice. What does *rational* mean in this framework? Rationality is defined by three requirements:[6]

1. *Transitivity:* choosing lottery A over lottery B, lottery B over lottery C implies choosing lottery A over lottery C.
2. *Independence axiom:* decisions between lotteries with identical parts depend only on the parts that *differ*.
3. *Monotonicity:* When comparing two certain payoffs, the higher payoff should be preferred.

Since all these requirements on preferences appear reasonable, we can say that decisions driven by preferences satisfying the requirements are rational. Von Neumann and Morgenstern proved that expected utility satisfies these three axioms—that is, we might say that it is rational. In the appendix, you can convince yourself that this is indeed true.

Note that in our argument for rationality we did not assume anything on the value function except that it is increasing. Hence, from this point of view the decisive difference between expected utility and prospect theory is the probability weighting function—the differences between the value and the utility function are inessential.

Before we pass to the next decision theory, it is worth mentioning that despite the strong normative appeal, people easily violate the expected utility hypothesis. The French Nobel Prize winner Maurice Allais gave the first example for this fact. It is called the *Allais paradox*. It was observed in an

---

[5] This general utility function includes the Bernoulli case of $\log(x)$ for the special case of $\alpha = 0$.

[6] In the literature one also finds the requirements called "completeness" and "continuity." Since these two requirements are usually met when the outcomes of the lotteries are monetary payoffs, we do not highlight them here.

experiment where people were asked to choose between a sure payoff and a lottery. When people are asked to choose between a sure payoff of \$3,000 and a lottery that with 80% chance pays \$4,000 while in the remaining case it pays nothing, most people choose the sure payoff. However, if the same people must choose between a lottery that with 10% chance pays \$3000 or a lottery that with 8% chance pays \$4,000, then they will choose the second lottery. The reason for the second choice is clear. If chances are small to obtain the payoff no matter what, then it does not matter much if they are 8% instead of 10% if one can increase the potential payoff to \$4,000 instead of \$3,000. However, these intuitive choices violate the expected utility principle: The first choice means that $u(3,000) > 0.8u(4,000)$ while the second choice means that $0.1u(3,000) < 0.08u(4,000)$.[7] Multiplying the second inequality by 10 reveals a contradiction to the first. Indeed, mixing the first two lotteries with a first chance move that gives nothing with 90% results in the second pair of lotteries. That is, the Allais paradox shows a violation of the independence axiom.[8] The Allais paradox shows that the essence of the independence axiom is that the decision criterion shall be *linear in probabilities*—it has the form $\sum_{i=1}^{n} p_i u(x_i)$ for whatever utility function $u$.

## 6.4 MEAN-VARIANCE ANALYSIS

Selecting and combining lotteries (such as single assets or market indexes) can be very complicated, as for each probability distribution resulting from holding single assets or portfolios an expected utility needs to be calculated. As suggested by Markowitz in 1952, the decision problem can be simplified if preferences are specified on the mean and the variance of the probability distribution instead on the whole distribution. Indeed, Markowitz recommended displaying each asset allocation in a mean-standard-deviation diagram. The investment decision then amounts to selecting an *efficient* portfolio, i.e., a portfolio with maximum return given a certain level of

---

[7]For simplicity we assume u(0) = 0.

[8]The first lottery in the second pair can be represented by $(p_i, x_i)_{I=1,...n}$ as (0.1,3000/0.9,0) while the second lottery is (0.08,4000/0.02,0/0.9,0). Thus, both lotteries have the common component (0.9,0), which—according to the independence axiom—should be ignored when choosing between them so that after normalizing the probabilities they sum up to one. The remaining pair of lotteries is essential the first pair.

risk. Investors with higher (lower) risk aversion then choose portfolios with a lower (higher) level of risk and return. Mean-variance preferences are "reasonable" if the utility increases with the mean, which corresponds to the maxim "more wealth is better," and if they are decreasing with the variance as the latter represents the risk of the lottery. The stronger the utility decreases with variance, the stronger is one's *risk aversion*. The stronger the risk aversion, the higher is the reward that the investor requires for taking risks.

Within the mean-variance framework, the investor's preferences are given, for example, by the utility function $u^i(\mu, \sigma^2) = \mu - \frac{\alpha^i}{2}\sigma^2$ where $\alpha^i > 0$ is a parameter describing the risk aversion of investor $i$. The higher this parameter, the higher is the *slope* of the utility function.[9] The higher the risk aversion, the higher is the required expected return for one unit increase in risk—that is, the required risk premium (see Figure 6.30).

Different investors have different risk–return preferences. Investors with a higher (lower) level of risk aversion choose portfolios with a low (high) level of expected return and variance, so their portfolios move down (up) the efficient frontier. This is displayed in Figure 6.31.

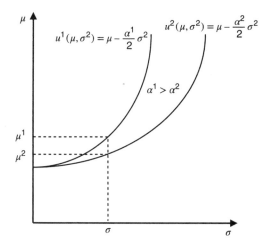

**FIGURE 6.30**   Risk aversion and risk premium

---

[9]The risk aversion concept is often discussed in the expected utility context, where the risk aversion is measured by the *curvature* of a utility function.

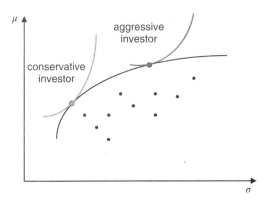

**FIGURE 6.31**   Mean-variance diagram with
efficient frontier and risk preferences

## 6.5   PROSPECT THEORY

Prospect theory is the most well-known theory describing the way actual
people make decisions under risk. Kahneman and Tversky developed it
through a series of experiments they performed with their students.
Presenting prospect theory step by step is easiest by reviewing these experiments. An excellent and detailed analysis of prospect theory is presented by
Wakker (2010).

The first property of prospect theory is that it is defined over changes
of wealth, that is, gains and losses, and not over final wealth. This has
been demonstrated in an experiment where individuals were asked to make
a choice between two lotteries. One group of participants was endowed
with $1,000, and another group was endowed with $2,000. The participants in the first group endowed with $1,000 had to make a choice between
a guaranteed gain of $500 or a 50:50 lottery to gain $1,000 or nothing.
The participants in the group endowed with $2,000 had to make a choice
between a guaranteed loss of $500 and a 50:50 lottery to lose $1,000 or
lose nothing. Typically, the first group preferred the sure payoff and the second group preferred the lottery, although from a total wealth perspective the
alternatives that the individuals in both groups faced were identical.

That changes in wealth (i.e., gains and losses), and not wealth are the
relevant quantities individuals consider, is an example of the editing phase of
prospect theory. As previously discussed, the editing phase describes possible
modifications of the original choice problem that allow people to simplify
their decision process. Coding payoffs as gains and losses reflect the way
people perceive payoffs, such as with respect to a given investment goal or
target return, and thus it simplifies processing payoffs.

The editing phase includes many operations people perform before evaluating the available choice alternatives. For example, people might frame a given decision problem in many ways, and this could lead to different choices. This is called the framing effect and has been extensively analyzed in the laboratory, but also referring to the choices of real-world investors (see Subsection 2.2.6). In financial decisions, investors usually look at historical performances, such as because these are often reported in fact sheets for investment products. Moreover, nowadays it is quite easy to access the historical performance of investment funds, asset classes and indexes, and one can also select different historical periods and focus on specific market events. Consequently, for many investors, the way they mentally represent the return distribution coincides with the historical return distribution. However, the historical return distribution can be framed in many ways, depending, for example, on the length of the historical period taken or the focus put on specific events. This is shown in Figure 6.32, where the historical performance of a fund is shown using different historical periods. Finally, having a specific frame for the historical performance leads to a specific mental representation of future returns (see De Bondt & Thaler, 1985), and this affects the subsequence evaluation phase, and thus also the chosen alternative.

Another example of editing refers to segregation or aggregation, such as whether subsequent portfolio returns over two periods are segregated and independently evaluated, or first aggregated to obtain the two-period portfolio return and then evaluated. As already seen in Subsection 2.2.12, segregation and aggregation typically lead to different results, and thus editing affects the subsequent evaluation.

Thaler (1985) proposes the *hedonic editing hypothesis* that states the people segregate or aggregate to achieve the highest perceived value. The following example presented by Thaler (1985) illustrates hedonic editing:

> *Mr. A was given tickets to lotteries involving the World Series. He won $50 in one lottery and $25 in the other. Mr. B was given a ticket to a single, larger World Series lottery. He won $75. Who was happier?*

Most respondents answered Mr. A, in line with the hedonic editing hypothesis, which implies that the additional win of $25, after having already won $50, delivers a higher perceived value when it is segregated (i.e., evaluated separately). However, the empirical evidence that the hedonic editing hypothesis holds when investors buy or sell stocks is rather weak (Lehenkari, 2009). Recently, Cillo & De Giorgi (2017) proposed that hedonic editing is applied when the cognitive effort it implies is not too

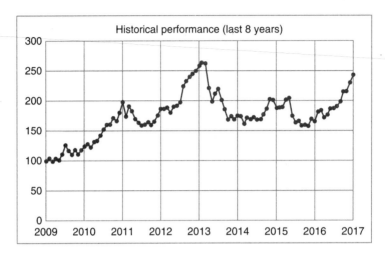

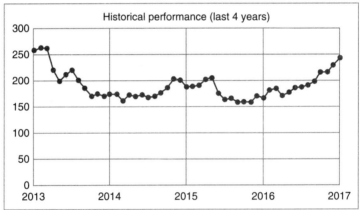

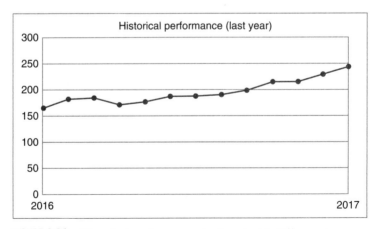

**FIGURE 6.32** Historical performance displayed with different time frames

high. An experiment shows that highly skilled individuals are more likely to apply hedonic editing compared to low-skilled individuals.

The second property of prospect theory is loss aversion—that is, the observation that losses loom more than for gains. Note that the loss aversion has an impact on the investment choice, if the payoffs involve gains and losses. If the payoffs involve only losses, then loss aversion is not relevant for the question of which alternative is more attractive. In this case, the decision on the attractiveness of the alternatives will depend only on the risk-taking attitudes.

The third property of prospect theory is the changing risk attitude in the context of gains and losses. In the context of gains, individuals show risk aversion. Thus, they prefer a sure payment to a lottery with the same expected payoff. But when confronted with losses, individuals are risk seeking—that is, they prefer to gamble rather than to accept a sure loss equal to the expected loss of the gamble.[10] Hence, one is willing to gamble in the face of sure losses.[11] This is observed in an experiment where participants have been asked to consider the following two alternatives: A: a 50% chance for winning $1,000 or nothing and B: a 50% chance of losing $1,000 or nothing. They were also asked to compare the alternatives A and B with a sure gain or loss of $500 and state their preference. When comparing lottery A with the sure gain of $500, most of the people decide to take the sure gain. They change, however, their risk attitude when facing the sure loss of $500 and compare it with the possibility to lose nothing in the context of losing $1,000. In this case, they decide to take the risk and try to avoid the losses.

The critical question is how to model the experimental findings explained above. This is, which calculus give the results consistent with those findings? In 1730, Isaac Newton blundered on the South Sea bubble and then said: "I can calculate the movements of heavenly bodies—but not the behavior of people." More than 200 years later, Kahneman and Tversky could achieve what Newton was looking for. Their prospect theory gives a mathematical calculus to describe the behavior of people. In this calculus, one distinguishes between probabilities of payoffs and the utility from payoffs. The latter is modeled by the so-called *value function*.

The experiments suggest that the value function $v(\Delta x)$ needs to be defined over gains ($\Delta x > 0$) and losses ($\Delta x < 0$), where $\Delta x$ is the difference

---

[10]This behavior is also called "gambling for resurrection" or "get evenitis."

[11]This behavior is typical in sports. For example, in ice hockey, a team replaces the goal-keeper with a field player when the score is against the team and there are only a few minutes left to play.

of the outcome x relative to the reference point RP. For example, suppose that under normal conditions the investors expect their portfolio will return 5%. Then, reference point would be RP = 5%. If the investment return $x$ is above 5%, say 7%, the investors consider this as a gain and $\Delta x = x - RP = 7\% - 5\% = 2\%$. The value of the function $v(\Delta x)$ expresses how much the investor likes the gain, and respectively, how much the investor dislikes the losses, when $\Delta x < 0$.

Moreover, the value function must be steeper for payoffs below the reference point (losses) than for payoffs above the reference point (gains) to reflect the loss aversion. Finally, the value function must be concave in gains and convex for losses. Tversky & Kahneman (1992) suggest the following piecewise power function[12] to model these properties:

$$v(\Delta x) = \begin{cases} (\Delta x)^\alpha & \text{for } \Delta x \geq 0 \\ -\beta(-\Delta x)^\alpha & \text{for } \Delta x < 0 \end{cases}$$

where $\Delta x = x - RP$ is a gain or a loss associated with the payoff $x$ relative to the reference point $RP$. The parameter $\beta$ reflects the steepness of the value function over losses or individual's loss aversion. An interesting case occurs when $\alpha = 1$, because then the exponent $\alpha$ vanishes and the value function has two linear pieces with the part in the negative domain being steeper (see Figure 6.33).

In general, the parameter $\alpha$ reflects the concavity (convexity) of the function. An illustrative example occurs for $\alpha = 0.5$. Then $(\Delta x)^\alpha = \sqrt{\Delta x}$, the square root of $\Delta x$. The square root function is increasing at a decreasing rate (i.e., it is concave). Now, if $\Delta x$ is negative, the square root cannot be computed directly. Instead, one flips the sign inside and outside the square—that is, one computes $-\sqrt{(-\Delta x)}$. Analogously, one proceeds for any other $\alpha$. The preferences of the median individual as observed by Tversky and Kahneman are given by the parameters $\alpha = 0.88$ and $\beta = 2.25$.

To demonstrate the properties of the value function, consider the following example. Suppose that there are two investors: Daniel Bernoulli and Daniel Kahneman. Both have two credit cards and two wallets in which to keep them. Suppose the chance of losing a wallet is 25% and it is independent of the chance of losing the other wallet. Further, suppose that the loss of one card is as bad as the loss of the other one. Who will put both cards into the same wallet and who will put one credit card into each wallet? Clearly, Daniel Bernoulli would diversify his risk by putting one credit card into each wallet. Daniel Kahneman, however, will put both credit cards

---

[12]The value function v($\Delta x$) has two parts. If $\Delta x$ is positive, a different rule how to compute the value is applied than when $\Delta x$ is negative.

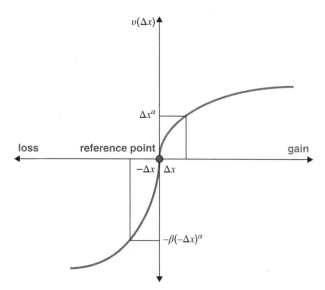

**FIGURE 6.33** The value function of Tversky and Kahneman (1992)

into one wallet to minimize the chance of losing some of the cards. Note that the decision of Daniel Kahneman is not driven by loss aversion but only by his risk-seeking attitude in the face of losses. This is because the alternatives that Daniel Kahneman has involve only losses. Note also that both Daniels are perfectly rational, because risk-aversion and risk-seeking is a matter of one's preferences.

In addition to the value function, the prospect theory specifies a probability-weighting function that should reflect the observation that people overweight small probabilities, as mentioned in the first chapter. This observation can be expressed formally by the function $w(p)$ that gives the decision weight the investor attributes to the probability $p$. Higher probabilities perceive a higher decision weight but smaller probabilities like 1% get more decision weight than their numerical value, i.e., $w(1\%) > 1\%$ while large probabilities like 60% get relatively less weight in the investor's decision, i.e., $w(60\%) < 60\%$. Tversky and Kahneman suggested that the psychological probability weight should be analytically calculated using the following *probability weighting function*:

$$w(p) = \frac{p^\gamma}{(p^\gamma + (1-p)^\gamma)^{1/\gamma}}$$

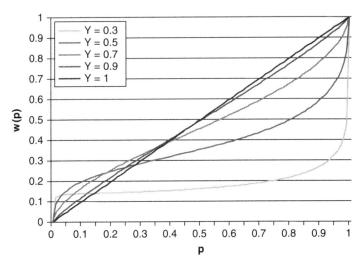

**FIGURE 6.34**   Probability weighting function

Overweighting of small probabilities and underweighting of large probabilities is captured by the parameter of $0.27 \leq \gamma \leq 1$. Note that for $\gamma = 1$ there is no probability weighting, and the lower the parameter, the stronger is the over- and underweighting. This is illustrated in Figure 6.34. In the experiments of Kahneman and Tversky, the average participant has a probability weighting parameter of 0.65.

Note that probability weighting can resolve the Allais paradox (see Section 6.3). Indeed, the two inequalities $u(3{,}000) > w(0.8)u(4{,}000)$ and $w(0.1)u(3{,}000) < w(0.08)u(4{,}000)$ are not in contradiction, for example, when $\alpha = \gamma = 0.5$. However, the fact that probability weighting resolves a paradox in the expected utility theory does not make the resulting decision rational. Forming expectations with respect to weighted probabilities may lead to a violation of the maxim "more wealth is better that less wealth." To demonstrate how this can happen, consider a lottery with 10 equally likely payoffs ranging from 99.0 to 99.9—that is, 99.0, 99.1, 99.2, . . . 99.9. If one weights the probabilities of 10%, multiplies them with the value of each payoff, and sum up the products, one will get a utility of 17.823, which is higher than the utility from receiving 100 for sure, which is $100^{0.5}$ = 10. Hence, probability weighting motivates one to prefer a lottery that pays for sure less than 100 to a sure payoff of 100! This is a contradiction to the maxim "more wealth is better than less wealth."

To cure the counterintuitive effect arising from probability weighting as demonstrated in this example, Tversky & Kahneman (1992) suggested the *cumulative prospect theory* that applies the probability weighting to the cumulative distribution function instead of the probabilities. In cumulative prospect theory, the outcomes are ranked and then the probability weighting is applied to the cumulative distribution function. This means that extreme events are overweighted. In asset return distributions, extreme events are also those events with small probabilities; thus, the difference to prospect theory is not as important as it could be with general lotteries.

An easier approach toormalize the decision weight $w(p)$ so that they add up to 1 and can again be interpreted as a probability distribution:

$$NPT(\Delta x) = \frac{\sum_{i=1}^{n} w(p_i)v(\Delta x_i)}{\sum_{i=1}^{n} w(p_i)} = \sum_{i=1}^{n} \frac{w(p_i)}{\sum_{i=1}^{n} w(p_i)} v(\Delta x_i) = \sum_{i=1}^{n} w_i^*(p)v(\Delta x_i)$$

where NPT denotes the normalized prospect theory utility and the term in the denominator is a simple normalization to make sure that the sum of all weighted probabilities is equal to 1. Using this normalization, one could introduce normalized probability weights as defined in the previous equation. But to simplify notation, from now on we understand the probability weights as being normalized.[13]

Figure 6.35 displays the annual returns of the S&P 500 from 1871 to 2010. We see that the return distribution of the index has slightly more negative realizations than a normal distribution with the same mean and standard deviation would have. We see that a prospect theory investor would overweight the probability for negative returns. Consequently, the investor might stay away from investing because he particularly dislikes negatively skewed distributions. This conclusion is supported by many studies showing that probability weighting generally leads to lower investments into stocks when the return distribution is negatively skewed, while the opposite applies when the return distribution is positively skewed (Barberis & Huang, 2009; De Giorgi & Legg, 2012).

Next, we show that probability weighting drives recommendations that explain the Allais paradox. The Allais paradox is one of the main issues discussed in decision theory, since it makes the point that people do not decide according to the expected utility hypothesis, which would imply that the so-called independence axiom is satisfied.

---

[13]For a binary lottery with outcomes $x_1 > RP > x_2$ occurring with probabilities $p$ and $(1 - p)$ the differences between PT, CPT and NPT are as follows: $PT(x - RP) = p\ v(x_1 - RP) + (1 - p)\ v(x_2 - RP)$; $CPT(x - RP) = w(p)\ v(x_1 - RP) + (1 - w(p))\ v(x_2 - RP)$ and $NPT(x - RP) = [w(p)/(w(p)+w(1 - p))]\ v(x_1 - RP) + [w(1 - p)/(w(p)+w(1 - p))]\ v(x_2 - RP)$.

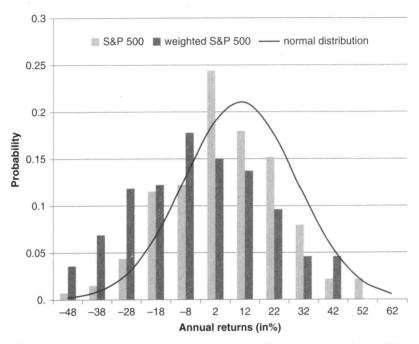

**FIGURE 6.35** Probability distribution with annual S&P 500 returns from 1871 to 2010, weighted probabilities and normally distributed returns

Based on the value function, $v$, and the normalized probability weighting function, $w$, the prospect theory decision criterion for the choice between two lotteries can be written as follows:

A lottery A with outcomes $x_1, \ldots, x_n$ occurring with probabilities $p_1, \ldots, p_n$ is preferred to a lottery B with outcomes $y_1, \ldots, y_n$ with probabilities $q_1, \ldots, q_n$ if and only if

$$PT(x) = \sum_{i=1}^{n} w_i(p)v(x_i) > \sum_{i=1}^{n} w_i(q)v(y_i) = PT(y)$$

Another puzzle that prospect theory can solve is related to risk taking. Investors typically do both: they take risk, e.g., on the stock market, and they insure against risk, e.g., they buy health insurance or insurance for their car. To explain this puzzling behavior, one should consider that risk taking, as seen by an outside observer, depends on the curvature of the decision maker's

**TABLE 4**  Fourfold pattern of risk taking behavior

|                              | Losses        | Gains         |
| ---------------------------- | ------------- | ------------- |
| Small probability            | No risk taking | Risk taking   |
| Moderate to high probability | Risk taking   | No risk taking |

value function *and* on the degree of probability weighting. In case of moderate probabilities, the curvature of the value function dominates risk taking so that in the area of gains a prospect theory investor does not take risk, while the investor does in the area of losses. However, for small probabilities, this risk-taking behavior is reversed. In the area of gains, the chance of gaining a high payoff dominates even when the probability for it is small. So, prospect theory investors pay more than the expected value for lotteries with small chances of high payoffs. While in the area of losses small chances of high losses stop the prospect theory investor from risk taking.

The *fourfold pattern of investor's risk taking behavior* in the face of gains and losses with small and high probabilities is then summarized in Table 4.

## 6.6  RATIONALITY OF MEAN-VARIANCE AND PROSPECT THEORY

Are the mean-variance analysis and the prospect theory consistent with the axioms of rational decision making? In the previous section, we saw that prospect theory may violate the axiom of monotonicity if the probabilities are not normalized. In the following, we show that mean variance analysis also has some severe restrictions.

Example 6.2 shows that the mean-variance analysis does not necessarily lead to rational decisions because some mean-variance decision makers violate the independence axiom.

### EXAMPLE 6.2: Mean-variance violating the independence axiom

Consider four lotteries A, B, A', and B' with payoffs in three states constructed in a way that in the third state the lotteries A and B and the lotteries A' and B' have the same payoff.

*(Continued)*

| Probability | State 1 10% | State 2 80% | State 3 10% | Mean | Variance | M/V |
|---|---|---|---|---|---|---|
| Lottery A | 75% | 50% | 30% | 51% | 1.02% | 49.39 |
| Lottery B | 40% | 60% | 30% | 55% | 1.05% | 52.38 |
| Lottery A' | 75% | 50% | 0% | 48% | 3.06% | 15.51 |
| Lottery B' | 40% | 60% | 0% | 52% | 3.36% | 15.48 |

By the independence axiom, the comparison between A and B and between A' and B' should be independent on the third state. If lottery B is more attractive than A and A' is more attractive than B', then the independence axiom will be violated. However, for some degree of risk aversion, the standard mean-variance utility function $\mu - \frac{\alpha}{2}\sigma^2$ leads to this choice.

The next problem of the mean-variance is known as the *mean-variance paradox*. To understand why it is a paradox, consider two assets: one that never gives any profit and one that pays a large amount with a small probability. A mean-variance investor would choose the first one because this investor does not like volatile payments. From the perspective of the real investor, however, such a choice is not optimal—after all, the chance for a gain is not a risk that one would like to avoid. Hence, for real investors, the variance cannot be a good measure for risk since it may lead to decisions that violate the principle that more wealth is better than less wealth.[14]

The mean-variance paradox might be hidden in the desire for diversification, as the following example shows. Consider two binary lotteries, $x$, $y$ paying off in equally likely states $s = 1,2$. The payoffs in state 1 are 10 for lottery $x$ and $-5$ for lottery $y$. In the other state, the payoffs are 5 and 0, respectively. One can easily see that the mean payoffs are 7.5 and $-2.5$, respectively, while the standard deviation is 2.5 in both lotteries. Thus,

---

[14]Formally, consider a lottery with two possible payoffs. With a probability $p > 0$ one can get the payoff $y > 0$. In the other case the payoff is 0. A mean-variance decision maker would calculate the expected value of the lottery, which is $\mu = py$. Assume that $p$ converges to 0 while the payoff $y$ increases so that the expected value of the lottery is constant. Then, the variance of the lottery $\sigma^2 = p(y - \mu)^2 + (1 - p)(-\mu)^2 = \mu y - \mu^2$ tends to infinity. As a result, any variance-averse investor will eventually prefer to get nothing rather than to play the lottery.

according to the Sharpe ratio one should chose lottery $x$. An expected utility and a prospect theory decision maker would avoid lottery $y$ at all since it never gains. However, a mean variance investor might be tricked by his desire into diversifying $x$ with the negatively correlated lottery $y$ and finds that a 90:10 portfolio of the lotteries $x$ and $y$ improves the Sharpe ratio of only investing in $x$ from 3 to 3.25.

A further problem with the mean-variance decision approach is the measure of risk. In the mean-variance framework, risk is measured by the variance of payoffs. Hence, assets with identical means and variances should be considered as equally attractive. Example 6.3 shows that if investors care about gains and losses, they would decide differently. Markowitz (1959) recognized this issue and suggested replacing variance with semi-variance, which only measure deviations *below* the mean—that is, losses when the reference point is set equal to the mean. However, semi-variance is theoretically less appealing as a risk measure, because differently from the variance, no explicit expression for how the semi-variance of a portfolio depends on the portfolio weights can be obtained.

---

### EXAMPLE 6.3: Variance as a risk measure

Consider the following lotteries:

Lottery A:

| Payoff | 27% | −20% |
|---|---|---|
| Probability | 0.57 | 0.43 |

Lottery B:

| Payoff | 85% | 0% |
|---|---|---|
| Probability | 0.08 | 0.92 |

Both lotteries have approximately the same mean (7%) and the same variance (23%). An investor applying the mean-variance analysis should be indifferent between them. However, an investor who cares about gains and losses might find lottery B more attractive, as it offers only gains.

---

The same point as in the example above can be made in a more realistic setting by comparing structured products. Since both products illustrated in Figure 6.36 have the same mean and variance, they are indistinguishable for a mean-variance investor. However, real investors would typically prefer the product with the unlimited gains since it has capital protection and

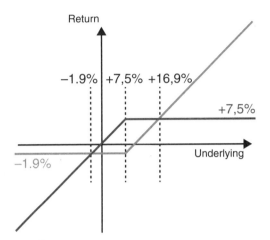

**FIGURE 6.36** Two different products with the same mean and variance

unlimited potential while the other has limited upside potential and unlimited downside potential.

Having demonstrated the shortcoming of mean-variance analysis one might wonder whether prospect theory is any better. To answer this question, recall the calculus for prospect theory. If probabilities are not weighted, i.e., if $w(p) = p$, then it coincides with the expected utility calculus:

$$PT(x) = \sum_{i=1}^{n} w(p_i)v(x_i) = \sum_{i=1}^{n} p_i v(x_i)$$

Certainly, the value function does not have the standard form $u(x) = \frac{x^\alpha}{\alpha}$. But the theorem of von Neumann and Morgenstern does not require this! Thus, prospect theory is rational when the probability weighting parameter $\gamma$ equals 1.

To finish the comparison of the three decision theories we note that one can also choose a form of the prospect theory value function so that in the special case of no probability weighting, no loss aversion and the same curvature in the gains and the loss area prospect theory coincides with mean-variance analysis. As we show in the appendix, this result is obtained for the piece-wise quadratic value function:

$$v(\Delta x) = \begin{cases} \Delta x - \dfrac{\alpha^+}{2}(\Delta x)^2 \text{ if } \Delta x \geq 0 \\ \beta\left(\Delta x - \dfrac{\alpha^-}{2}(\Delta x)^2\right) \text{ if } \Delta x < 0 \end{cases}$$

where $\Delta x$ is defined as the change relative to the investor's reference point. Note that for $\alpha^+ > 0$ and $\alpha^- < 0$ the function is s-shaped; that is, concave for gains and convex for losses as the piece-wise power function of Kahneman and Tversky. Moreover, the parameter $\beta > 1$ indicates again the degree of loss aversion.

An important property of the piecewise quadratic value function is that for $\beta = 1$ and $\alpha^+ = \alpha^-$, the prospect utility of an investor is depending only on the mean and the variance of the payoff $x$. Thus, in principal mean-variance is a special case of prospect theory when the value function is piecewise quadratic. This observation is important since it nails down the difference between prospect theory and mean-variance. Mean-variance is the special case of prospect theory when the latter does not weight probabilities, does not lead to get-evenitis, and has no loss aversion.

## 6.7 THE OPTIMAL ASSET ALLOCATION

So far, we have seen that prospect theory is well founded by actual decision behavior and that it is consistent with rational choice if there is no probability weighting. The question of this section is how we can compute asset allocations based on prospect theory. Moreover, it would be useful for communicating the results to private investors if prospect theory can be displayed in a *reward-risk diagram* as, like the mean-standard-deviation diagram of Markowitz.

In this section, we consider the two-period optimal asset allocation and the multiperiod or dynamic asset allocation. In the two-period case, it is assumed that investors buy and hold the assets irrespective of what happens in between. This is well justified if the two periods are not too far apart. In the case of the dynamic asset allocation, investors can adjust their asset allocation to the events that happen along the investment path. Finally, we consider a very long investment horizon—so long that the optimal investment path must be considered together with the optimal consumption path. This approach is called life-cycle planning.

Before we analyze the strategic asset allocation of a prospect theory investor, we briefly recall the well-known case of mean-variance analysis. As Tobin (1958) has shown in the presence of a risk-free asset, the optimal asset allocation is particularly simple, since it follows the *Two Fund Separation Theorem*. The theorem says that differently risk-averse investors with same beliefs should diversify between the risk-free asset (e.g., certificates of deposit or cash) and a single optimal portfolio of risky assets that is the same for all investors. The *tangent portfolio* gives this optimal mix of risky assets. The tangency portfolio only depends on investors' beliefs, or their estimations of expectations and covariances. Therefore, it is the same for all investors with the same beliefs and corresponds to the portfolio on the efficient frontier at the point of tangency between the efficient frontier and a line starting at the risk-free rate of return. When all investors possess the same beliefs, the tangency portfolio corresponds to the market portfolio, and this line is called the *Capital Market Line* (CML). The slope of the CML is $\frac{\mu - R_f}{\sigma}$, which is called the *Sharpe ratio*.

Thus, according to the two-fund-separation theorem, different attitudes toward risk result in different combinations of the risk-free asset and the tangent portfolio. All investors can improve on the mean-variance trade-off given by the efficient frontier. More conservative investors, for example, should put a higher fraction of their wealth in the risk-free asset; respectively, more aggressive investors should borrow capital on the money market (go short in risk-free assets) and invest it in the tangent portfolio (see Figure 6.37). The following well-known formula for the mean-variance asset allocation encompasses this property:

$$\lambda = COV^{-1} \frac{(\mu - R_f)}{\alpha},$$

where $\lambda$ is the vector of the risky assets' proportions, $\mu$ the vector of the risky assets' expected returns and COV the covariance matrix of returns. For the special case of a single risky asset we get:

$$\lambda = \frac{(\mu - R_f)}{\alpha \sigma^2}.$$

The so-called asset allocation puzzle shows, however, that advisors do not follow the two-fund-separation theorem. Instead, they adjust the recommended mix of risky assets according to the risk preferences of their clients. This can be seen in Table 5. In the advice given by the *New York Times,* for example, the ratio of the portfolio weight of S&P 500 to bonds changes from 0.25 to 1.0 in aggressive, moderate, and conservative portfolios. This is in contradiction to the two-fund separation theorem that says that the asset allocations of investors with different risk attitudes should differ only by the percentage of wealth invested in the mix of risky assets. However, the mix of risky assets should be the same for everyone. The question that arises, then, is, "Who is right? Tobin or the practitioners?" As we see Table 5, while traditional finance sides with Tobin, behavioral finance gives support to the practitioners.

Having defined a utility function that represents the preferences of a prospect theory investor, we now look for a suitable risk–reward representation of investment opportunities. From the investor's point of view, the

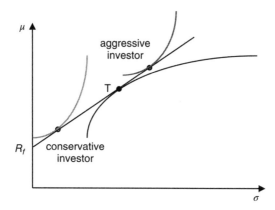

**FIGURE 6.37**    The two-fund separation theorem

**TABLE 5**    The asset allocation puzzle

| Advisor and Investor Type | Percent of Portfolio | | | Ratio of Bonds to Stocks |
|---|---|---|---|---|
| | Cash | Bonds | Stocks | |
| A. Fidelity[a] | | | | |
| Conservative | 50 | 30 | 20 | 1.50 |
| Moderate | 20 | 40 | 40 | 1.00 |
| Aggressive | 5 | 30 | 65 | 0.46 |
| B. Merrill Lynch[b] | | | | |
| Conservative | 20 | 35 | 45 | 0.78 |
| Moderate | 5 | 40 | 55 | 0.73 |
| Aggressive | 5 | 20 | 75 | 0.27 |
| C. Jane Bryant Quinn[c] | | | | |
| Conservative | 50 | 30 | 20 | 1.50 |
| Moderate | 10 | 40 | 50 | 0.80 |
| Aggressive | 0 | 0 | 100 | 0.00 |
| D. *The New York Times*[d] | | | | |
| Conservative | 20 | 40 | 40 | 1.00 |
| Moderate | 10 | 30 | 60 | 0.50 |
| Aggressive | 0 | 20 | 80 | 0.25 |

*Source*: (Canner, Mankiw, & Weil, 1997)

reward of an investment is not its expected return as in the mean-variance analysis but the expected utility over the reference point or its *average gain*. It is defined as the utility from the sum of all portfolio returns over the investor's reference point, weighted with the corresponding probabilities as perceived by the investors. More precisely, the average gain is defined as

$$pt^+ = \sum_{i=1, R_i > RP}^{n} w(p_i)v(R_i - RP)$$

where $R_i$ is the return of the portfolio in state $i$.

Respectively, the risk of the investment is not the deviation from the expected return as in the mean-variance analysis but the expected portfolio return below the investor's reference point. This is the portfolio's *average loss*:

$$pt^- = -\frac{1}{\beta} \sum_{i=1, R_i < RP}^{n} w(p_i)v(RP - R_i)$$

where $\beta$ is the investor's loss aversion. Therefore, the utility over the average gains and losses is $PT = pt^+ - \beta pt^-$. Graphically, the reward–risk perspective can be represented as the behavioral efficient frontier (BEF), as shown in Figure 6.38.

Thus, prospect theory can also be used to do a reward–risk diagram. The two measures $pt^+$ and $pt^-$ are specific to the investor with value function $v$, probability weighting function $w$, and reference point $RP$. Therefore, the corresponding reward–risk diagram and BEF are customized to each

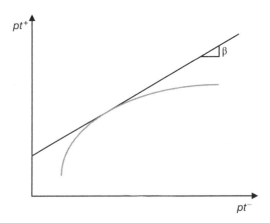

**FIGURE 6.38** Behavioral efficient frontier (BEF)

investor and allow emphasis on how the optimal allocation varies with the most important ingredient of prospect theory, loss aversion. However, if one prefers to work with standardized measures of reward and risk—measures that are the same for all their clients—the reward–risk representation of prospect theory still suggests that mean and variance should be replaced by other measures, such as lower and upper partial moments defined as

$$LPM(RP) = \sum_{i=1, R_i < RP}^{n} (RP - R_i)^{\alpha}$$

and

$$UPM(RP) = \sum_{i=1, R_i \geq RP}^{n} (R_i - RP)^{\alpha}$$

respectively, and the Sharpe ratio should be replaced by the ratio

$$\Omega(RP) = \frac{UPM(RP)}{LPM(RP)}$$

known as the Omega ratio or simply as the gain-loss ratio when $\alpha = 1$ (Shadwick & Keating, 2002).

The question now is, what is the optimal asset allocation of the prospect theory investor? To give the intuition we consider the simple case with one risky and one riskless asset. The return of the riskless asset is $R_f$. The risky asset has two possible returns, $R_u$ and $R_d$. The probability that $R_u$ realizes is $p$. Let now $\lambda$ be the percentage of wealth invested in the risky asset. Thus, the portfolio return can be either $R_f + (R_u - R_f)\lambda$ or $R_f + (R_d - R_f)\lambda$. As shown in the appendix, for the piecewise quadratic value function we get the optimal asset allocation as

$$\lambda = \frac{w(p)(R_u - R_f) + \beta(1 - w(p))(R_d - R_f)}{\alpha^+ w(p)(R_u - R_f)^2 + \beta\alpha^-(1 - w(p))(R_d - R_f)^2}.$$

Note that the percentage of wealth invested in the risky asset increases with the expected return of the risky asset—that is, $\mu = pR_u + (1 - p)R_d$, and decreases with the investor's loss aversion but also with the investor's risk aversion for gains and losses if the latter is not too negative.

Finally, as De Giorgi, Hens, & Mayer (2011) have shown, the optimal asset allocation of a prospect theory investor could be in line with the two-fund separation theorem if (1) the investors' preferences are described by the piecewise power value function of Tversky and Kahneman (1992) and (2) the reference point is the return of the riskless asset. This is, however, not very likely. Thus, as shown by De Giorgi (2011), prospect theory would resolve the asset allocation puzzle shown in Table 5 by siding with the practitioners. That is, the asset allocations they recommend violate the two-fund separation property because they might come from a prospect theory interpretation of risk and reward!

Example 6.4 demonstrates how important the theory of choice is when recommending an asset allocation to a particular client (that this example is generally true is shown in Hens & Mayer, 2017).

---

### EXAMPLE 6.4: A comparison of asset allocations based on mean-variance, expected utility, and prospect theory

Suppose that there is a client looking for an optimal asset allocation among five risky asset classes: bonds, stocks, commodities, and two hedge funds. The advisor has four scenarios regarding the expected returns of these classes: u-shape, v-shape, double-dip, and war scenario. Table 6 summarizes the expected returns of the asset classes under the four scenarios.

**TABLE 6**   Expected returns

| Scenario | Probability | Bonds | Stocks | Cdty | HF1 | HF2 |
|---|---|---|---|---|---|---|
| u-shape | 40% | 3% | 10% | 5% | 2% | −6% |
| v-shape | 40% | −5% | 20% | 20% | −6% | −2% |
| double-dip | 19% | 7% | −30% | −50% | 1% | 2% |
| war | 1% | −50% | −50% | 20% | 2% | 10% |

The risk preferences and the optimal asset allocation are determined within three theories: mean-variance, expected utility, and prospect theory. To make sure that the estimated risk preferences and the resulting optimal asset allocation depends only on the theory, the risk preferences of the client is elicited with the same question:

*"An investment offers a 50% chance to double the initial wealth (100% gain). Which negative return are you ready to accept in the other case?"*

The answer of the client to this question is the same, but it has different meaning in dependence on the theory used to interpret it.

Suppose, finally, that the client expresses willingness to accept a loss of 20%. Then the utility of the investor with mean-variance preferences $u(x) = \mu - \alpha\sigma^2$ will be $u(x) = 0.4 - \alpha \times 0.36$. To determine client's risk aversion, we solve $0.4 - \alpha \times 0.36 = u(0)$, where $u(0)$ is client's utility from not investing and get $\alpha = 1.11$. Now we look for a portfolio that maximizes the client's utility.

When searching for the optimal portfolio, we apply the following restrictions in all theories:

- The weights of the asset classes need to sum to 1.
- No short sales are allowed (weights must be greater than 0).
- The maximum portfolio weight of a hedge fund is 5%.[15]

For the case of mean-variance preferences with a risk aversion of 1.11, we get an optimal asset allocation with 71% stocks and 29% bonds (see Figure 6.39).

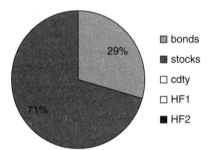

**FIGURE 6.39** Optimal asset allocation with mean-variance

Suppose now that the advisor assumes that the client maximizes the final wealth as in the expected utility theory. Under this assumption, the client's answer to the lottery question gets a different meaning. Under the expected utility, a client ready to lose 20% has a risk aversion of −2.76. It is estimated by solving the equation $0.5 \times 2^\alpha + 0.5 \times (1 - 0.2)^\alpha = 1^\alpha$, where the left side of the equation is client's expected utility from playing the lottery based on the final wealth in each scenario and the right side of the equation is client's initial wealth of 1. The optimal asset allocation assuming expected utility is now different: it contains 44% stocks, 46% bonds and the maximum allowed weight of hedge funds (Figure 6.40). *(Continued)*

---

[15] We use this restriction to account for the *uncertainty* in the return distributions of hedge funds.

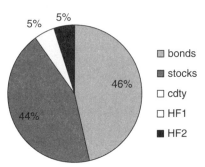

**FIGURE 6.40** Optimal asset allocation with expected utility

Suppose finally that the advisor believes that client's preferences are best estimated when using prospect theory. The advisor wants to consider client's loss aversion in the calculation of an optimal asset allocation. The advisor assumes also that the client's risk aversion and probability weighting are like those of the median investor. From client's answer to the lottery question, the advisor estimates that client's loss aversion is 4.12. This is the solution of the equation $w(0.5) \times 1^{0.88} + w(0.5) \times (-\beta)(0.2^{0.88}) = 0$ under the assumption the client's reference point is 0%, which means keeping the initial wealth. The optimal asset allocation based on prospect theory contains fewer stocks and more bonds compared to the asset allocations based on mean-variance and expected utility (see Figure 6.41). Note that this result does not change if one uses the piecewise quadratic value function instead of the piecewise power function.

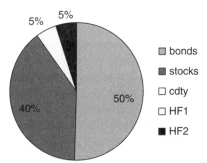

**FIGURE 6.41** Optimal asset allocation based on prospect theory

The example illustrates two important aspects. First, optimal asset allocations vary depending on the theory used to calculate them. For example, the behavioral efficient frontier (BEF) typically differs from the mean-variance efficient frontier. This means that asset allocations that are optimal for some investors with mean-variance preferences, could be suboptimal for *all* investors with preferences according to prospect theory. Therefore, the way the strategic asset allocations are obtained should consider which underlying theory is applied to evaluate clients' preferences.

In the special case where assets' returns are normally distributed, Levy & Levy (2004) show that the BEF and the mean-variance efficient frontier almost coincide. The implication of this result is that under normality of returns, prospect theory investors can optimally choose their asset allocations from the mean-variance efficient frontier. However, here we emphasize the second important aspect illustrated by the previous example. The same answer to a question designed to estimate client's risk preferences gives rise to different expose to risky assets in dependence on the theory used to interpret the client's answer. For example, if advisors neglect loss aversion and only consider aversion to volatility as in the mean-variance model, they would underestimate the psychological ability of the client to confront with losses and recommend an excessive exposure to risky assets. The result will be that the client will give up on the recommended allocation as soon as losses realize.

Briefly, advisors should be very careful when choosing a theory for evaluating clients' preferences and calculating their optimal asset allocations. The wrong theory will lead to unsatisfied clients (De Giorgi & Hens, 2009) so that the long-term relation between clients and advisors will be affected.

An important concept related to asset allocation is diversification. Diversification is understood as the reduction of the overall portfolio risk by investing in a wide variety of assets. Mean-variance preferences and diversification are strongly connected, as the mean-variance investor combines assets that are not positively correlated to reduce risk. In expected utility theory, diversification is equivalent to risk aversion. That is, risk-averse expected utility maximizers prefer a combination of assets to holding single assets. Even though diversification is a cornerstone of traditional finance, empirical evidence shows that individuals' portfolio lack diversification (Goetzmann & Kumar, 2008). Example 6.5 shows that the diversification behavior of investors with prospect theory preferences differs from the predictions of traditional finance and thus prospect theory could explain underdiversification.

### EXAMPLE 6.5: A comparison of the diversification behavior under mean-variance, expected utility theory and prospect theory

We consider the allocation among two risky assets. Because for mean-variance investors the highest diversification potential arises when assets' returns are negatively correlated, we assume that if asset 1 pays off $R$, then asset 2 pays off $-R$. In this case, if an investor equally splits his wealth among the two assets, then the portfolio return is $0.5 \times R + 0.5 \times (-R) = 0$. That is, equally splitting the wealth among the two assets implies the highest possible reduction of risk, because it leads to a risk-free payoff.

Table 7 reports the distribution of returns of assets 1 and 2:

**TABLE 7**   Distribution of assets' returns

|            | Scenarios and Probabilities | | |
|------------|:-------------------:|:-------------------:|:-------------------:|
|            | Scenario 1<br>20%   | Scenario 2<br>50%   | Scenario 3<br>30%   |
| Asset 1    | −30%                | 0%                  | 60%                 |
| Asset 2    | 30%                 | 0%                  | −60%                |

Asset 1 has expected return and standard deviation of 4% and 20%, respectively, while asset 2 has expected return –4% and the same standard deviation of asset 1. Therefore, asset 1 is clearly better than asset 2 for a mean-variance investor, and thus, the only reason the investor might want to invest into it is because it allows diversification of risk. Indeed, for a wide range of values for risk aversion, the mean-variance investor will optimally hold both assets. If risk aversion further increases, then the allocation to asset 2 constantly increases as well and reaches 50% when risk aversion become very high (see Figure 6.42). The intuition for this result is that highly risk-averse investors optimally chose allocation with low variance, and this can only be achieved by holding both assets. The extreme case in our example is when variance is 0, which is obtained by equally holding both assets.

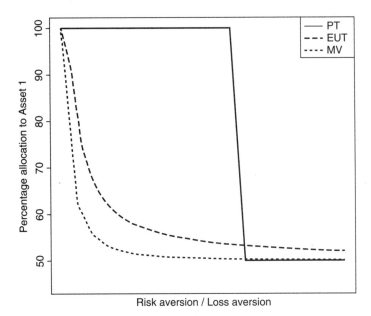

**FIGURE 6.42**   Optimal allocation to asset 1 in Example 6.5 for prospect theory (PT), expected utility theory (EUT), and mean-variance investors (MV)

The same result holds for an investor with expected utility preferences. For a wide range of values for risk aversion, the investor always allocates a percentage of his wealth to both assets. As risk aversion increases, the portion invested into asset 2 constantly increases as well. Again, if risk aversion becomes very high, he will finally equally split his wealth between assets 1 and 2 (see Figure 6.42).

The prospect theory investor behaves differently. Because the returns of asset 1 are positively skewed, while the returns of asset 2 are negatively skewed, the prospect theory investor strongly prefers asset 1 to asset 2. This is due to probability weighting that further overweights the right tail of the distribution of asset 1 as well as the left tail of the distribution of asset 2. Mixing the two assets will always lower skewness compared to asset 1 alone, so combining assets 1 and 2 is not convenient to the prospect theory investor unless he becomes very averse to losses. In this latter case, the equal split between assets 1 and 2 suddenly looks better, simply because of no losses. Therefore, in this example, the prospect theory investor either holds asset 1

(*Continued*)

only or equally split his wealth between assets 1 and 2. Empirical evidence supports the result for the prospect theory investor, as it has been shown that underdiversified portfolios generally display higher skewness compared to well-diversified portfolios—that is, households tend to invest in a lower number of assets with positive skewness (Mitton & Vorkink, 2007).

## 6.8   COMPARING THE DECISION THEORIES

In this chapter, we have outlined expected utility theory, mean-variance analysis and prospect theory and compared them along the following criteria:

- Does the theory lead to rational decisions?
- Is the theory close to realistic behavior?
- Is the theory intuitive?

The first criterion is mandatory for every advisor. If advisors use theories that lead to irrational recommendations, they will eventually get complaints from clients and from the regulator. Moreover, advisors should recommend investments that best suit the investor's preferences—that is, the way the investor approaches situations of risk. These two criteria, rational decisions and behaviorally sound decisions, are in conflict as the long list of behavioral biases shows. However, these biases refer to the framing phase of decision theory, and here we analyze the evaluation phase. That is, here we assume that the investor has the choice between lotteries like return distributions of assets. The last criterion is whether the recommended decision is intuitive so that the advisor can explain it to the client. Clients are more likely to follow an intuitive decision than a "black box" recommendation that they do not understand. Table 8 summarizes the findings of this chapter along those criteria.

Expected utility theory is rational since it satisfies the axioms of choice. However, as the Allais paradox shows, people systematically violate the axioms of choice. Thus, expected utility theory is not behavioral. Also, the expected utility calculus is not easy to understand and conduct. Mean-variance scores highest exactly in that respect. It is very intuitive as it uses the old Christian idea of good and evil. However, as our previous examples show, mean-variance is not behavioral. People prefer certain lotteries among others even though they should be perceived as equivalent since they have the same mean and variance. This happens, of course,

**TABLE 8** Comparison of expected utility, mean-variance, and prospect theory

|  | Rational | Behavioral | Intuitive |
| --- | --- | --- | --- |
| Expected utility | Yes | No | No |
| Mean-variance | No | No | Yes |
| Prospect theory | No | Yes | Yes |

because the two lotteries have different loss characteristics. Finally, as we have already shown, mean-variance analysis is not rational, as it neither satisfies the independence nor the monotonicity. Prospect theory is only rational if the reference point is kept fixed and probabilities are not weighted. But it is certainly behavioral since prospect theory describes well how investors choose among lotteries. Finally, one can display prospect theory in a reward–risk like the mean-variance diagram, so that it is also easy to explain. Based on this analysis, advisors should use prospect theory with a fixed reference point and no probability weighting that is then explained by a reward–risk diagram highlighting the prospect theory measure of gains and losses.

## 6.9 CONCLUSION

Decision theory is at the foundation of finance and has therefore always been an active research area. It allows formalizing many aspects of observed behavior and it suggests how to make rational decisions. The current state of the art is prospect theory, since it is the most general decision theory that describes most observed behaviors. Moreover, avoiding probability weighting can be used to construct better risk measures than volatility, which is standard in traditional finance.

All this sounds unequivocal. However, it assumes that the probabilities are known or can at least be estimated with good confidence. Banks use investment committees to solve this problem—that is, to figure out good probability estimates of scenarios so that they can deliver optimized portfolios, based on mean-variance or other decision criteria. Individual investors do not have those resources and one would think that they are damned to systematically underperform the optimized portfolios of banks. However, a recent study by DeMiguel, Garlappi, & Uppal (2009) shows that simple heuristics like equally distributing wealth among groups of stocks are not worse than optimized portfolios. We will come back to this new view on portfolio construction in Chapter 11, where we discuss style investing.

# CHAPTER 7

# Product Design

## 7.1 INTRODUCTION

In the previous chapter, we studied decision theory as a foundation of the strategic asset allocation. The purpose of this chapter is to show which application it delivers for the evaluation and the design of structured products.

In the recent past, structured products have been very popular, particularly in Europe and East Asia. By the end of 2007 in Switzerland, there were more than 340 billion Swiss francs invested in structured products. This corresponds to 6.5% of all assets under management invested in traditional asset classes (e.g., equities and funds). Also, there were more than 20,000 listed structured products on the Swiss stock exchange, which is an increase of 87% compared to the previous year. The immense popularity of structured products is amazing since they are derivatives sometimes based on rather complicated constructions. For example, the most popular structured product in the Swiss market are reverse convertibles whose payoff might depend on a basket of assets in a nonlinear way since knock out barriers are defined.

After the collapse of Lehman Brothers and its subsequent default on its structured products, the popularity of the structured products decreased substantially. Moreover, some regulators acted and intervened in the market for them. In Norway, for example, these investment vehicles were essentially banned for private investors. Other countries are considering similar actions. But do investors really act irrationally when buying structured products, and do they need such kind of "protection"? The answer to this question depends on the investors' psychology. As we have seen in the previous chapter, some motives may lead to rational and others to irrational decisions.

From traditional finance's point of view, investors do not need structured products. As we have shown in the previous chapter, their optimal portfolio consists of the market portfolio and a riskless asset. Hence, banks taking care of the financial wealth of their clients should offer them only the market portfolio at a minimum cost (e.g., in the form of an exchange-traded fund (ETF)).

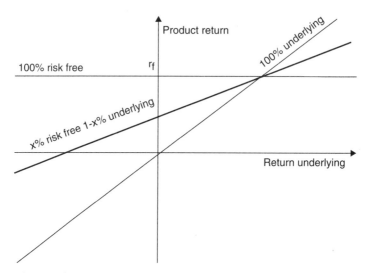

**FIGURE 7.43** Optimal traditional portfolio from the perspective of a structured product

To see the limitations of the traditional portfolios that might arise for more general utility functions, it is instructive to look at them from the point of view of a structured product. The standard description of a structured product uses the payoff diagram, in which the return of the structured product is shown as of the return of the underlying of the structured product (see Figure 7.43).

In terms of a payoff diagram the standard traditional portfolio is a linear function of the market payoff and the risk-free return (see Figure 6.31). Its slope depends on the risk aversion of the client—that is, clients with a lower risk aversion should choose a higher percentage of the market portfolio so that the payoff line of the product gets steeper. Hence, the portfolio construction in the traditional portfolio limits the shape of the payoff diagram severely. In general, one might want to design payoff diagrams that have capital protection, floors and caps, as well as changing degrees of participation. Figure 7.44 shows the payoff diagram with these three components that best suits a behavioral investor.

We see that in principle, structured products could be used to generate quite flexible payoffs. So, was the strong demand for structured products caused by a misperception of the risks (caused, for example, by aggressive marketing) or by preferences for payoffs, which are not directly available on the market? To answer this question, we first consider a structured product

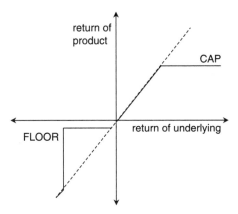

**FIGURE 7.44**   Possible components of a
payoff diagram for a structured product

as a case study and ask whether clients with different preferences prefer
the product to direct investments. Afterward, we analyze the question of
how the payoff of a structured product should optimally look. Based on this
analysis, we will conclude whether the most popular products offered on the
Swiss market serve investors' needs or rather exploit investors' misperception
of risk and reward.

## 7.2   CASE STUDY

In the following case study, we consider a structured product called "Ladder
Pop" offered on the Swiss market and analyze whether it serves investors'
needs better than direct investments on the stock and the bond market.[1]
The Ladder Pop is a typical structured product that was very popular
after the meltdown of the internet bubble in the beginning of the new
millennium.

### 7.2.1   Product Description

The Ladder Pop was constructed to follow the Swiss Market Index (SMI)
over almost 4.9 years (issue date: January 22, 2002, expiration date: December 12, 2006). The minimum investment was CHF 5000 and the floor was

---

[1]The product was offered by Bank Wegelin&Co, Privatbankiers.

set at 80%. That is, at maturity, investors get at least 80% of their money back. Additionally, investors participate in the upward movements of the SMI according to the following formula given in the product sheet:

$$5000 \left( 0.8 + N * 5\% + max \left( 0\%; \frac{S_{final} - S_{initial}}{S_{initial}} - N * 5\% \right) \right)$$

where $S_{final}$ is the closing price of SMI at maturity and $S_{initial}$ is the index value at the issuance day. The factor $N$ is the number of levels achieved by the underlying over the whole period, while each level is equal to 10%.

By taking a closer look on the product's payoff, we can conclude that it depends basically on two factors:

- The *maximal* underlying value achieved over the 4.9-year period
- The underlying value at the end of the period

To understand the construction of the first return factor, let $a$ be the return of the underlying achieved when the underlying achieves 10%. By construction of the product, the buyer of the Ladder Pop gets half of it. For example, if the SMI return is 10%, then the investor gets 5%; if SMI breaks the next level and achieves 20%, then the investor gets 10%. Thus, $a = N * 5\%$, where $N$ is the number of levels achieved by the underlying. The underlying reaches the next level every time when it realizes an additional 10% return. Hence, the factor $a$ can be interpreted as half of the maximum underlying return over the whole period truncated to the lower decimal level (if e.g. the SMI maximum return is 45%, then $N = 4$ and $a = 20\%$).

The second return factor of the structured product is the percentage increase of the underlying over the whole period, which we define as $b$. This is equivalent to the buy-and-hold return of an investor holding only the underlying.

By simplifying the formula given in the product's fact sheet, we get that the nominal value of the Ladder Pop is equal to $5,000[0.8 + a + max(0; b - a)]$, where 5,000 is the nominal of the Ladder Pop at the beginning and the investor starts at a floor of 80%. This is logically equivalent to $5,000[0.8 + max(a, b)]$. Hence, starting at 80%, the investor obtains the higher of the two returns at maturity. Figure 7.45 summarizes the payoff of the Ladder Pop *at maturity*.

The dashed line represents the payoff of Ladder Pop, given that the buy-and-hold return $b$ of the index is higher than half of the maximum index return over the whole period (truncated to the lower decimal level). In this scenario, the Ladder Pop pays 20% less than the return achieved by

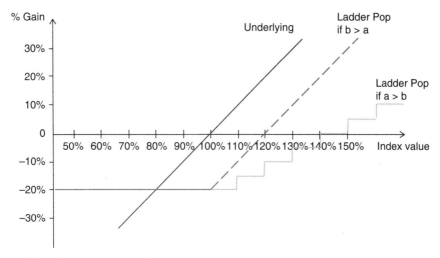

**FIGURE 7.45** Payoff of Ladder Pop at maturity

the index. However, if the index is very volatile (i.e., it reaches high levels before maturity but it falls at the time of maturity), then half of the maximum index return achieved over the whole period may be larger than the buy-and-hold return. In this case, the number of levels achieved over the holding period determines the payoff of the Ladder Pop. For example, if the maximum index return over the whole period is 65% (index value of 165%), then $N = 6$ and $a = 30\%$ so that the payoff of the Ladder Pop is 10%. That is, $100(0.8 + 0.3) - 100$.

The product takes the maximum between $a$ and $b$, and adds it to the floor of 80%. Hence, paying 20%, the investor gets the return of the SMI to maturity or if it is higher, the investor gets half the maximal increase during the next 4.9 years.

From today's perspective, investors who decided to buy the Ladder Pop on January 22, 2002, and then held it until maturity were not lucky. During the first year until spring 2003, the SMI lost up to 40%, whereas the loss of Ladder Pop investors was limited to 21% (see Figure 7.46). However, over the whole period of 4.9 years, the Ladder Pop investment was worse than a buy-and-hold strategy. The return of the latter was 38.2%. In contrast, Ladder Pop investors paid 20% disagio in the hope of getting half of the maximum return over these 4.9 years. Unfortunately, the SMI was not so volatile, so that the maximum index's return up to maturity was lower than the buy-and-hold payoff. At maturity, Ladder Pop investors got the buy-and-hold return minus 20%, or 18.2%

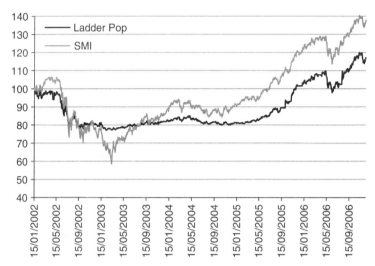

**FIGURE 7.46**  SMI and Ladder Pop prices (indexed) from January 15, 2002, to December 12, 2006
*Source*: Bank Wegelin&Co.

Note that investors who wanted to sell the Ladder Pop could not have achieved at least the 80% in the period of January to July 2003. The floor of 80% is guaranteed only *at maturity*.

To understand why the value of the structured product may fall below the floor before maturity, consider the following example. Suppose that one invests 10,000 in a bond for two years. The interest rate per year is 4%. If one does not need to sell the bond, the account at the end of the first year will show 10,400 and after the second year 10,816. Suppose now that one must sell the bond after the first year and thereafter the interest rates increases to 10%. In this case, there will be a loss of 167.27, which is a gain of 400, comprised of interest from the first year minus a capital loss of 567.27. Why? At the end of the first year, one has two options to continue: either one sells the bond and reinvests for 10% or one keeps going with 4%. Hence, (10,400 − 567.27) appreciating at 10% equals the alternative to hold the 10,400 in the form of the bond paying 4% interest. That is, the combination of market to market and no-arbitrage leads to a negative time value before maturity. Structured products are like bonds: before maturity, their value can fall below the guaranteed floor.

### 7.2.2  Product Evaluation

Clearly, in advance, when the market is unpredictable so is the payoff of the Ladder Pop. However, evaluating different scenarios allows us to draw conclusions on at least two questions.

1. Does the bank make a profit?
2. What type of investors would buy this product?

To answer these questions, consider two scenarios for the underling (SMI) and a riskless bond as an alternative with the following payoffs.

|  | $t = 0$ | $t = 1$ | $t = 2$ | $t = 3$ | $t = 4$ |
| --- | --- | --- | --- | --- | --- |
| SMI positive | 100 | 110 | 140 | 178 | 170 |
| SMI negative | 100 | 105 | 120 | 90 | 85 |
| Bond | 100 | 102.4 | 104.9 | 107.4 | 110 |

The payoff of the bond is determined under the assumption that it pays 10% over the whole investment period of 4.9 years.

The value of the Ladder Pop with a nominal value of 100 at maturity is either $100(0.8 + 0.7) = 150$ in the positive scenario or $100(0.8 + 0.1) = 90$ in the negative scenario. In the positive scenario, the value of the Ladder Pop is driven by the buy-and-hold return $b = 70\%$, since in this scenario $a = 35\%$. In the negative scenario, the value of the Ladder Pop is driven by $a = 10\%$, as the buy-and-hold return of the underlying is negative $(-15\%)$.

To answer the first question, whether the bank makes a profit, we assume that asset prices are determined in a way that arbitrage is excluded. Then, we get that the bank offering the Ladder Pop at 100 does not run a deficit, as intuitively assumed. To see this, calculate a hedge portfolio as the combination of the underlying ($S$) and the bond ($B$) so that $170S + 110B = 150$ and $85S + 110B = 90$. Taking the difference of both equations gives $S = 0.706$. Inserting this result in the first equation, we get $B = 0.273$. Given that the underlying and the bond cost each 100, the hedging costs of the bank are equal to 97.86. Hence, the bank does not run a deficit by selling the product for 100. The bank hedges the risk of the product and earns 2.14 (since $100 - 97.86 = 2.14$) on each unit sold.

Would an investor without hedging possibilities buy this product? To answer this question, we can apply the expected utility or, more generally, the prospect theory approach. We expect to see differences in the valuation of the product for the following reasons. In both cases, we assume that the investors evaluate the Ladder Pop separately from possible other assets. The marketing of most structured products suggests that this is the typical client's point of view.

While expected utility maximizers integrate gains and losses to their total wealth, prospect theory investors are very sensitive to losses. Moreover, from their point of view, a loss is a shortfall behind a reference point that itself is a crucial aspect of their preferences.

The second major difference in the preferences of investors is that expected utility investors focus on their returns independent of the market returns or the bank's profit, while a real investor has a clear sense of fairness from which the investor derives a sense of how returns on a certain investment should be divided between him and the bank.

Finally, an expected utility investor either likes to take or to avoid risk while the risk taking of a prospect theory investor depends on whether pay-offs below the reference point are possible and on how probabilities are weighted.

Consider first an investor with a constant relative risk aversion (CRRA); i.e., investor's risk aversion and choice do not change with the wealth: $u(w) = w^\alpha/\alpha$, where w is the final wealth and $\alpha$ is a parameter indicating the investor's risk aversion. If we assume that the probability for the positive scenario is 35%, we can calculate the expected utility $Eu$ of this investor with the different investment alternatives. The willingness to pay for an investment is then determined by $WTP = (\alpha Eu)^\wedge(1/\alpha)$. In dependence of the risk aversion $\alpha$, the CRRA investor would invest either in the underlying or in the bond but not in the Ladder Pop, as Table 9 shows.

Would a loss-averse investor decide differently? To answer this question, we assume that the investor's choice is determined by the normalized prospect theory with the piecewise power value function with $\alpha = 0.88$ and the probability weighting function with $\gamma = 0.65$. Additionally, we assume that the investor's reference point is 100 (the nominal value of the assets at the beginning of the investment).

With these assumptions, we first calculate the expected PT-utility with each asset and then use the results to calculate the investor's willingness to pay. Since the investor's PT-utility (PT) with each asset is always positive, the investor's willingness to pay for an asset is given by $WTP = (PT)^{1/\alpha} + 100$. We observe that if the investor is loss neutral ($\beta = 1$), the investor will hold the underlying. If he is loss-averse ($\beta > 1$), the investor will prefer the bond, as Table 10 shows.

So, is there a contradiction to our previous intuitive judgment that the structure product offering a capital protection is attractive for loss-averse investors? The answer is no because people make judgments within classes

**TABLE 9** Willingness to pay of an investor with a constant relative risk aversion

|  | SMI | Ladder Pop | Bond |
|---|---|---|---|
| $\alpha = -1$ | 103.0 | 104.7 | 110.0 |
| $\alpha = 0$ | 108.3 | 107.6 | 110.0 |
| $\alpha = 0.5$ | 111.4 | 109.3 | 110.0 |

**TABLE 10**  Willingness to pay of a prospect theory investor

|           | SMI   | Ladder Pop | Bond  |
|-----------|-------|------------|-------|
| $\beta = 2$   | 104.6 | 104.1      | 110.0 |
| $\beta = 1.5$ | 109.3 | 107.2      | 110.0 |
| $\beta = 1$   | 114.2 | 110.6      | 110.0 |

such as *riskless assets* and *assets with upside potential*. We could therefore assume that when deciding to invest in a structured product, investors usually compare the product with its underlying but not with a riskless alternative. For the prospect theory investor comparing only the risky alternatives, the structured product appears more attractive than the underlying.

Referring to the dynamic of returns, the structured product is more attractive than the underlying because it provides a certain protection during periods of big losses, as, for example, in year 2003, at the costs of lower returns in good times (see Figure 7.47). As described in the roller coaster illustrated in Figure 2.01, this perspective is important for investors with a limited loss tolerance. Supposing that the investor cannot stand to lose more than 25%, the best investment for him is the Ladder Pop. If the investor chooses the Ladder Pop, the investor holds through the investment and ends with a 15% gain. If the investor chooses the underlying, the investor jumps out of the boat at a 25% loss. Also, the bond would not be better for the investor, because the investor would then end up with a 10% gain.

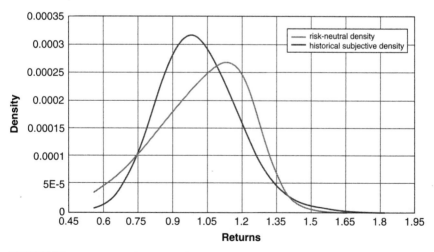

**FIGURE 7.47**  State price density and subjective density for the DAX in April 2000

## 7.3  THEORY OF PRODUCT DESIGN

In the previous section, we have seen that with structured products one can generate very flexible payoffs that in principle could be chosen to tailor them to the utility function and the beliefs of the investor. The general problem of designing structured products involves the following ideas:

- One needs to determine the price of payoffs as a function of the underlying.
- One needs to combine those payoffs to achieve the highest utility given a certain budget to be spent.

The standard methods for determining the price of the payoffs use option pricing. Consider, for example, a position of two call options one with strike $X$ and one with strike $X + a$. If one holds the first and sells the second then one has essentially bought a payoff for the state that the underlying ends up in the interval $[X, X + a]$. Moving $X$ from very low to very high prices of the underlying determines the prices of all those elementary states. Naturally, the less likely the price of the underlying is, the cheaper the payoff of a structured product in that case will be. However, the resulting state prices also reflect economic principles such as scarcity of resources and risk aversion. Thus, the distribution of state prices (the state price density, also called the risk-neutral density) is typically distinct from the probabilities the investor beliefs with which those states occur (the subjective density of the historical density if the investor beliefs the future is like the past). Figure 7.47 shows both densities for the DAX in April 2000. We observe that payoffs in states with very low returns of the underlying are more expensive than the probability with which they occur because payoffs in those states are needed desperately. On the other hand, state prices for high returns of the underlying are a bit cheaper.

Revisiting the simple scenarios used in the Ladder Pop case study, we can derive the risk-neutral probabilities and then design the optimal product for expected utility and for prospect theory investors. The risk-neutral probabilities are given by the equation $\pi^*u + (1 - \pi^*)d = 1 + r$, where $u$ and $d$ are the gross returns of the underlying in the up and down state, respectively, and $1 + r$ is the gross rate of interest. For the previous example, we get $\pi^* = 0.294$. The risk-neutral probabilities define the budget restriction[2]

---

[2]To keep the results comparable with the real case we assume that the budget is equal to 0.97861.

so that we get the design of the structured product from the maximization problem:

$$\max_{x,y} w^*(p)v(x - RP) + (1 - w^*(p))v(y - RP)$$

$$\text{s.t. } \pi^*x + (1 - \pi^*)y = 1 + r$$

We get the following optimal structured product for the various parameters of the expected and the prospect utility.

| CRRA utility | x | Y | WTP (SMI) | WTP (Bond) | WTP (Ladder Pop) |
|---|---|---|---|---|---|
| $\alpha = -1$ | 117.64 | 103.48 | 103.03 | 110.00 | 108.03 |
| $\alpha = 0$ | 128.10 | 99.10 | 108.33 | 110.00 | 108.42 |
| $\alpha = 0.5$ | 150.18 | 89.92 | 111.43 | 110.00 | 109.27 |

As before, the optimized Ladder Pop remains unattractive for CRRA investors as compared to a direct investment in the SMI or to a bond investment.

| Prospect utility | x | Y | WTP (SMI) | WTP (Bond) | WTP (Ladder Pop) |
|---|---|---|---|---|---|
| $\beta=1$ | 366.000140 | 0.000000 | 114.2394 | 110.0 | 130.1975 |
| $\beta=1.5$ | 124.843379 | 100.481984 | 109.2840 | 110.0 | 109.2551 |
| $\beta=2$ | 124.843335 | 100.482002 | 104.6382 | 110.0 | 109.2551 |
| $\beta=2.5$ | 124.843375 | 100.481985 | 100.5711 | 110.0 | 109.2551 |
| $\beta=3$ | 124.843385 | 100.481981 | 99.1364 | 110.0 | 109.2551 |

We see for a mildly loss averse investor we can design a structured product that is better than the market and the bond. Generally, investors who are more loss averse require a higher payoff in the negative scenario and less in the positive scenario than investors who are less loss averse. Again, the optimized Ladder Pop remains more attractive for prospect investors as a direct investment in the underlying and prospect investors are ready to pay more for the optimized product than for the real Ladder Pop.

Now, if the investor does not overweight small probabilities and if the investor were risk neutral (i.e., if in prospect theory with the piecewise power value function we have $\alpha = 1$, $\beta = 1$ and $\gamma = 1$ for the probability weighting function), then the investor would sell payoffs in those states in which the subjective beliefs are below the state price and finance this with the receipts from those states in which the opposite holds true. In general, however, the investor will typically also suffer more when the underlying has very bad returns so that the general solution to the optimal design problem gets quite complicated. Therefore, we now give a couple of examples to see how optimal structured products look like for investors with different preferences. In these examples, we assume that the investor evaluates the structured product independently from other assets[3] and that the state price density is consistent with the capital asset pricing model (CAPM).[4] For an investor with a utility having constant relative risk aversion (CRRA) (e.g., an investor with the power utility function $u(x) = \frac{x^{\alpha}}{\alpha}$ the optimal payoff of the structured product is convex, i.e., it exhibits a "smooth" capital protection and an increasing participation in gains (see Figure 7.48).

Consider, now, an investor with a piecewise quadratic utility function. In the special case where this investor behaves as a mean-variance investor, that is, (in the notation of our quadratic prospect theory model) with $\alpha^{+} = \alpha^{-}$, $\beta = 1$, and $\gamma = 1$, the optimal payoff of the structured product is linear with decreasing participation in the gains as well as the losses of the underlying (see Figure 7.49). Thus, as we could have expected from the two-fund separation theorem for a quadratic utility the traditional asset allocation is indeed the optimal structured product.

In contrast, if this investor is loss averse with $\beta = 2$, the structured product is optimal only if it protects the investor from losses of the underlying. The stronger the investor's loss aversion, the stronger the capital protection should be (see Figure 7.50). As in the previous case, the optimal participation in gains of the underlying is decreasing.

Consider now an investor with a probability weighting (e.g., with $\gamma = 0.5$). This investor overweighs small probabilities and underweights high probabilities. From this perspective, the best-structured product is one with a strongly increasing payoff as the return of the underlying becomes greater or lower than the average (see Figure 7.51). As the probability of very likely payoffs is underweighted, the investor is ready to accept a lower than average payoff of the underlying.

---

[3]In the next section, we see that this behavior might be the result of separating assets in different mental account.

[4]In the CAPM the ratio of the state prices to the subjective density is a linearly decreasing function of the underlying.

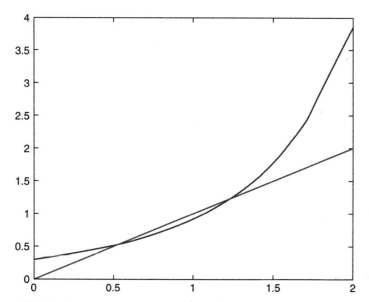

**FIGURE 7.48** Optimal structured product for a CRRA investor with $\alpha = 0.8$

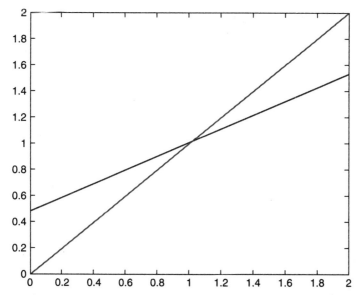

**FIGURE 7.49** Optimal structured product of a quadratic value function

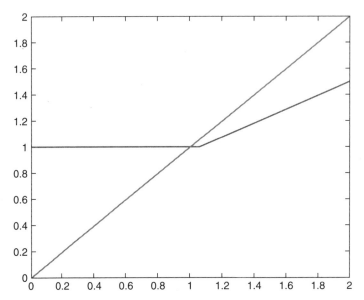

**FIGURE 7.50** Optimal structured product for a prospect theory investor with $\beta = 2$

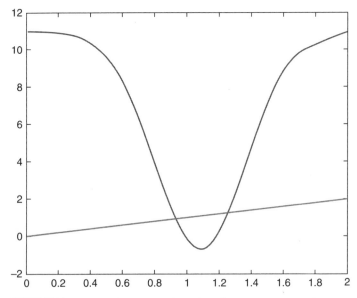

**FIGURE 7.51** Optimal structured product for an investor with probability weighting

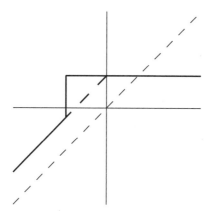

**FIGURE 7.52**  Payoff of a barrier reverse convertible

Now we want to reverse the point of view and ask what could be the reason for investors to buy into the most popular structured product in Switzerland, a barrier reverse convertible. The product pays a fixed interest ("coupon"). Moreover, the invested amount is fully returned at maturity unless the price of the underlying falls at some point below a predefined barrier level. In this case, at maturity only the value of the underlying (plus the coupon) is paid back. Figure 7.52 illustrates the payoff structure of the product.

The underlying could be also a basket with assets. The payoff of a worst-of-basket product, a variant of the barrier reverse convertible, depends then on the worst-performing asset in the basket. Example 7.1 demonstrates this.

## EXAMPLE 7.1: Worst-of-baskets certificates

Consider a worst-of-basket product with two underlyings in the basket, A and B. Suppose that the price of the underlyings develops over time as in Figure 7.53.

In this case, the barrier has been touched, since underlying B was below the barrier at some point. The final payoff is given by the worst underlying in the basket at maturity, which is underlying A. If none

*(Continued)*

of the assets in the basket hits the barrier, the payoff is the initial investment.

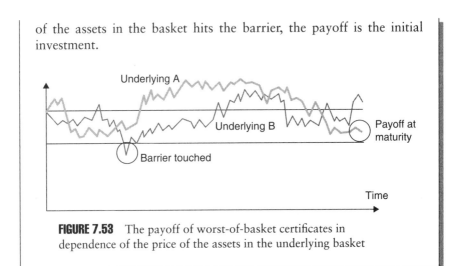

**FIGURE 7.53**   The payoff of worst-of-basket certificates in dependence of the price of the assets in the underlying basket

To explain the attractiveness of these products Rieger (2011) asked participants in an experiment to estimate probabilities related to the payoff of such products (the probability that a certain barrier will be reached) and to combine this with hypothetical investment decisions on structured products. He found that barrier reverse convertibles seem attractive to investors because investors underestimate the relative probability that the barrier will be hit. The relative probability is the difference in the probabilities that the barrier is hit at some point of time and at maturity. Further, worst-of-baskets seem attractive for investors because they do not consider that the probability for a barrier to be hit increases when the assets in the basket have a low correlation. In fact, in the experiment, participants assessed the probability that one of the assets in a basket hits the barrier as lower as the probability that the barrier is hit if there is only one asset as an underlying. The finding that investors buy barrier reverse convertibles because they do not really understand the probability of the payoffs is, unfortunately, typical for complicated structured products.

## 7.4   STRUCTURED PRODUCTS DESIGNED BY CUSTOMERS

A direct way to find the payoff that a client would like most is to let him design the product's payoff by himself. Before the client does so, the client needs to understand well what a structured product is. For example, investors might not be aware that it is not possible to construct a product that always pays more than an underlying. To help clients understand the trade-offs in constructing structured products, a group of researchers at the University of Zurich developed an interactive tool called *multitouch table*. The tool demonstrates how structured products work and visualizes their construction. At the heart of the device is a payoff diagram that the client and the advisor can change with their hands and discuss the pros and cons of capital protection or upside potential, to cite an example (see Figure 7.54). The client will understand that there are trade-offs since whenever the client raises the payoff for some returns of the underlying, the program readjusts the payoffs in all areas so that the same budget is spent for the structured product. Having an initial idea of the structured product the client likes most, one can then back-test its performance in relation to the underlying in various market scenarios.

The tool was used during a public exhibition on the event of the 175th anniversary of the University of Zurich. Visitors could try the device and design their personally structured product. More than 600 people took part. Afterward, a rough categorization of their products was assembled. The

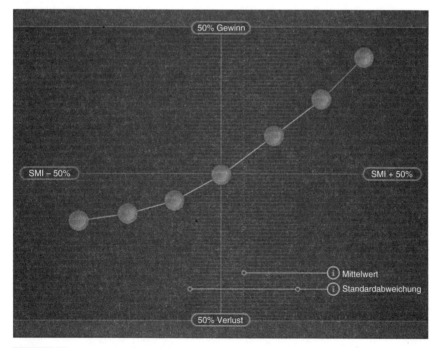

**FIGURE 7.54** A screen-shot of the interactive multitouch table

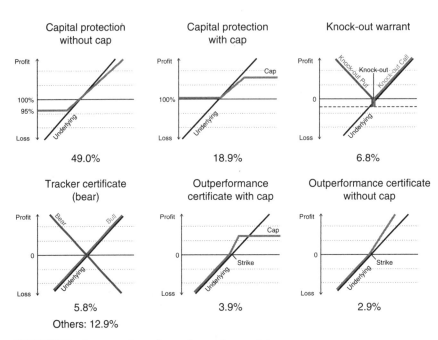

**FIGURE 7.55** Structured products chosen by participants

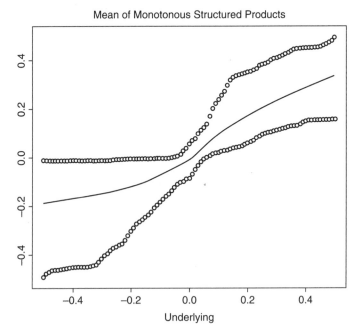

**FIGURE 7.56** The average structured product as designed by the participants in the experiment (line) with 95% confidence intervals (circles)
*Source*: Rieger & Hens (2012)

most popular types are shown in Figure 7.55 (see previous page). The fact that the most frequently designed types resembled capital protected products (with or without cap) underlines the importance of loss aversion in investment decisions of private investors.

The payoff of the average favorite product is illustrated in Figure 7.56. The payoff looks like the payoff of a capped capital protected product and has features of a *covered call,* which had been found to be popular among investors buying options.

## 7.5   CONCLUSION

Product design is about structuring assets in a way that serves the needs of the client soon or over the client's life cycle. The desired payoff can be achieved either with derivative instruments, as structured products are, or with traditional assets such as bonds and equities. The main advantage of the structured products is that they can offer capital protection with a fair participation on the performance of the underlying. These criteria are particularly important for prospect theory clients who are ready to give up some gain potential to prevent losses that they would need to realize with a direct investment in the underlying. An experiment with real investors provides further support for the existence of such preferences.

At first glance, structured products with capital protection appear attractive for clients with prospect theory preferences. In our case study, however, for the average prospect theory client it would be better to buy and hold the underlying unless the client expects that its return will be too volatile. In this case, the structured product may be a better alternative. A dynamic perspective shows that structured products with capital protection are better than stocks and bonds because they avoid a high drawdown along the investment path and yet achieve a higher payoff at the end.

# CHAPTER 8

# Dynamic Asset Allocation

**W**e have seen how to find the optimal asset allocation for different investors. In this chapter, we will discuss whether and how the asset allocation changes over time. We will answer the following two questions:

1. Does the length of the investment horizon matter for the optimal asset allocation? For example, should younger investors (with a longer investment horizon) hold more risky assets than older investors?
2. Should investors care about the ups and downs of the markets? How should they adjust their asset allocation optimally to the market movements?

In the theoretical literature, we find clear answers to these questions. Two of the best-known theorists in economics and in finance, the Nobel Laureates Paul Samuelson and Robert Merton, prove the "No time diversification theorem" (Merton, 1969; Samuelson, 1969)—that is, that in an efficient market, asset allocation is independent of the investment horizon.[1] Moreover, in this case the optimal response to the ups and downs of the efficient market is to hold the proportions of the asset allocation fixed (i.e., to rebalance). A market is efficient when it is not predictable—that is, the odds of having a good or a bad market in the future are independent from the past. Rebalancing implies that one should buy more of those assets that depreciated while those appreciating should be sold so that along the investment process one holds the percentage of wealth invested in the various asset classes fixed.

In practice, however, we find very different recommendations. Typically, the recommendation is to increase the percentage of risky assets in the strategic asset allocation when the investment horizon increases. This is reasonable because risky assets have a positive expected return and over time, good years will offset bad years so that the risk to fall below a certain benchmark will decrease with the investment horizon. One example based on

---

[1]The researchers assume that the investor is an expected utility maximizer with constant relative risk aversion and constant beliefs. See the appendix for a more details.

these ideas is the so-called *age rule* according to which the percentage of stocks held should be the retirement age minus the age of the investor. Some fund providers (e.g., Fidelity), have implemented this type of investment scheme in a retirement fund.[2] Additionally, in practice we find various recommendations how to change the asset allocation over time. One prominent recommendation is to do nothing and just buy and hold the assets. As an effect, after each appreciation of risky assets, the amount of wealth invested in risky assets increases. The opposite holds true after depreciations. Also, there are a vast amount of active funds suggesting strategies that react to indicators or news. Thus there is a clash between rational theory and practice and we will show that behavioral finance can combine the two.

## 8.1 TIME DIVERSIFICATION

According to time diversification, the attractiveness of a risky investment increases with the length of the investment horizon. If one can wait longer, good times would compensate for bad times. But should long-term investors hold more risky assets than short-term investors? The famous *no time diversification theorem"* (Merton, 1969; Samuelson, 1969) says that under certain conditions, the optimal asset allocation does not depend on the investment horizon. The conditions refer to the investors' preferences and the predictability of asset returns. The optimal asset allocation does not depend on the investment horizon if the investors maximize their final expected wealth while having a constant relative risk aversion (CRRA) and the investment returns are unpredictable.[3] What if the first assumption does not hold and the investor is the typical prospect theory investor? Example 8.1 deals with this possibility.

---

### EXAMPLE 8.1

We consider an initial investment of 1,000 over two periods on a random walk with two equally likely states; one giving a 20% gain the other a 10% loss. After one year, there is a 50% chance that the investor gains 20% and a 50% chance for a loss of 10%.

---

[2]See Fidelity's Freedom Fund: http://personal.fidelity.com/products/funds/content/ DesignYourPortfolio/freedomfunds.shtml.cvsr
[3]See Appendix 15.5. for a mathematical proof.

If this is a typical prospect theory investor who is therefore loss averse by a factor of 2.25 (and to keep the example simple, the investor is not risk averse), the investor will not want to invest since the possible gains after one year cannot compensate for the possible losses ($2.25 \times 10\% > 20\%$). However, if the investor intends to invest for two years, then the investor would face a 75 percent probability of making a gain and the investor achieves a positive prospect utility from investing: ($0.5 \times 8\% + 0.25 \times 44\% - 2.25 \times 0.25 \times 19\% > 0$). Thus, the investor will invest. This shows that the willingness to take risks depends on the investment horizon.

The effect that with an increase of the investment horizon loss averse investors allocate more toward risky assets was first observed by Benartzi & Thaler (1995). A closer look reveals that the effect is driven by the property that more risky assets have a higher expected return than less risky assets. Therefore, we need to look at data to see whether this holds true for typical asset classes. The following figure is based on the long-term stock market and bond market data that Kenneth French updates on his webpage.

Figure 8.57 shows that the longer the investment horizon, the more likely it is that the less risky assets will be beaten by the riskier assets. On a one-year investment horizon, bonds are better than stocks in only one out of three years. On a 10-year investment horizon, bonds are better than stocks in only one out of seven decades. Thus, loss-averse investors will allocate more to stocks the longer their investment horizon is.

To see how the attractiveness of strategies varies with investors' risk and loss aversion and the investment horizon, Dierkes, Erner, & Zeisberger (2010) compared the attractiveness of six investment strategies (pure stocks, pure bonds, buy-and-hold (bah), constant mix, protective put (pp), and best-of-two (bot))[4] for various behavioral investors with an investment horizon ranging from 1 to 60 months. The attractiveness of the strategies is illustrated in Figure 8.58 in dependence of investor's loss aversion (vertical axes), the risk tolerance (horizontal axes), and the investment horizon

---

[4]Pure stocks (bonds) is a portfolio with 100% stocks (bonds). Buy and hold means to initially form a portfolio with 50% stocks and 50% bonds, which is then never changed, while constant mix means that a 50:50 asset allocation of stocks and bonds is rebalanced. Finally, the protective put strategy is like a stock portfolio with some capital protection while the best-of-two strategy converts stocks into bonds and vice versa, depending on the previous period's success.

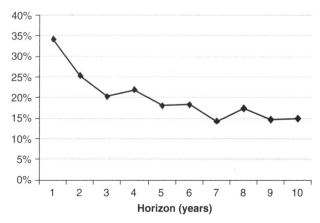

**FIGURE 8.57** Relative frequency of bonds outperforming stocks on various investment horizons
*Data source*: http://mba.tuck.dartmouth.edu/pages/faculty/ken.french/data_library.html

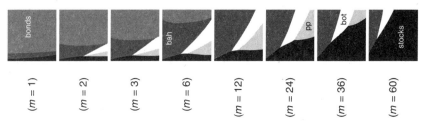

**FIGURE 8.58** Attractiveness of investment strategies in dependence of investor's preferences and investment horizon
*Source*: Dierkes, Erner & Zeisberger (2010)

($m = 1, 2, 3, 6, 12, 24, 36, 60$). The results show that for investors with short investment horizon (left side) the pure bond strategy is preferred. For these investors, the pure stock strategy (black area) is optimal only if they are not loss averse. As the horizon increases, the buy-and-hold (bah) strategy (in dark gray) replaces the pure bonds strategy. Moreover, with the investment horizon, the attractiveness of the pure stocks strategy increases. For the median investor, the pure stock strategy is the most attractive for horizons from 18 months onward. Interestingly, the constant mix strategy is inferior for almost all analyzed preferences and investment horizons.

How does the asset allocation of the mean-variance investor respond to changes in the investment horizon? The answer to this question depends on whether the mean and the variance of the returns increase proportionally with the length of the time horizon. With logarithmic returns, assuming efficient markets the expected return and the variance increase proportionally with time, so that the time horizon does not matter. With simple returns, time diversification is not possible as well, because the variance does not increase proportionally with time so that the optimal risk exposure decreases with the investment horizon.[5] Hence, for mean-variance investors there is no time diversification.

So, to rationalize the age rule that calls for reducing the risk exposure over time, one needs behavioral finance. The rule can be justified by the asymmetry between gains and losses that investors perceive. In traditional finance, this is not possible.

To be fair we should mention that traditional finance gives a different reason for the impact of the time horizon on the asset allocation. If an investor derives income from financial and from human capital, then, as the investor ages, the net present value of the income from human capital decreases relative to that of the financial capital. Thus, to hold the risk in the overall portfolio constant while the human capital decreases, the investor should also decrease the fraction of the risky assets in the financial capital. But this reasoning is a bit cynical in an advisor–client relationship. It means the following: If the advisor does a bad job and the investment loses a lot, then a young client can still work long enough to recuperate the losses.

## 8.2 REBALANCING

A long time ago, the Talmud recommended the following asset allocation: "One third in business (buying and selling things), one third kept liquid (e.g., gold coins), and one third in land (real estate)." Many other recommendations have followed. For example, Harry Markowitz recommended using mean-variance analysis and we have recommended using the more general prospect theory. The question then arises how one should change the asset allocation once the ups and downs of the markets have impacted it. A simple answer is to rebalance—that is, to restore the original weights one wanted to hold. Rebalancing implies investing countercyclically, which is not easy psychologically because people prefer conforming decisions. Thus, it is

---

[5] See Section 15.5.

important that the investors understand the logic behind it and the limitations of it.

### 8.2.1  The Case for Rebalancing

Suppose, as we assumed in Chapter 2, the investor frames the investments in terms of the returns that can be achieved over the given investment horizon. The investor also has a reference point below which investment results are considered as losses and above which results are considered as gains. Moreover, the investor might be loss averse and have an s-shaped value function that turns from being convex to becoming concave in the reference point. These features of the value function determine the optimal asset allocation, as shown in Section 8.1. If the value function does not change over time and the market view of the investor does not change, there is no need for the investor to reconsider the investments in a later period. That is, the investor should rebalance so that the asset allocation has the same risk and return characteristics as before. Note that if the investor does not rebalance, the actual asset allocation might shift away from the optimal point on the behavioral efficient frontier, as Figure 8.59 shows.

### 8.2.2  The Case Against Rebalancing

In this section, we show that three rational reasons can imply departing from rebalancing. One reason is that the investor has a specific goal so that the ups and downs of the market bring him closer to it or further away from it. The second reason is that the investor builds the asset allocation focusing on the risk ability, which changes due to the ups and downs of the market. Third, the investor might be good in analyzing indicators and news and thus

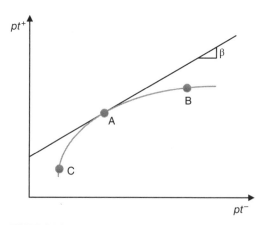

**FIGURE 8.59**  The asset allocation without rebalancing when the market goes up (point B) or down (point C) compared to the optimal asset allocation with rebalancing (point A)

wants to base the asset allocation on their changes. As before, we start with an illustration, provided in Example 8.2.

---

### EXAMPLE 8.2

Berta has a current wealth of 1 million Swiss francs and wants to buy a cottage in the Swiss Alps two years from now, which costs at least 1.2 million Swiss francs. Berta is loss averse—that is, falling short of her target by 0.1 million is equivalent for her to exceeding the target by 0.2 million. Moreover, Berta is not greedy. She has a strictly decreasing marginal utility from exceeding the target; precisely, she evaluates those gains by the square root of them. This also implies that she has a decreasing marginal rate from suffering when missing the target (i.e., she evaluates losses also by the square root of them). Berta can invest her wealth in two assets: a risk-free asset and a risky asset that with equal probability can either appreciate by 20% or depreciate by 10%. Suppose Berta plans to hold through a simple investment strategy (either investing all or nothing over both periods). What shall she do? Invest fully in the risky asset or stay in the risk-free asset?

The answer depends on the risk-free rate. If that rate is sufficient to achieve the target of 1.2 million in two years, then it is better for her to "play it safe" and invest fully in the risk-free asset than to fully invest in the risky asset, as the following computation shows.

If the risk-free rate is 10% then $PT(\text{risk-free}) = (1.21 - 1.2)^{0.5} = 0.1$, which is larger then

$$PT(\text{risky asset}) = 0.25 \times (1.44 - 1.2)^{0.5} - 0.5 \times 2 \times (1.2 - 1.08)^{0.5}$$
$$- 0.25 \times 2 \times (1.2 - 0.81)^{0.5} = -0.5362.$$

If the risk-free rate is 2%, then $PT(\text{risk-free}) = -2 \times (1.2 - 1.0404)^{0.5} = -0.799$, which is smaller than $PT(\text{risky asset})$. Hence, if Berta invests only in the risk-free rate, she will not be able to reach her target (i.e., she better invests risky).

Continuing this example, assume the risk-free rate is insufficient (2%) and Berta has fully invested in the risky asset for one period and then reconsiders the situation. Will she continue to invest?

The answer to this question depends on whether the risky asset has gone up or down in the first period. After a good market, her prospect utility from staying invested is:

$PT(\text{risky asset}) = 0.5 \times (1.44 - 1.2)^{0.5} - 0.5 \times 2 \times (1.2 - 1.08)^{0.5} = -0.10146$, while switching to the risk-free asset obtains: $PT(\text{risk-free}) =$

_(Continued)_

$(1.224 - 1.2)^{0.5} = 0.154919$. Thus, Berta should "take profits" and secures the goal instead of risking it once more.

After a bad market, her prospect utility from staying invested is: $PT(\text{risky asset}) = -0.5 \times 2 \times (1.2 - 1.08)^{0.5} - 0.5 \times 2 \times (1.2 - 0.81)^{0.5} = -0.97091$, while switching to the risk-free asset obtains: $PT(\text{risk-free}) = (1.2 - 0.918)^{0.5} = -1.06207$. As Berta has a decreasing marginal utility from suffering, she decides to stay invested in the risky asset and keep a chance reducing the losses.

The effect can also be seen by calculating the optimal asset allocation in the risky asset at the beginning of the investment and comparing it with the asset allocation after good times and after bad times. Table 11 illustrates the effect using different reference points. If the reference point is not too high, Berta should always reduce the optimal exposure to the risky asset after good times and keep or increase it after bad times.

**TABLE 11**   Optimal exposure to the risky asset over time with an investment goal

| Reference point | Optimal exposure to the risky asset at the beginning | Optimal exposure to the risky asset good times | Optimal exposure to the risky asset after bad times |
|---|---|---|---|
| 1.1 | 71% | 17% | 100% |
| 1.2 | 100% | 6% | 100% |
| 1.3 | 100% | 88% | 100% |
| 1.4 | 100% | 100% | 100% |

With respect to our main theme, *rebalancing*, Example 8.2 shows that an investor with a fixed goal should not keep the strategy fixed but take profits or stay committed, depending on what has happened before. Of course, if Berta had adjusted her reference point to the status quo attained after the first year, then looking ahead for one more period would be the same as initially investing for one period and she would rebalance, which in this case means she will keep her extreme asset allocation being either zero or 1 for the share of the risky asset. Finally, one may argue that it is sometimes better to reflect one's goals before focusing too much on them. Increasing risk to increase the chance of a fixed goal might be inferior to reducing the appreciation level embodied in the goal.

A second reason for not rebalancing is that one has lost the risk ability after a bad market. The next example illustrates the effect.

## EXAMPLE 8.3

Suppose Berta can afford losing 10% of her wealth but not more. In this case, her reference point would be 0.9. If we allow Berta to split her wealth among the assets optimally, we can see that the optimal plan is to first invest 38% of the wealth in the risky asset and then increase it to 54% when the value of the risky asset increases and reduce it to 27% when the value of the risky asset decreases in the second period.[6] The reason for decreasing the exposure to the risky asset is that when the investor loses and gets close to the risk ability constraint as defined by the reference point, the investor will try to avoid further losses by reducing the risk. When downside markets may challenge the risk ability, the optimal investment behavior becomes pro-cyclical: after gains one should increase the share of risky assets, while after losses one should reduce it. Table 12 illustrates the effect on Berta with different risk ability constraints (reference points). In all cases, the optimal exposure to the risky assets decreases after bad times, as compared to the optimal exposure at the beginning of the investment. This is exactly the case against rebalancing.

**TABLE 12** Optimal exposure to the risky asset over time with a liability constraint

| Reference point | Optimal exposure to the risky asset at the beginning | Optimal exposure to the risky asset after good times | Optimal exposure to the risky asset after bad times |
| --- | --- | --- | --- |
| 0.6 | 100% | 100% | 98% |
| 0.7 | 91% | 100% | 70% |
| 0.8 | 65% | 88% | 47% |
| 0.9 | 38% | 54% | 27% |

---

[6]The optimal allocation can be calculated with the Solver in MS Excel.

Finally, we want to point out that if the investor believes in market timing (i.e., if the expectations change along the investment process), the investor should not rebalance, either. An interesting case is if the investor believes in momentum. Then, after a good market, the investor might not take profits but increase the position, while after a bad market the investor might reduce the share of risky assets. The extent to which this happens depends on the size of the changes in the beliefs. If the investor believes in momentum from the very beginning, the belief in momentum would offset the degree of rebalancing the investor would otherwise do and the investor would effectively follow a buy-and-hold strategy. See Example 8.4.

---

**EXAMPLE 8.4**

To give a numerical example, investigate once more the case where the investor would take profits after a good market. If at the beginning, the investor believes that both states are equally likely but after a good market the investor gets more optimistic, the investor will stay invested. The smallest probability for the good state $(p^*)$ after the market has gone up so that the investor stays fully invested is given by the equation:

$$PT(\text{risky asset}) = PT(\text{risk} - \text{free asset})$$

$$p^* \times (1.44 - 1.2)^{0.5} - 2 \times (1 - p^*) \times (1.2 - 1.08)^{0.5}$$

$$= (1.224 - 1.2)^{0.5},$$

which gives $p^* = 0.717$.

For beliefs below this value, the investor will fully disinvest. For beliefs above this value, the investor will fully invest.

---

## 8.3  CONCLUSION

In this chapter, we have seen that loss-averse investors should increase the proportion of risky assets with their investment horizon. Moreover, we argued that any investor with constant views on the risk return characteristics of the markets should rebalance the portfolio. Exceptions to the rebalancing rule can arise for investors with fixed goals, investors focusing on their risk ability, and confident investors who believe they can change their market views successfully along the ups and downs of the markets. Being obsessed with one's goals might not be wise, and one should rather reflect on whether adjusting them to what can be reasonably expected from the continuation of the investment is a wiser decision. Focusing on the risk ability leads to a pro-cyclical investment style, and one might rather take other means to take care of the risk ability (e.g., by applying the asset split that we explain in the next chapter). Finally, given the many biases in forming good expectations, it will be hard to outperform a passive rebalancing strategy. Thus, our conclusion is that rebalancing should be the benchmark against which more sophisticated strategies should be measured.

# CHAPTER 9

# Life-Cycle Planning

So far, we have mainly dealt with investment situations, where the investors do not need to withdraw wealth for consumption before the ultimate investment result is revealed. If the investors want to make a long-term plan (e.g., along their life-cycle), then it is evident that the consumption and the investment decision must be integrated. Moreover, it is natural in life-cycle planning to assume that the reference consumption level is updated over time. This leads to the effect of *habit formation*; that is, one gets used to a previously high consumption level. Finally, we will discuss how future consumption is discounted to present consumption. The rational way is exponential discounting—like taking compounded interest—while behavioral agents might discount the future against the presence even more, which is the concept of hyperbolic discounting. In addition to the previous chapter, we now have to consider an exogenous flow of wealth (human capital or labor income) that is hump-shaped (highest in the middle period).

The following questions will be addressed from a rational (intertemporal expected discounted utility maximizer) and a behavioral (prospect theory maximizer with hyperbolic discounting adjusting the reference point over the life-cycle) investor:

- What is the best consumption/savings path along the life cycle?
- What is the best proportion of risky assets to financial capital over the life cycle?
- Does it make sense to lock in the investor in a life-cycle product?

The following case study shows what could go wrong when investors plan their consumption and investments along the life cycle.

## 9.1 CASE STUDY

Widow Kassel died in 2007 at the age of 92. She left 30 million euros to the University of Frankfurt. In 1975, she had inherited 2 million euros in the form of 30 to 40 German stocks. She never touched these stocks—she

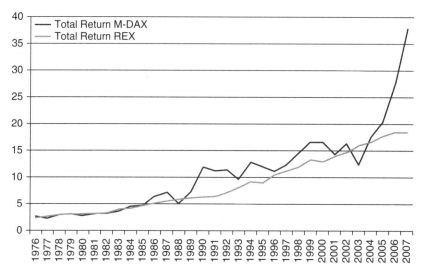

**FIGURE 9.60**  Performance German stocks (DAX) versus bonds (REX)

lived on the dividends in a small rented apartment in Frankfurt Lerchesberg. The performance of her portfolio roughly aligned with the performance of the M-DAX.

Let's first analyze whether Widow Kassel could have achieved a higher final wealth by investing in bonds instead of stocks. The answer of this question depends on the expected investment horizon. In 1974, Mrs. Kassel was 60. If her life expectancy at the time was more than 10 years, then the best investment consisted of 100% stocks (see Figure 9.60).

But could Mrs. Kassel have achieved higher consumption by investing in bonds? The answer to this question depends again on the expected investment horizon. From 1974 to 2007, dividend yields of stocks were smaller than the interest on bonds but stocks appreciated faster. Since Mrs. Kassel decided not to "dip into the capital" and to live from the dividends, we see that her consumption could have been higher if she had lived from the interest on bonds than from the dividends on the stocks (see Figure 9.61). Thus, given her choice—her mental accounting rule—to only live from the cash flows of the investments (dividends or interest payments), bonds would have been better with respect to her consumption and stocks would have been better with respect to final wealth. Hence, the moral of this case study is that the University of Frankfurt benefited from the mental accounting of Widow Kassel while a financial advisor trained in behavioral

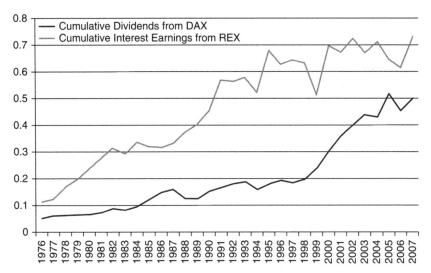

**FIGURE 9.61**   Dividends from DAX versus interest from REX

finance could have helped Widow Kassel to improve on her simple mental accounting rule.

In the following, we consider life-cycle planning problems like that of Mrs. Kassel in a more general setting.

Over time, each agent should make two types of decisions. First, one needs to decide about the savings/consumption, and second, one needs to choose among different investments to save: certificate of deposit, bonds, stocks, but maybe also real estate or durable goods. The higher the savings today, the lower is the current consumption, and the higher is the income (and consumption) in the future. In the end, everything is either consumed or inherited. We will assume that the investors also derive utility from final wealth and do not distinguish here whether this utility results from consuming or passing on their wealth.

## 9.2   CASE STUDY WERNER BRUNI

On April 28, 1979, Werner Bruni became the first lotto millionaire in Switzerland. He successfully bet the numbers 11, 40, 29, 2, 33, 15, and 31, resulting in a prize of CHF 1,69 million. Taxes reduced that to CHF 729,386. In his memories, he wrote that no bank approached him with suitable advice on how to save and invest his winnings for the long term. He was so happy about his jump in wealth that he was very vocal about his newfound fortune, and in a short time he had many new friends and spent everything on houses, cars, holidays, entertainment, and other extravagances. Soon, he was poor again, and today lives from social benefits. But he continues to bet his lucky numbers. He learned at least one lesson: those numbers are winning numbers.

While Widow Kassel and Werner Bruni had the opposite reaction to the sudden increase in wealth, for both, a middle way between not digging into capital and spending everything in a short time would have been best. In the following, we show how traditional finance suggests computing such a golden middle way and how behavioral biases hinder people from pursuing it.

## 9.3 CONSUMPTION SMOOTHING

One of the main empirical observations on consumption behavior is the so-called *permanent income hypothesis*. It asserts that consumption (and saving) responds to *permanent* changes of income and almost not to transitory ones. Further, households do care about having a *smooth* consumption over their whole life so that transitory income changes have little impact on their consumption (and savings) path. Consider, for example, two brothers identical in any aspect; one earns most of his money early in his life (e.g., tennis professional), the other earns most of his money late in his life (e.g., a manager). If they plan their consumption over the life cycle, the tennis professional should save to increase consumption later in his life and the manager should borrow from his future income to finance consumption today.

Why do households care about a smooth consumption? The reason is that—as already suggested by Bernoulli—individuals have a diminishing marginal utility of consumption—that is, the additional utility gained from one unit of consumption decreases with the consumption level. To get an intuition on the link between consumption smoothing and the utility of consumption, consider Example 9.1.

---

### EXAMPLE 9.1

Consider two alternative consumption plans:

1. equal amount of consumption in each of two periods
2. consuming all in one period and nothing in the other

Which consumption plan is more attractive for individuals with a diminishing marginal utility of consumption (concave utility function)?

Agents with a concave utility function would be better off by transferring some consumption from the period of plenty to the period of starvation. This is because the loss in the utility in the period of plenty is more than compensated by the gain in utility in the period of starvation. This is illustrated graphically in Figure 9.62. The dotted arrows indicate the consumption transfer. Let $C_2$ be the consumption in the period of plenty and $C_1$ be the consumption in the period of poverty. We can easily see that the reduction of utility $u(C_2) - u(C_{smooth})$ in the period of plenty is smaller than the increase of utility $u(C_{smooth}) - u(C_1)$ in the period of poverty.

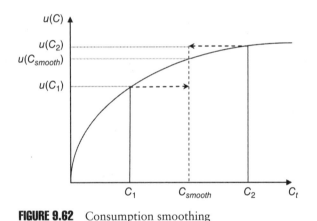

**FIGURE 9.62** Consumption smoothing

## 9.4 THE LIFE-CYCLE HYPOTHESIS

The idea that people have unequal income over time that they try to smooth is the basis of the life-cycle hypothesis developed in the 1950s and 1960s. It deals with the question of why people save. One answer to this question is that people live longer than they can work and generate income. If people want to keep spending, they need to save and accumulate assets during the period they work so that they can reverse the saving process (sell the assets) when they retire. Example 9.2 illustrates the point.

---

**EXAMPLE 9.2**

---

Suppose a 20-year-old man plans to retire at 60 and expects to die when he is 70 years old. His yearly income is $30,000. Thus, over the period of 40 years when he works, he will be able to generate $1,200,000.[1] If the person wants to be able to spend the same amount over his whole life (also after retirement) and does not want to leave wealth after his death, he needs to restrict his spending to $24,000 each year. To be able to spend this amount also after he retires, he will need to save $6,000 per year (or 20% of his yearly income) during the 40 years of working.

Suppose, now, that when he is 20, the man wins $200,000 from playing the lottery. Then, his total income at retirement will be $1,400,000 and over the 50 years of living he will be able to spend $28,000 per year—that is, $4,000 more compared to the case without the win.

Thus, consumption can be financed through income (or through the sale of assets), and its increase should increase consumption.

---

If the economic agent smooths consumption over the whole life span, as suggested by the life-cycle hypothesis, one should not observe any changes in people's spending after retirement. The observed behavior of retirees seems not to accord with these theoretical implications. Elderly people seem to reduce consumption after retirement. They do not appear either to decumulate their wealth at all or to reverse their savings at a rate fast enough to hold up consumption. Whereas according to standard theory investors decide once and for all on holdings of bonds and stocks and then stick to this ratio, common investment advice[2] suggests that the investment behavior depends on the investment horizon. Young people with a long investment horizon should invest more in risky assets, and as people age and have a shorter investment horizon, they should switch more and more to the nonrisky asset.

To understand why people do not behave according to standard economic models, one needs to enrich them by behavioral elements such as

---

[1] Assume for simplicity the income is held in cash and does not earn any interest.
[2] A prominent rule is the "age rule" according to which the share of equity in one's portfolio should be equal to a hundred minus the age of the investor.

self-control, mental accounting, and framing. Hyperbolic discounting can cause investors to spend more today at the expense of saving tomorrow. As a result, they become not prepared for retirement and by myopic loss aversion the degree of risk in their portfolios is inappropriate and the portfolios cannot make up for the lost time. A contrasting problem is when people apply simple rules like "consume from dividends but do not dip into capital" to overcome self-control problems, such that their asset allocations are not balanced and there are too many income-producing assets. Moreover, investors with a self-control bias have a loose sight of financial principles such as compounding of interests and in general, they are unable to deal with the financial aspects of retirement questions.

In the following, we show how these behavioral aspects of life-cycle planning affect investors' decisions by using the behavioral life-cycle hypothesis of Shefrin and Thaler (1988).

## 9.5   THE BEHAVIORAL LIFE-CYCLE HYPOTHESIS

In the behavioral life-cycle hypothesis of Shefrin and Thaler (1988), households have difficulties postponing consumption until retirement because of a lack of self-control. Furthermore, they treat components of their wealth as nonfungible or noninterchangeable. Households are observed to divide wealth into three mental accounts: current spendable income, current assets, and future income. The accounts are important because households feel differently tempted to spend from them.[3] At a given time, the marginal propensity to consume is typically highest out of income ($I$), lowest out of future income ($F$), and somewhere in between for current assets ($A$). This is illustrated graphically in Figure 9.63.

At the beginning, the consumption is financed from the current income account ($I$). As consumption increases, the psychological costs of resisting temptation (willpower effort) decreases so that the total utility $Z$ (equal to the pleasure from consumption + pain from willpower effort) increases but at diminishing rate. When the entire balance of the current income account is consumed, the next marginal unit of consumption is financed out of the asset account ($A$). However, when invading this account, the consumer needs to pay an entrance fee, which reduces the total utility $Z$ at the beginning. Similar remarks apply when the next account $F$ is invaded.

---

[3]This contrasts with the permanent-income hypothesis that says that wealth and income should be treated in the same way if they are permanent.

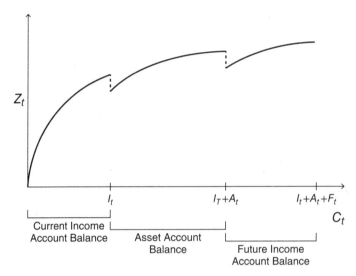

**FIGURE 9.63**   Mental accounts
*Source*: H. M. Shefrin & Thaler, 1988

An application of the different marginal propensity to consume out of the mental accounts is that the saving rate of the households can be affected by the way wealth is framed. An income paid in the form of a lump sum bonus is treated differently than a regular payment, even if the bonus is expected.

People's inter-temporal decisions of consumption and saving (investing) are additionally influenced by the discount factors used to determine the current value of future consumption. Laboratory and field studies find that discount rates used by decision makers are much greater in the short run than in the long run, which contradicts the predictions of utility function with stationary fixed discount rates. This explains why some people prefer "one apple today" to "two apples tomorrow" but at the same time they prefer "two apples in one year and one day" to "one apple in one year." To express these time-inconsistent preferences in a formal way, economists assume that individuals make decisions based on the following utility function.

$$u(c) = u(c_0) + \beta[\delta u(c_1) + \delta^2 u(c_2) + \cdots + \delta^T u(c_T)]$$

where $0<\beta<1$ is the hyperbolic and $0<\delta<1$ is the exponential discount factor. To see the effect of the hyperbolic discounting compare the utilities of consumption between two subsequent periods over time. For example, the

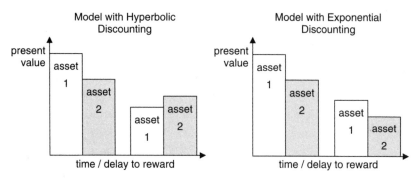

**FIGURE 9.64** Hyperbolic versus exponential discounting

utility of current consumption $u(c_0)$ is $\beta\delta$ times greater than the utility of consumption one period ahead $u(c_1)$ but the utility of consumption in period 2 $u(c_2)$ is only $\delta$ times greater than the utility of consumption one period ahead $u(c_3)$. As a result, the consumption $c_1$ is discounted stronger than the consumption $c_3$ compared to a period before. Consequently, in period 0 the agent would prefer to consume immediately but after arriving in period 2, the agent would prefer to postpone consumption for the next period. Such preferences are called *time-inconsistent*. Figure 9.64 illustrates the effect. If at the beginning the agent prefers to consume asset 1 to asset 2, that is received in one period; later, the agent prefers to wait one period and take asset 2. If agent's time preferences were exponential and not hyperbolically discounted, there would be no preference reversal.

Inter-temporal decisions are additionally influenced by habit formation. Habitual behavior can be defined as a behavior displaying a positive relation between past and current consumption. A higher level of consumption in the previous period results in a higher level of consumption in the current period, holding wealth constant. For example, a given standard of living usually provides less utility to persons who got accustomed to a higher standard in the past.

To consider the effect of habit formation, we assume that client's utility is:

$$u(c) = u(c_0) + \beta[\delta(u(c_1)(1 - h)) + hv(c_1 - c_0)$$
$$+ \delta^2((1 - h)u(c_2) + hv(c_2 - c_1)) + \dots]$$

where $0 < \beta \leq 1$ is the hyperbolic discount factor, $0 < \delta \leq 1$ is the time-consistent discount rate, $h$ is a coefficient determining whether the utility is driven by habit formation and $v$ is the prospect theory value function.

From the habit formation perspective, the reference point is the previous period consumption. In dependence on the coefficient $h$, the client's utility depends on the one hand on the current consumption and on the other hand on the consumption growth. For $h = 0$, only the consumption level matters; for $h = 1$, only consumption growth is important.

So, to motivate people to save (and invest) more, one should probably focus on product design. Benartzi and Thaler, for example, suggest a program called Save More Tomorrow (SMarT) (Thaler & Benartzi, 2004). The basic idea of the program is to give workers the option of committing themselves to increase their savings rate later, each time they get a raise. The plan has the following ingredients: First, employees are asked to increase their contribution rates a considerable time before their scheduled pay increase. Because of hyperbolic discounting, the lag between the time when they sign up and the start-up date should be feasible.

Second, if employees join, their contribution to the plan is increased beginning with the first payment after a raise. This feature mitigates the perceived loss aversion of a cut in the payment employees can take home. Third, the contribution rate continues to increase on each scheduled raise until the contribution rate reaches a predefined maximum. In this way, inertia and status quo bias help to keep the employees in the plan. Fourth, the employee can opt out of the plan at any time. This feature makes employees feel more comfortable joining the program. According to the authors, the initial experience with the SMarT plan has been remarkably successful. Most of the people decided to use it and to stick with it. As a result, their saving rates tripled (see Benartzi and Thaler, 2004).

## 9.6 CONCLUSION

Life-cycle planning is complicated since it requires to integrate investment and consumption decisions. Case studies show that people need advice on it. While the rational solution is based on the idea of consumption smoothing behavioral biases like mental accounting, hyperbolic discounting and habit formation are huge hurdles. As Nobel laureate Richard Thaler has suggested cleverly designed contracts can help people to overcome those obstacles.

# CHAPTER 10

# Risk Profiling

This chapter combines all insights of behavioral finance that we laid out previously. In the first chapter, we explained which typical behavioral biases hinder investors to achieve the best possible performance. As we showed, a diagnostic tool helps detecting those biases and suggests ways moderating them. Thereafter, we laid the foundation for this chapter by outlining the most up-to-date decision theory: prospect theory. Given all this the advisor must recommend an asset allocation that yields the optimal combination of reward and risk and that the client can hold through during the ups and downs of the markets. As the study of Brinson, Hood, & Beebower (1995) and Brinson, Singer, & Beebower (1991) have shown, the asset allocation determines 90% of the investment success—but to achieve this success the investors must also be able to hold through the strategy. Thus, risk profiling is one of the key elements of investment advice. Besides this important conceptual aspect of risk profiling it is also important for legal reasons. In a sense, risk-profiling means that the advisor and the client write a contract that protects both sides if a dispute arises sometime later. Finally, in some countries the regulator requires using a risk profiler that satisfies some minimal standards and in some countries the regulator might even mystery shop to check whether a risk profiler is used appropriately in the advisory process.[1]

Used appropriately, *risk profiling* (together with diagnostics) is a process by which investors can achieve the logical consistency between the set of investment possibilities, their goals and constraints, and preferences. Only after this has been achieved should implementation of the optimal asset allocation with products be addressed. Risk profiling has four main steps:

1. *Questionnaire*: collecting information from the client
2. *Risk cube*: evaluating information collected from the client

---

[1]Mystery shopping reveals that some advisors first seduce the client to buy an investment product that seems attractive for the client but is only good for the advisor since he earns a high margin on it and finally the advisor tells the client how to fill the risk profiler so that the agreed product can be sold.

3. *Portfolio construction*: delivering an investment strategy for the client
4. *Reporting*: explaining the characteristics of the investment solution to the client

In this chapter, we discuss how behavioral finance can be used to develop a risk profiling process, focusing on these four steps. We will present an example of a risk profiler based on behavioral finance. While the logical sequence of the process is "Questionnaire," "Risk cube," "Portfolio construction," and "Reporting," our description will follow a different order, since the choice of the evaluation model (the design of the risk cube) obviously affects the way the questionnaire is constructed. Therefore, Section 10.4 presents the risk cube and its characterization under behavioral finance and classical finance. Section 10.5 describes a behavioral risk profiler based on prospect theory. The discussion will benefit from a case study that is first presented in Section 10.3 and then carried through the whole chapter.

## 10.1   RISK-PROFILING METHODOLOGIES

There are several methodologies that one can use to define a risk profiler. The *ad-hoc methodology* is the most common (and at the same time most rudimental) approach used in the financial industry. The risk profiler is mostly based on a basic questionnaire created by a team of client advisors, business developers, and maybe also experts with a quantitative background. The composition of the questionnaire is mainly driven by intuition and experience. It is further intended to fulfill the basic legal and supervisory requirements. The main advantage of this method is that the questions are close to the needs in business practice. For example, the advisor knows from his experience which questions the client is willing to answer. However, the ad-hoc methodology is likely not able to assess risk preferences in a reliably way. Furthermore, some basic desirable requirements such as reliability or validity are not necessarily fulfilled.[2] Research conducted at

---

[2] Reliability is a measure of how consistent a test result is when the test is repeated. In this context, the interrelatedness of questions is important and should be proven with a statistical test. The validity looks at how well a test measures what it is intended to measure (e.g., that the students with the highest test score are the best ones in the class).

the University of Zurich has also demonstrated that questions in typical bank questionnaires do not lead to optimal investment decisions (Bradbury, Hens, & Zeisberger, 2014 and Bachmann et al. 2017). Thus, doing an ad-hoc risk profile is very risky for the bank since it will be hard to defend it when clients claim that they were misled by advice based on the risk profiler.

The *psychometric methodology* aims at measuring psychological concepts such as knowledge, abilities, attitudes, or personal traits. It needs to be combined with other questions that determine the needs and the risk ability. The information is normally collected with a long questionnaire that asks similar questions multiple times. Once very many respondents have answered the questions one can group the answers into clusters, which can be interpreted as the psychological concepts just mentioned. From this clustering, a scoring method is derived. The answers to each question are given a certain score, which add up to a total score. The total score is then mapped to a risk profile, which is often linked to a general investment strategy. Of course, the scoring cannot account for nonlinear dependencies between different questions, which might lead to considerably inaccuracies. But the most disturbing feature of the psychometric approach is that the psychological concepts might be fictitious. This is, the psychometric approach has no external validity by which its predictions can be validated or rejected. The questionnaire might also be perceived as too "psychological."

The *utility methodology* attempts to derive an individual utility function for each client based on a scientifically state-of-the art decision theoretical model (e.g., expected utility theory or prospect theory). As in the case of prospect theory, the utility function is determined by different elements, such as loss aversion, risk aversion, and a reference point. Prospect theory is currently the most successful and important decision theoretical model in the behavioral economic literature. Mostly quantitative questions are used to derive the utility function (e.g., what is the willingness to pay for a given investment). The approach has the advantage that it is scientifically founded and that optimal asset allocations can be calculated based on the previously derived utility function. Consequently, it is also possible to explicitly connect the characteristics of the proposed investment solution with client's risk preferences and needs. This way, the proposed investment solution can be illustrated and explained to clients referring to their characteristics. Depending on the theory used, various aspects of risk preferences can be modeled, as, for example, loss aversion, which has been demonstrated to be a very robust preference. The utility method thus represents a very powerful tool and does not have to rely on rules of thumb as most other methodologies. The disadvantage of the methodology is that quantitative questions are more difficult to answer for the client. This problem can be overcome by using qualitative questions that approximate the more precise quantitative questions.

The *socioeconomic methodology* focuses on the client's socioeconomic characteristics such as age, gender, income, wealth, marital status, number of children, and job position. It is empirically justified by identifying correlations between socioeconomic factors, client's personality traits, and risk preferences. For example, it is known that men are on average more willing to take financial risks than women or that older people are less willing to take risk than younger people. The main advantage of the socioeconomic approach is that the data are relatively easily available, which implies further advantages like a quick and easy evaluation of the results, and it is thus relatively inexpensive and easy to administrate. Some of the data might also be already available as financial institutions must gather this information for legal reasons anyhow. Of course, the limits of this approach—if implemented in a pure manner—are that it relies on average relations between socioeconomic variables and risk preferences. Due to heterogeneity between the clients among a group with similar socioeconomic characteristics, the risk tolerance might well be quite different.

The *biological–neurological methodology* comprises physically measurable characteristics such as brain activity or genetic analysis. Research findings have shown that some common brain areas are affected when an individual is confronted with a specific financial situation (e.g., gain or losses). The use of the biological–neurological methodology has the advantage that the results of the analysis are based on concrete observations (e.g., brain activities or genetic findings) so that one does not have to rely on revealed preferences (stated answers). The acquisition of the required information is, however, expensive and relatively impractical.

All methodologies outlined above have in common that they indirectly map gathered information to investment advice in a multistep approach. Alternatively, it is possible to derive optimal investment strategies or asset allocations directly by asking clients what their preferred strategy or allocation is. The major disadvantage is that these questions might have little meaning to many investors and answers might not be robust. A way to circumvent this problem is to enable clients to experience possible outcomes of financial decisions. This is the *experience sampling methodology*. In academic literature, this approach is called *experience sampling* because experience is simulated from an underlying model describing the payoff distributions of the relevant investment solutions. Research findings in psychology and decision making have recently demonstrated that people who are exposed to experience sampling have significantly improved awareness for real-world risk-return trade-offs. Interestingly, studies also have shown that people are more willing to take risks and, importantly, despite this higher risk-taking are not less satisfied with their investment decisions after receiving return feedback (Kaufmann, Weber, & Haisley, 2013 and Bradbury, Hens, & Zeisberger, 2014). People also reported feeling better informed and confident about their investment decision. The research is ongoing—for example, we still need to test the persistency of the effect.

Experience sampling intends to align perceived and actual risk and serves as an effective tool for expectations management. The disadvantage of the methodology lies in the necessity of using return distributions for the experience sampling. These distributions can be based on empirical data or expectations about future returns, but might not resemble actual future returns. Furthermore, the derivation of optimal strategies might take longer than for other methodologies, and the method requires the use of an adequate electronic device (computer, notebook, or tablet).

Nowadays, the growing quantity of data available to financial institutions allows for a detailed analysis of clients' behavior. In principle, clients' transactions and trading behavior, for example, can be analyzed to develop emotional and risk profilers, such as methodologies to describe of how clients typically react to the performance of their investments or, more generally, to the market environment. With the use of *artificial intelligence (AI) techniques* (e.g., machine learning techniques), banks can use past observations to identify typical patterns in clients' behavior, and thus to predict how clients will react in the future when confronted with risk (e.g., losses and volatility). AI-based profiling tools are potentially powerful, but they require big datasets and very detailed information for each client. Moreover, AI-based profiling tools could be misleading, because they might fail to disentangle risk tolerance from other personality traits and from behavioral biases. Thus, AI-based methodologies might also fail to distinguish between past behavior and optimal behavior.

## 10.2 COMPARING RISK-PROFILING METHODOLOGIES

As we have shown, the various risk profilers were growing out of different research silos (behavioral finance, psychology, sociology, neurology, etc.). Therefore, it is not surprising that they use different methodologies and lead to different questionnaires and evaluation methods. The obvious question to ask is which risk profiler is best suited for the practical purpose it needs to solve. Unfortunately, not much research has addressed this interdisciplinary question. A long time ago, Rice (2005) showed that for the same client applying different risk profilers leads to a different assessment of his risk tolerance. More recently, Hens & Mayer (2017) demonstrated that for the same client and the same market view of the bank, applying different decision theories leads to different asset allocations. Thus, combining these two results we know that selecting carefully the most appropriate methodology indeed matters for risk profiling. Moreover, Dorn & Huberman (2005) compared the recommended risk profiler asset allocations with actual behavior of investors and concluded that there is a difference between what they say and what they do.

This motivated Bachmann et al. (2017) to compare risk tolerance questions and methods along a learning ladder like the advisory process in practice. The idea was to filter out those questions that can be used to predict the risk taking of investors once they have understood the various aspects of the investment problem. Some questions used in practice could predict the initial risk taking behavior, which was however revised later. In other words, it would not have been a good advice to recommend an asset allocations based on those questions. Bachmann et al. (2017) find that risk taking can be predicted by some questions on individuals' risk tolerance, but it is not related to self-reported investment experience. Although simulated experience as part of their study design improves the risk awareness and leads to higher risk taking, it cannot substitute the assessment of the risk tolerance and more precisely the assessment of individual's loss aversion. In contrast, self-assessed risk tolerance measures are not suitable for predicting risk taking in any stage of the decision process. This first comparative study gives support for the prospect theory-based approach in general and for loss aversion in particular.

## 10.3   A CASE STUDY

Sabine Fisher (25 years old) lives in New York and is single. She just inherited $500,000. She wants to use this amount to finance her own company in 8 years, when she will have completed her MBA in marketing, gained extensive experience in public relations, and created a professional network. According to her assessment, the *minimum* capital needed to start her business is $650,000 and she will consider not being able to reach this amount in 8 years as a loss. She decided to ask for advice from Bank BF to find a suitable investment strategy. She has never invested in any asset class, but has read from time to time the finance section in the newspaper. Therefore, she is aware of the trade-off between risk and reward offered by asset classes.

While she is completing her MBA, Sabine works part time, and her yearly income is just enough to cover the regular expenses. To face unexpected expenses, she wants to put aside at least $200,000 from her inherence as a reserve.

Sabine is very loss averse with respect to her investment goal, since she really wants to have her own company. She has dreamed about this since when she was 15 years old. By contrast, she is less concerned about volatility and can stand through some fluctuations in her wealth. However, in case of a large temporary drawdown, she would consider changing her strategy almost immediately.

## 10.4 THE RISK DIMENSIONS

Risk is the possibility that undesirable events happen. Undesirable events are not uniquely defined. First, each investor can have a different view on what is undesirable and this view shapes the *risk preference*. For example, Sabine Fisher considers the possibility that she will not be able to start her company as an undesirable event; thus, from her perspective, risk is the possibility of missing the target of $650,000. However, this view is specific to her investment objectives, ambitions and preferences. Second, even if two investors agree on what is an undesirable event, they could have different perceptions of the possibility that an investment strategy delivers an undesirable outcome. This perception shapes the *risk awareness*. Finally, two investors may face different constraints, which determine the *risk ability*. For example, Sabine Fisher needs to put $200,000 on the side to face unexpected losses, since she doesn't have any additional capital she could use in this case.

This leads us to the definition of risk along three different dimensions:

- Risk preference
- Risk awareness
- Risk ability

To evaluate risk, one should define a way to measure or describe the three risk dimensions. Here classical and behavioral finance propose two different paradigms. Traditional finance builds on the assumption of rationality and assumes that investors possess risk preferences that are normatively acceptable—that is, consistent with the set of requirements that lead to expected utility theory and, under some conditions, to mean-variance analysis. Moreover, investors are assumed to possess a correct perception of risk; that is, their risk awareness is not affected by behavioral biases and misjudgments. Finally, risk ability is described using a value-at-risk constraint—that is, a constraint on the probability of extremely unfavorable events.

By contrast, behavioral finance builds on prospect theory. Risk preferences are characterized by coding payoffs in term of gains and losses with respect to a reference point (which corresponds, e.g., to a given target payoff, to a benchmark, or to the current wealth level), by loss aversion, by extreme aversion to large temporary losses (investment temperament), and by uncertainty aversion. Risk awareness can be affected by behavioral biases, investment experience, and financial knowledge (see Chapter 2 for a discussion). Finally, risk ability is addressed using mental accounting—that is, investors split their asset into two different mental accounts: one refers to dedicated assets, for which the risk tolerance is typically very low, while the other refers to free assets, for which the risk tolerance is usually higher.

Table 13 summarizes the behavioral and traditional finance paradigms to characterize the risk dimensions.

Concerning risk preferences, the difference between the behavioral and the classical finance paradigms is visualized in Figure 10.65. The figure shows the prospect theory and the mean-variance value functions on final wealth. The main differences are: (i) a change in slope at the references point ($RP$) for the prospect theory value function, which captures loss aversion; and (ii) a change of slope for the prospect theory value function at a given target level $W_{min}$, which captures aversion to large losses (investment temperament). It is clear from Figure 10.65 that the mean-variance value function arises as special case of the prospect theory value function, as already discussed in Chapter 6.

**TABLE 13**   Risk dimensions under behavioral and classical finance paradigms

|  | Behavioral Finance | Traditional Finance |
| --- | --- | --- |
| Risk preference | Gains and losses (with respect to reference point) Loss aversion Uncertainty aversion Investment temperament | Expected returns and volatility |
| Risk awareness | Behavioral biases Financial knowledge (Experience) | Rationality No misperception |
| Risk ability | Asset split | Value-at-risk constraint |

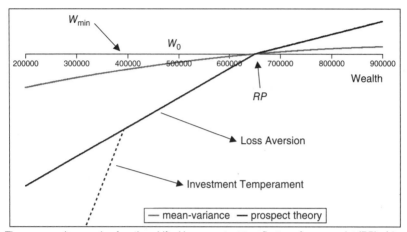

The mean-variance value function shifted by a constant to reflect a reference point (RP) of 0, which can facilitate the comparison with the prospect theory value function. $W_0$ = 500,000 USD is the initial wealth, $RP$ = 650,000 USD is the reference point and $W_{min}$ = 400,000 USD is a target level which define large losses.

**FIGURE 10.65** Prospect theory and mean-variance value functions on final wealth to characterize risk preferences

## 10.5 BEHAVIORAL RISK PROFILER

The questionnaire is used to collect information from clients. In this section we present a questionnaire, which is built on the behavioral finance paradigm, used to characterize the different dimensions of risk, as discussed in the previous section. As an illustration, we apply the questionnaire to the case of Sabine Fisher.

### 10.5.1 Investment Goals

As discussed in the introduction, investment goals affect the way an investor perceives the investment universe, as goals act as reference points to code payoffs in terms of gains and losses. Investors' investment goals should be addressed in the context of an individual financial planner, where goals' priorities should also be reported. Sometimes attributing a monetary value to goals is difficult, specifically for goals far away in the future. In this case, one can also access specific databases where the monetary values of goals are estimated (e.g., based on previous goals of other clients).

The question about the investment goals enters in the evaluation model, as it determines the reference point the client applies to evaluate the performance of the investment strategy (see later the discussion on expectations).

**FIGURE 10.66**    Question on the investment goals
*Source*: BhFS Behavioral Finance Solutions.

Moreover, asking about investment goals is extremely useful because it helps clients to think about what they expect from their investment. It is also necessary for reporting. The purpose is to keep a record of what the client's goals are in general to be aware of this at an organizational level and to be consistent with regulation requirements.

**Our Case Study**    Sabine Fisher wants to start her own business. This investment goal is illustrated in Figure 10.66.

### 10.5.2   Investment Amount and Investment Horizon

This question determines the amount the investor is looking to invest. Moreover, the question also specifies how much of the investment amount the client anticipates needing during the investment period (i.e., a reserve amount). This can also be obtained from an individual financial planner that describes the financial situation of the client, including income, assets, liabilities, and goals. The reserve amount defines the asset split. Thus, it sets a constraint on the optimal asset allocation to make sure that the clients future liabilities will be protected. The constraint corresponds to a minimum investment in cash. Finally, the question also asks about the investment horizon, which sets the relevant distribution of returns to determine the optimal asset allocation (see Figure 10.67).

**Our Case Study**    Sabine Fisher is looking to invest $500,000 and put $200,000 in reserve. This implies a minimum allocation to cash of 40%. The investment horizon is 8 years, as this is the time when she wants to start her own business.

The questions that follow refer to the whole investment amount, including dedicated assets. As discussed, the asset split determines a constraint on the minimum investment in cash.

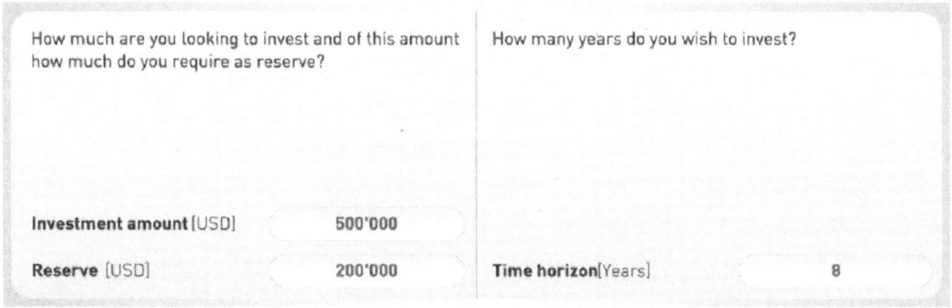

| How much are you looking to invest and of this amount how much do you require as reserve? | How many years do you wish to invest? |
|---|---|
| Investment amount [USD]  500'000 | |
| Reserve [USD]  200'000 | Time horizon[Years]  8 |

**FIGURE 10.67** Question on the investment amount and the investment horizon
*Source*: BhFS Behavioral Finance Solutions.

### 10.5.3 Expectations

Even before the client enters the advisory discussion, the client often has return expectations. To satisfy clients with their portfolios, it is sensible to ask what they expect from them. Moreover, the clients might be sensitive to returns below a certain level, which they consider as losses, and will be disappointed with their portfolios if the return is below that level. This is their reference point, and it can be larger than a 0% return level, such as if the clients have a specific investment goal they want to reach. The question on the expectations collects the information about the expected return and the reference point, as illustrated in Figure 10.68.

**Our Case Study** Sabine Fisher wants to reach her investment goal in 8 years. The *minimum* capital needed to start her business is $650,000—that is, a return of at least 30% over 8 years. This implies a minimum yearly return $R$ such that $(1 + R)^8 = 1 + 0.3$; that is, $R = (1 + 0.3)^{1/8} - 1 = 3.35\%$. While 3.35% is the minimum return, Sabine expects to obtain a higher payoff from her investment. She expects a final capital around $750,000, which is an annual expected return of around 5%.

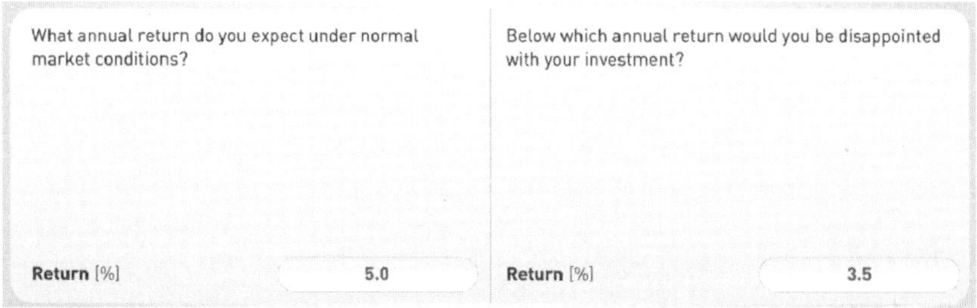

| What annual return do you expect under normal market conditions? | Below which annual return would you be disappointed with your investment? |
|---|---|
| Return [%]  5.0 | Return [%]  3.5 |

**FIGURE 10.68** Question on expectations
*Source*: BhFS Behavioral Finance Solutions

### 10.5.4   Experience, Knowledge, and Constraints

The question determines the level of experience and knowledge that the client has in the listed asset classes. We emphasize that experience is not simply a matter of years but refers to the direct involvement of the clients in its investments (i.e., his knowledge). For each asset class, the client may have no experience, or a low, medium, or high level of experience that should be stated as illustrated in Figure 10.69.

Experience plays a crucial role in forming risk preferences. Clients without any investment experience may overestimate their risk tolerance and may give a biased description of their risk preferences. As an example, suppose that clients never experienced a market downturn. How well can they judge their tolerance to large temporary losses? Therefore, the question on experience can be used to adjust the assessment of the clients' risk attitude, specifically their attitude with respect to temporary losses, what we call the *investment temperament*.

**Our Case Study**   Sabine has no experience with financial markets. She never invested in any asset class, but doesn't have any strong preference to exclude a specific asset class from her investment strategy. She has some understanding of the trade-off between return and risk the several asset classes can offer, since she sometimes reads the finance section in the newspaper.

### 10.5.5   Attitude toward Losses

To capture loss aversion, we consider a simple, hypothetical investment decision between a risky product and a risk-free product. The risky product offers a 50% chance of a gain and a 50% chance of loss. The risk-free product (cash) offers a certain return. These two alternative investment opportunities are described in Figure 10.70. The potential

| | | | | | |
|---|---|---|---|---|---|
| Global Bonds | None | Low | Medium | High | ✖ |
| Global Equities | None | Low | Medium | High | ✖ |
| Hedge Funds | None | Low | Medium | High | ✖ |
| Global Real Estate | None | Low | Medium | High | ✖ |
| Commodities | None | Low | Medium | High | ✖ |
| Private Equity | None | Low | Medium | High | ✖ |

**FIGURE 10.69**   Question on investment experience
*Source*: BhFS Behavioral Finance Solutions.

**FIGURE 10.70** Question on the attitude toward losses
*Source*: BhFS Behavioral Finance Solutions.

loss of the risky product is decreased until the client weakly prefers the risky product to cash. When this happens, the clients reveal their personal trade-off between gains and losses, that is, their attitude to losses, or loss aversion.

**Our Case Study** Sabine is very loss averse, since her project to start her own business is of vital importance to her. Therefore, she requires an upside potential, which is 10 times higher than the downside potential.

### 10.5.6 Attitude toward Uncertainty

To capture her attitude toward uncertainty, we again consider a simple, hypothetical investment decision between a risky product and a safe deposit. The risky product offers a 50–50 chance of two returns. The returns are specific for each client (i.e., their range includes the return expectations of the client). The safe deposit offers a risk-free return. These two alternative investments are described in Figure 10.71. The risk-free return of the safe deposit must be changed until the client weakly prefers the safe deposit to the risky product. When this happens, the clients reveal their personal attitude to uncertainty, that is, clients who are less concerned about uncertainty will require a higher return on the safe deposit to be willing to switch from the risky product to the safe deposit. By contrast, clients who are very averse to uncertainty will prefer the safe deposit even though its risk-free return is low.

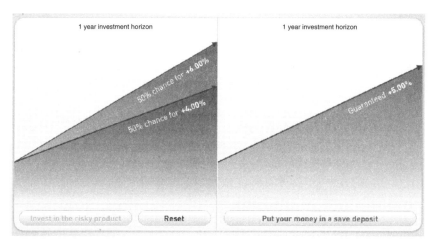

**FIGURE 10.71**    Question on the attitude to uncertainty
*Source*: BhFS Behavioral Finance Solutions.

**Our Case Study**   Sabine can tolerate uncertainty with respect to the final performance of her investment. She can start her business if at least $650,000 is available in 8 years, and she is not very concerned about fluctuations of her final wealth above this amount. The investment goals defined the annual return that Sabine needed to achieve with her investment, which is 3.5%. Therefore, when she is asked to choose between a risky product that gives either 4% or 6%, and a safe deposit, she would require at least a guaranteed return of 5% on the safe deposit to prefer the deposit, since in the worst case the risky option would pay 4% while Sabine needs 3.5% to avoid a disappointment.

### 10.5.7   Investment Temperament

The question on the investment temperament determines how strongly a client reacts to a large temporary drawdown. What is meant by a large drawdown depends on client's expectations and attitude to losses, which have been determined in the previous questions. The question on the investment temperament asks for how long a drawdown is acceptable for the client (see Figure 10.72). This is used to specify the aversion to large losses, as discussed in Section 10.2.

**Our Case Study**   Sabine is very concerned about a large temporary drawdown. She will change her investment strategy within a few months if a loss of 5% occurs.

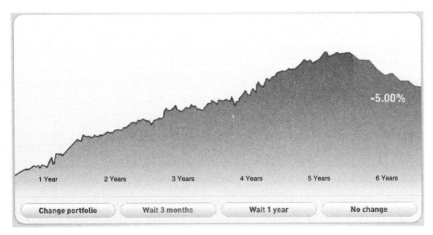

**FIGURE 10.72** Question on the investment temperament
*Source*: BhFS Behavioral Finance Solutions

### 10.5.8  Portfolio Construction

The questionnaire is used to determine risk ability (asset split, investment constraints) and risk preferences (reference point, attitude to losses, attitude to uncertainty) of a client. Under the behavioral finance paradigm, risk preferences are described by the prospect theory value function:

$$v(x) = x^\alpha \text{ if } x \geq 0 \text{ and } v(x) = -\beta(-x)^\alpha \text{ if } x < 0$$

where $0 < \alpha < 1$ and $\beta \geq 1$ and the answers to the questionnaire deliver a set of client's specific conditions on the value function $v$. In this way, the value function can be specified—that is, the parameters $\alpha$ and $\beta$ can be determined.

As an example, consider a client who is indifferent between a 50–50 risky product that delivers 2% or 6% and a safe deposit that delivers 4% (similarly to the question on the attitude toward uncertainty). Under the assumption that risk preferences for the client are described by the prospect theory value function $v$, we obtain the following condition (ignoring probability weighting):

$$0.5 \times v(2\%) + 0.5 \times v(6\%) = v(4\%)$$
$$\Longleftrightarrow 0.5 \times 0.02^\alpha + 0.5 \times 0.06^\alpha = 0.04^\alpha$$

which implies $\alpha = 1$. Similarly, also the parameter of loss aversion $\beta$ can be derived.

Having specified the value function $v$ and the portfolio constraints, we can derive the risk profile and the optimal asset allocation, as explained in Section 6.7.

**Our Case Study**   Sabine Fisher has a conservative risk profile (see Figure 10.73). She has high tolerance to uncertainty, but only moderate tolerance for losses and is very sensitive to large temporary drawdowns. Nevertheless, the attitudes toward losses and uncertainty have the highest impact on her risk profile. The asset allocation contains more than 50% of cash. This is mainly given by her requirement to have $200,000 in reverse, which implies that 40% of her assets are dedicated and safely invested in cash. The yearly expected return of the recommended asset allocation is 4.47%, below the return of 5% expected by Sabine Fisher. The probability of missing the investment goal is around 25% (see Table 14).

The portfolio construction based on a risk model like prospect theory also allows analyzing what happens if the clients want to overrule the proposed asset allocation. For example, suppose that Sabine Fisher is unhappy with the proposed asset allocation and aims for a higher expected return (i.e., at least 5%), as she indicated in her questions on the expectations.

Having a risk model as the building block of the risk profiler, one can easily analyze how the portfolio characteristics changes if the asset allocation is forced to deliver 5% expected return per annum (the so-called overruled asset allocation) and connect the new characteristics to the client's risk profile. This is shown in Figure 10.75 and in Table 15. We see that with the

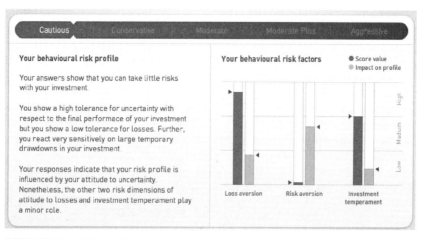

**FIGURE 10.73**   Risk profile
*Source*: BhFS Behavioral Finance Solutions.

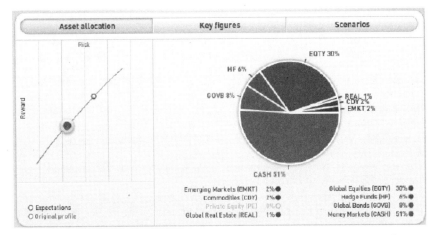

**FIGURE 10.74** Asset allocation on the behavioral efficient frontier (BEF) and its characteristics
*Source*: BhFS Behavioral Finance Solutions

**TABLE 14** Key figures for the proposed asset allocation

| Key Figures | Proposed Portfolio |
|---|---|
| Expected Return p.a. | 4.47% |
| Expected Volatility p.a. | 6.17% |
| Probability of Loss p.a. | 24.22% |
| Expected Gain p.a. | 7.15% |
| Expected Loss p.a. | 4.07% |
| Maximum Drawdown | 17.32% |

*Source*: BhFS Behavioral Finance Solutions

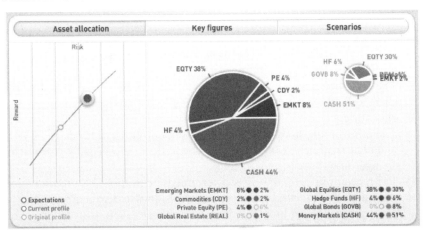

**FIGURE 10.75** Overruled asset allocation versus the original asset allocation
*Source*: BhFS Behavioral Finance Solutions

**TABLE 15**   Key figures of the overruled asset allocation and of the original asset allocation

| Key Figures | Proposed Portfolio | Overruled Portfolio |
|---|---|---|
| Expected Return p.a. | 4.47% | 5.01% |
| Expected Volatility p.a. | 6.17% | 9.57% |
| Probability of Loss p.a. | 24.22% | 30.86% |
| Expected Gain p.a. | 7.15% | 9.97% |
| Expected Loss p.a. | 4.07% | 6.23% |
| Maximum Drawdown | 17.32% | 28.31% |

*Source*: BhFS Behavioral Finance Solutions

overruled allocation the percentage invested in cash decreases from 51% to 44% and global equities increase from 30% to 38%. The overruled asset allocation now delivers an expected return of 5%. However, this comes at the cost of a higher probability of missing the investment goal (from less than 25% to almost 31%) and a higher maximum drawdown (from slightly more than 17% to almost 30%).

The analysis of the overruled portfolios is very useful, since it allows, for example, connecting client's expectations with portfolio characteristics, and this further improves the understanding of the proposed asset allocation. Specifically, in the example of Sabine Fisher, it is clear from the analysis of the overruled portfolio that an expected return of 5% requires a much higher level of risk in terms of probability of missing the investment goals, and this is exactly what Sabine Fisher wants to avoid.

### 10.5.9   Reporting

Reporting the results of the risk profiling process is important for at least the following reasons:

- It clarifies the connection between the proposed asset allocation, risk preferences, and risk ability, and facilitates feedback opportunities. The characteristics of the optimal asset allocation can be linked to the client's risk profile, improving the client's understanding of the proposed allocation.
- The information used to make an investment decision needs to be documented so that it can be double-checked later, especially in light of changes in opinion.
- The relevant information that determined the proposed asset allocation should be documented to help avoiding cognitive dissonances—that is, the irrational regret after the decision has been taken. Moreover, it prevents hindsight bias from occurring.

These reasons are particularly important from a behavioral perspective. The behavioral client is unlikely to commit to an investment strategy if the client doesn't understand its characteristics. Moreover, for a behavioral client, it is particularly important to visualize the properties of the proposed asset allocation in terms of scenario analysis—that is, what happens if the investment strategy faces specific market conditions, such as upward or downward trends. This scenario analysis could be further be extended with an experience sampler that allows clients to experience (through simulation) possible outcomes of the proposed asset allocation. As previously discussed experience sampling improves risk awareness.

As an illustrative example, we again consider our case study. How does the proposed allocation of Sabine Fisher perform under a normal trend, or an upward trend, or a downward trend? This question is answered in the scenario analysis shown in Figure 10.76 and reported to Sabine Fisher. This type of feedback illustrates the properties of the asset allocation, improves the understanding of it, and clarifies how it links to the risk profile.

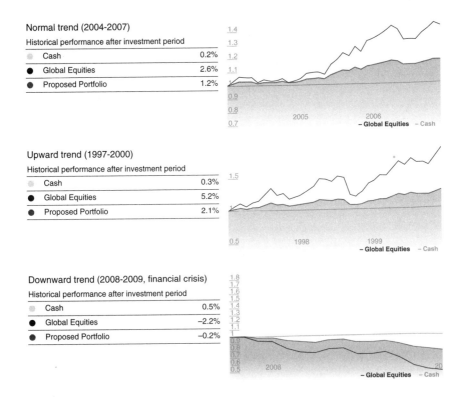

**FIGURE 10.76** Investment performance under different scenarios
*Source*: BhFS Behavioral Finance Solutions

## 10.6   RISK PROFILING AND ITS REGULATION

The risk profiler helps clients to decide how to invest their wealth but there are many other decisions that the clients need to take to implement the recommendation. These decisions refer to the delegation of the wealth management to a discretionary mandate, getting advice on the whole wealth in form of an advisory mandate, asking for advice on one single asset and getting assistance in the execution of trades. Figure 10.77 shows these categories and indicates what the regulator in Switzerland requires for these different services.

Depending on the depth of the financial services, the Swiss regulator requires a suitability or an appropriateness test. The suitability test is the most encompassing test that considers the clients' goals, financial situation, risk tolerance[3] and knowledge and experience. The appropriateness test only requires the knowledge and experience of the client. On the other hand, if the client asks the financial advisor only to execute a trade, then no test is required. These rules are like those in Europe, where they can be found in the MiFID-law.

The Swiss law, however, has one extra case, which is partial advice and not all-encompassing advice. If the client only wants advice with respect to one position in his portfolio, the advisor only needs to do an appropriateness test. Thus, he does not need to check whether selling a certain asset is

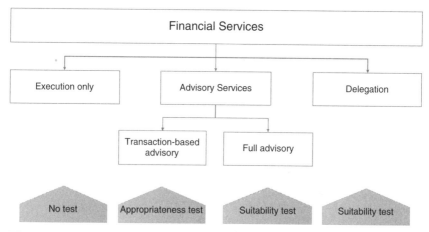

**FIGURE 10.77**   Various financial services and their regulation in Switzerland

---

[3] Even though risk tolerance is not mentioned in the Swiss law, called FIDLEG, it is included in the official commentary given by the regulator, the "Botschaft."

in line with the goals or the financial situation of the client. This rule sounds like a convenient simplification, but it can be problematic if the single asset that is sold is a hedge against certain risks, such as the foreign currency risk in the portfolio. Moreover, some advisors offer a "one-stop shopping" opportunity in which a client can buy a single asset (or fund) when he reveals his age and declares his risk tolerance. As Bachmann et al. (2017) show, the self-assessed risk tolerance is not a good measure for the true risk tolerance that clients have once they understand better what investing means. If one wants to insist on using it, it should be combined with the experience and not with the age of the client. This is justified under the assumption that more experienced clients are better at assessing their risk tolerance.

These examples show that neither the regulator nor the financial advisors—or their lobby talking to the regulators—care enough about the scientific evidence on risk profiling. Laws are not designed by research studies but by a lobbying process in which money counts more than wisdom!

## 10.7 CONCLUSION

While some advisors see risk profiling as a disturbing interference in their business, which they try to trick by backfilling in accordance with the products they want to sell, this book on behavioral finance sees risk profiling as a chance to improve the dialogue with the client and ultimately to improve the advice. Financial advisors who share this view have a unique chance for differentiating themselves from the rest of the industry. Before we conclude, we should note that there are many risk profilers competing for this task—very few of them, however, having a sound scientific background. The risk profiler presented here is based on prospect theory—the Nobel Prize awarded decision theory of Kahneman and Tversky that includes all previous decision theories as special cases. Moreover, this risk profiler has been tested and successively improved scientifically in an experimental laboratory and is in use by financial advisors in Switzerland, Austria, Germany, Luxembourg, Denmark, and Norway.

# CHAPTER 11

# Structured Wealth Management Process

Managing wealth is a difficult task since assets traded on a financial market never offer bargains, only trade-offs. To find the best solution, one should combine the trade-offs that the market offers with the preference of the investor, given the constraints of the personal financial situation. Study of behavioral finance is worthwhile in this respect, since it makes one aware of the typical mistakes in investing. It is difficult to say which mistakes are the most severe because a major disaster typically results from the combination of many aspects, which in isolation may not even be mistakes in other circumstances. For example, reference point behavior and mental accounting may be useful in some circumstances, but when applied simultaneously, they may lead to a loss of money. The following list attempts to order the behavioral traps, from fundamental factors to the more sophisticated ones[1]:

1. *A lack of planning of wealth management.* The most fundamental mistake in wealth management is not to plan your wealth-related decisions. Of course, planning consumes time and asking for advice may be expensive. Consequently, many clients try to hitch a free ride by imitating what others are doing, or they prefer to postpone the planning to another time. As the concept of hyperbolic discounting has shown, in the short run this looks attractive but ultimately, without proper planning, one will end up in an unfortunate situation.

2. *Incorrect framing of the situation.* Framing a decision is a powerful skill once you master it. For example, marketing specialists make money from providing a frame that influences the customers' decisions in whichever way the firm wants them to be. Frames in wealth management should be based on the stocks and flows of money, the risk scenarios and the alternatives one has. The frame should be forward-looking—that is, previous decisions (like at which price you

---

[1]See Chapter 2 for a more comprehensive list of behavioral biases.

bought an asset) should not be used as a reference point for future decisions. Moreover, frames should not be too narrow. The wealth should not be split up into many mental accounts and changes of wealth over time should be integrated so that myopic loss aversion can be avoided.

3. *Inefficient risk management, e.g., false diversification.* Diversification is the most powerful tool to master the ups and downs of the financial markets. A well-diversified portfolio will always lose on some assets but also always win on others. It is possible to diversify in such a way that on average your wealth grows. Single bets like buying stocks of only one company might be exciting, but they are not worth risking a large amount of your wealth on. Mental accounting may hinder good diversification and quantitative tools should be used to avoid naïve diversification.

4. *Not following a strategy.* One should be aware that during investing, things will happen that could not have been anticipated. These things will always happen, so there is no need to overreact to them. To avoid being swept away by the hectic nature of the markets, you should follow a strategy of future investments in what has already been proven to achieve the characteristics that suit your preferences and constraints. Moreover, one should not believe that you can find a perfect response to the ups and downs of the markets. A good strategy is typically less volatile than the markets are. Whenever something happens, double-check whether your fundamental investment premises and your constraints are still satisfied in a long-run perspective.

5. *Wrong performance attribution.* The best investors also have had luck, know that they have had luck, and set moderate goals for the future. Success carries the risk of making you proud and overconfident so you do not perceive risks so effectively. Finding a correct performance attribution is important for improving your strategy. Emotions like greed and fear, pride and regret may hinder a balanced evaluation of the situation.

These five points seem obvious on a general level. But when it comes to more specific situations, this is less so. The structured advisory process outlined in this chapter should help you to avoid most of the traps. The main ingredients of such a process can be summarized as follows:

- *Needs analysis*: Which goal(s) does the client have? How should the goals be ranked in terms of importance?
- *Risk ability*: Comparing the assets and the liabilities of the client, how much risk can the client take financially?

- *Risk awareness*: Does the client understand the meaning of risk measures like volatility? Is the client aware of the risk of all the assets the client considers investing in?
- *Risk tolerance*: Does the client have the psychological risk capacity to hold through the investment strategy you recommend?
- *Investment style*: Which investment style (passive, core-satellite, active, etc.) is most suitable for the client? Are certain assets ruled out?
- *Monitoring*: Are the client's goals, risk awareness, risk ability, and risk awareness still valid? Did the risk–reward trade-off on the financial markets change? Is the actual asset allocation in line with the optimal asset allocation?

Independent wealth managers must carry out all these steps on their own. They may try to get some support by using a questionnaire as a checklist for assessing the client's risk preference and risk awareness, they may purchase an asset liability tool, and they should apply a portfolio optimization tool. They also must form a good understanding of the future risk–returns the various asset classes offer.

All these tasks are quite ambitious if they are to be carried out by a single advisor. In a large organization, some specialization reflecting the comparative advantages of various specialists can be exploited. Here we will argue that for a large organization, a high degree of standardization is required in the wealth management process to guarantee good-quality advice to all clients and to benefit from this specialization.

The purpose of private banking is to bridge the gap between the client and the market. The client advisors therefore need to have a double talent. They need to understand their clients and the market. Since time is a scarce resource to any client advisor, allocating time to the client and to the market is a delicate balance. In the traditional approach, the client advisor is a market specialist who mostly concentrates on understanding the market. This approach is based on the wrong idea that there is something like "the best investment strategy" that is the same for all clients. Indeed, most financial news sources give the impression that the art of investing is to find this universal best investment strategy. Experts can easily be classified as being pro stocks, pro bonds, or pro hedge funds. The same is true for client advisors. Some advisors are more interested in stocks, others in bonds, and still others in hedge funds, for example. Hence, it should not come as a surprise that client advisors make biased recommendations according to their personal style of investing. The truth, however, is that the market offers trade-offs: The more return one desires to achieve on a market, the higher the risk one must take. Hence, there is nothing like "the best investment strategy" that can be found independently from knowing the risk tolerance and the risk preference of the client.

The right approach to private banking is therefore to reveal these trade-offs to the clients and then to assess the client to find the best balance of investments. Since there are very strong economies of scale in understanding the market, the time of the client advisor should mainly be reserved for understanding the client. Many specialists can easily work together to understand the market, but only a few people (the client advisor and some specialists on taxes, inheritance, etc.) can work together to understand the client. This fact calls for a clear division of labor in which client advisors devote most of their time to understanding the client. Understanding the client goes beyond having a good personal relationship with the client, which is a necessary prerequisite for doing private banking. It also involves assessing the clients' risk ability and their risk preferences in a systematic way. These important characteristics of the clients determine their asset allocations.

## 11.1  BENEFITS

A structured process clearly reduces the freedom of the client advisors. Moreover, it makes the client advisors more controllable, and it requires from them the filling in of forms, data sheets, and the ability and willingness to handle new information technologies (IT). This involves high costs. But they are worth paying, because without a structured process, the high degree of heterogeneous advice as found in many mystery shopping studies, as the Bilanz study that will be presented in Chapter 13, will erode the client's trust in private banking. Clients will then focus only on the costs they must pay and they might ultimately all end up with low-cost "solutions" such as the Internet. A structured process, on the other hand, guarantees service quality through standardization, and it exploits economies of scope by focusing on comparative advantages. Finally, only with a structured process is an organization able to learn and improve collectively. This last aspect will become the competitive edge in an ever more rapidly changing world.

To illustrate the idea of comparative advantages, consider the trade-off faced by client advisors. They could either spend most of their time in understanding the market or in understanding the client. A client advisor must allocate time and effort so that the total value the advisor is able to create from these two activities is maximized. Now, even if the investment committee (IC) is worse in both activities of understanding the client (which is certainly true) and understanding the market (which may not be true), then it would still make sense for the client advisor to specialize in understanding the client. This is illustrated in Figure 11.78.

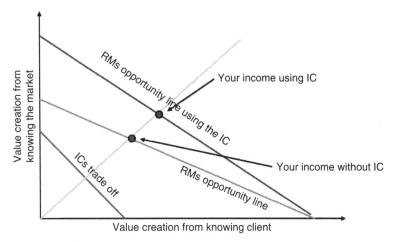

**FIGURE 11.78** Exploiting the comparative advantage of the relationship manager (RM)

The same argument can, of course, also be made by showing that the IT department should specialize in providing a good IT platform and by showing that the analysts should specialize in giving effective appreciation of stocks and bonds. But since we are used to these specializations, we might have forgotten that they originate from the same principle according to which client advisors should specialize in understanding clients.

Finally, we should say that only a structured process allows an organization to learn collectively. Using the data provided to the IT system by the client advisor, the bank can do systematic studies to spot possible problems. Concerning the individual client, one must check the individual risk ability and risk tolerance regularly, since the gains and losses obtained through the investment process change the client's free assets. Additionally, gains and losses will make the client more experienced.

## 11.2 IMPLEMENTATION

Client advisors and their clients must optimally adjust to a given process. The transition requires some effort on both sides. Most likely, one would expect to experience the usual J-curve effect: first, things will become worse and eventually things will improve a lot.

One should be aware that some participants would seek "the easy way out." That is, they will fill in the required forms without involving the client, and they will try to complete them in such a way that the advice they have given before still turns out to be optimal.

Further, when structuring the wealth management process, one should be aware that this might change the possible conflicts between the parties involved and could cause implementation problems. Concerning the client advisors and the bank as parties, a structured process restricts the freedom of the client advisors; it redefines their core competences and it requires them to fill in forms and handle a new IT system. On the other hand, the client advisors will get a good IT system, which also helps in the client reporting. Finally, a structured process binds the clients more to the bank and less to the client advisors. Concerning the clients and the bank as parties, the former can be sure of getting less random advice. However, the IT system may also introduce more trading. Finally, concerning client advisors and specialists, one must find a way of making sure that using the service of specialists to the client advisors is not for free, since this may result in an inefficient overuse of this free good.

## 11.3  REGULATORY REQUIREMENTS

Before going through a structured wealth management process based on behavioral finance, it is useful to know what legislation the regulator requires. This depends, of course, on the regulator. In Europe, the Markets in Financial Instruments Directive (MiFID) was issued well before the financial crisis and now a revised version MiFID II is ready to be rolled out. The Swiss Parliament is on the way to passing its own version "Finanzdienstleistungsgesetz" (FIDLEG). Even though regulations need to be adjusted to a country's culture—and Switzerland has a different financial culture than Europe (Bachmann & Hens, 2016), the FIDLEG has many aspects in common with the MiFID regulation because Europe insists that for its citizens the European laws apply even when they get advice in Switzerland!

The following regulations are being considered in Switzerland:

- Registration of financial advisors
- Revealing retrocessions earned by the financial advisor
- Duty to inform the customers properly
- Duty to document the advice given
- Duty to inquire properly about the clients' needs, their risk ability and risk tolerance
- Suitability of the products one recommends

### 11.3.1 Registration

Each financial advisor, working in a bank or independently, shall be registered at FINMA. The cost for the registration is small, but once a year an auditor will check whether the financial advisor is still suitable to be registered. This check costs considerable money per advisor and includes the properness of the advice given in the previous year and the auditor will also check whether the education of the advisor is still up-to-date. A consequence of these costs might be that many financial advisors get out of business and less wealthy clients will be directed to cheap digital banks. Also, some countries now require a certification of client advisors. This means that they should take courses to make sure they have the necessary knowledge acting as an advisor.

The other aspects of the regulation can only be understood if one knows that the regulator sees the financial advisor as a product seller or product pusher. The regulator does not necessary share the view that a financial advisor gives holistic advice, in which selling financial products is only one part.

### 11.3.2 Retrocessions

In many industries, the producers of products grant the sellers a sales commission. These incentivize the sellers to sell the products the producer wants to be sold. Sometimes to the extent that a product is sold, even though a different product would have been better for the client. In some countries like England and Germany, it is now forbidden for financial advisors to accept those retrocessions in the financial industry. In Switzerland, it is required to reveal the retrocessions to the client.

### 11.3.3 Key Investors Information Document (KIID)

The regulators also require that the financial advisors inform their clients properly about the risks of the financial products recommended. For each product, an information sheet (Key Investors Information Document, KIID) of at most two pages needs to be designed. The regulators give some hints about what the KIID shall contain—but ultimately, they will use the principle of negative screening. When someone claims that the KIID was misleading then the regulators will investigate this—case by case. Only recently, there is research emerging on how to design KIIDS. For example, Stössel and Meier (2015) find that bar charts are most appropriate to communicate the risks of investments.

### 11.3.4 Documentation

In Switzerland, some clients could not sue the bank for bad advice since that bank did not reveal the documents collected during the advisory process. This was ultimately ruled as illegal and is now included in the new regulation. Now the bank has the duty to properly document the reasons for each advice it gives and FIDLEG also requires that in case of disagreement the bank will have to prove that she did not give bad advice. This latter part is, however, contested by the banks and it might not be part of the final version of FIDLEG.

### 11.3.5 Risk Ability

Whenever a product is sold, the bank must check whether the client has the risk ability to deal with the potential losses involved in that product. To do this the bank must assess the goals of the investor and compare them to the assets that the client currently has. The question, then, is whether a financial product can close the gap between the goals and the existing assets or whether it could deepen this gap so much that very important goals are endangered. A delicate issue arises when the client does not want to reveal all assets to the same financial advisor. Some lawyers read the regulation such that in this case the financial advisor is not allowed to give advice.

### 11.3.6 Risk Tolerance

As MiFID II now shows, the regulator has understood that besides the pure financial aspect of risk ability there is the psychological aspect of risk tolerance. Interestingly, the regulator does not think of risk tolerance in terms of volatility of the client's wealth but in terms of the maximal losses the client can tolerate. This prospect theory view has made it into MiFID II and into FIDLEG!

### 11.3.7 Product Suitability

The view of the regulator is that in general, consumer products can be categorized so that clients and products can be matched to be suitable for a client. For example, alcohol is not suitable for kids and pregnant women should limit their intake of things like caffeine and canned tuna. However, the portfolio view is more important in finance than the product view. According to this view, each product must be seen in combination with all other products and not considered in isolation as whether they are suitable for clients. But MiFID II seems to be moving in this direction. These aspects need to be considered when designing a structured wealth management process.

## 11.4 STRUCTURING THE WEALTH MANAGEMENT PROCESS

Each bank has its own way to structure the wealth management process: some go through four steps (e.g., Merrill Lynch[2]); others use a five-step analysis (e.g., Credit Suisse). As the number of different stages is not decisive for the quality of the provided advice, we illustrate how to structure the wealth management process by outlining the wealth management process suggested by BhFS Behavioral Finance Solutions since this process has been developed based on scientific research; see Figure 11.79.

### 11.4.1 Needs Analysis

Good advice starts with an assessment of a client's needs. These are closely related to the client's life cycle and to some turning points such as unemployment, a move to another country, marriage, children, or inheritance. These turning points are important because they can trigger the client's decision to

**FIGURE 11.79** Recommended wealth management process

---

[2]In the first step, the client advisor establishes the client's objectives. The second step sets an investment strategy. The third step implements a solution, and in the last step the progress is reviewed.

ask for investment advice. Therefore, it is strongly recommended that client advisors understand which needs arise at which stage of the client's life cycle to be able to keep the current clientele and acquire new customers.

The aim of the needs analysis is to check whether the client can benefit from professional advice and, if so, whether the advisor can provide solutions. The question of whether the client can benefit from an advice depends on client's financial knowledge and competence to deal with emotions when investing. Investors with low competence in these areas are more willing to decide autonomously and less willing to delegate decisions to an advisor as Bachmann & Hens (2015) find. The form of the advice depends further on client's preferences: some clients may prefer to invest some assets over a certain time, others may prefer to receive financial planning advice over their life cycle.

If the client wants financial advice, then the outcome of the needs analysis is a list of goals that the client wants to achieve with the investments (e.g., "financing children's education," "retirement") as well as a ranking of the importance of these goals. The latter can be considerably influenced by biases related to time (as discussed in Chapter 9). In particular, some goals (e.g., "retirement") may receive a lower ranking than other (e.g., "buying a new car") just because they need to be achieved later in time. Additionally, habit formation and mental accounting can influence the size of the financial needs in terms of the returns that need to be achieved. In particular, habit formation makes goals that need to be achieved later in the future more expensive than short-term goals. Mental accounting can be used to reduce these costs. For example, advisors could use mental accounting to support client's willingness to save. Stronger savings reduce the return that an investment needs to achieve to finance the investment goal. This reduces the investment risks that need to be taken and thus the likelihood for a mismatch with the personal willingness to take risks. Stronger savings are most beneficial for long-term goals with lower stated ranking. The easiest way to achieve stronger savings for these goals is to "book" them in one account with income that is not available yet. For example, the goal "retirement" may be ranked as less important as the goal "buying a new car" because it needs to be achieved later in the future. If this time lag motivates a lower stated ranking, then advisors need to take this into account and motivate clients to save more for the later goal, even if its stated importance is low.

### 11.4.2 Risk Ability: Personal Asset and Liability Management

The next stage of the wealth management process requires a careful assessment of the clients' personal assets and liabilities. Professionals describe this approach as *personal assets and liability management* (PALM). Examples of assets are the current financial wealth of the client, and wealth in terms of illiquid assets (e.g., real estate). Liabilities might be mortgages to be paid. The PALM is based on the notion that from a financial point of view a person is like a firm—that is, the personal financial situation can be described using a balance sheet of assets and liabilities and a cash flow overview, usually called a profit and loss statement, P&L. In the case of households, the P&L is the balance between the income and the expenses. Since we are not interested in detailed financial planning[3] but in the best way to invest the client's assets, we integrate the PALM and the P&L by determining a restriction from the P&L for the assets the client wants to invest. The way we suggest handling this is to look ahead for the investment horizon of the client and identify possible gaps between income and expenses. The (discounted) cumulative sum of these gaps will be a liability to be considered when investing the assets. The market evaluates the financial assets, the illiquid assets might have to be appraised and the current and future income needs to be discounted back to the present. The liabilities need to be measured similarly. Debt borrowed from a bank and all future payments must be represented by their present value. Finally, the investor shall try to prioritize the goals—that is, the liabilities as well as plans and wishes. Example 11.1 provides an interesting case study.

---

### EXAMPLE 11.1: PALM

Mr. Bush has assets worth CHF 15 million (13 million in financial assets and a house worth CHF 2 million), a regular annual income of CHF 250,000, and some fluctuating extra income of usually CHF 100,000 per year. He needs to repay his mortgage of CHF 1.25 million, eventually wants to buy a nicer house (CHF 4 million estimated), and might need money to set up a business venture. His annual expenses are CHF 250,000 but when he sets up his own business he will quit his job, so CHF 250,000 annually are at stake. He sets the following priorities: Continue with current lifestyle and repay mortgage is his first priority, while buying a nice family home and continuing to send his kids to

*(Continued)*

---

[3]In the needs analysis of section 9.7.1., the demand for a detailed financial planning must be assessed. In the PALM, which is part of the investment process, we assume the need of the client "simply" was to invest some money with the bank.

private schools comes second. Finally, quitting his job and setting up his own business venture would be nice to have but not necessary for the near future.

A first look at Mr. Bush's PALM balance sheet shows that the status quo is in a stable balance. His assets exceed his first-order priorities by almost 9 million CHF and his income exceeds his first-ordered expenses. Even going to the second-order priorities (nicer house and education of children), he is still doing fine. However, the goals he prioritized third (quitting the job and setting up a business venture) imply some liability on his assets since in that case his income would not be sufficient for his expenses (Figure 11.80). Thus, we can identify the following liabilities attached to his wealth:

1. A mortgage of CHF 1.25 million
2. The wish to climb up the property ladder by CHF 2 million
3. The plan to set up a business venture of CHF 150,000 a year

|  | Assets | Liabilities |  | Priority |
|---|---|---|---|---|
| Financial wealth |  | Financial liabilities |  |  |
| - Cash | 2,000,000 | - Debt |  |  |
| - Bonds | 5,000,000 | - Mortgage 1 | 1,250,000 | 1 |
| - Stocks | 6,000,000 | - Mortgage 2 |  |  |
| - Other |  | - Other |  |  |
| Real estate |  | Wishes |  |  |
| - Private | 2,000,000 | - Family home | 4,000,000 | 2 |
| - Commercial |  | - Business venture | 1,000,000 | 3 |
| Total | 15,000,000 |  | 6,250,000 |  |
| Annual income |  | Annual outflows |  |  |
| - Main source | 250,000 | - Living expenses | 200,000 | 1 |
| - Extras | 100,000 | - Education of children | 50,000 | 2 |
|  |  | - Quitting job | 250,000 | 3 |
| Total | 350,000 |  | 50,000 |  |

**FIGURE 11.80**   Example of a personal balanced sheet

Suppose Mr. Bush wants to invest for 10 years; then the third liability amounts to CHF 1.5 million.

The PALM is important in determining the agent's risk ability. The risk ability sets a constraint for the optimization of the agent's utility, which embodies the risk preference of the agent. In general, one should aim to find an asset allocation that maximizes the agent's utility while ensuring that the agent is able to finance any liabilities. In this respect, the advisor needs to find out two important things: first, how to determine client's preferences (i.e., the risk profile). An important step forward is done when the client can structure the liabilities in, say, hard liabilities (e.g., necessary wealth to keep up the lifestyle) and soft liabilities (e.g., wealth to accomplish plans and wishes that would enhance the life style). Based on this distinction, one can then also split the assets accordingly.

Consider, for example, the case of Credit Suisse. In the meltdown of the TMT bubble, Credit Suisse had to confess to many clients that the remaining assets were not sufficient to finance hard liabilities like the future education of their children. As one can imagine, this was a shock to the clients of Credit Suisse, which subsequently lost many of them to their competitors. The management reacted by introducing the asset split. The total bankable assets were split into dedicated assets and free assets. The hard liabilities are now matched with safe dedicated assets. The free assets can then be invested in more risky assets. That is, Credit Suisse introduced two mental accounts, in one of which is applied the safety-first principle and in the other Credit Suisse applies the concept of value at risk. The idea is illustrated in Figure 11.81.

The asset split gives the clients a higher utility since they know that their hard liabilities are no longer in danger. Moreover, it could be a risk management technique, as the following argument shows.

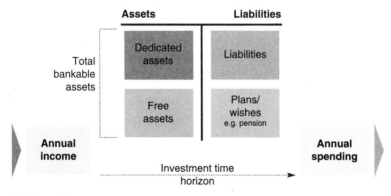

**FIGURE 11.81** Assets split
*Source*: Credit Suisse

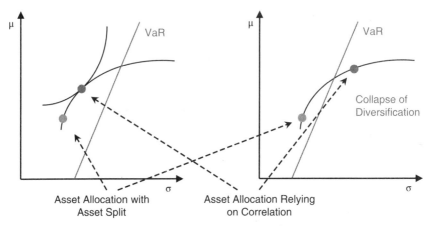

**FIGURE 11.82** The asset split protects the client from a collapse of diversification

Instead of splitting the liabilities, one could integrate free and dedicated assets into one class, trying to exploit the fact that typically different assets are not perfectly correlated. For example, using the classical mean-variance diversification, the liabilities could be handled by a value at risk (VaR) constraint. In a mean-variance diagram, the intended solution can be displayed as on the left in Figure 11.82.

If assets are more highly correlated than one thought, then the solution that looks safe from a mean-variance perspective turns out to be treacherous because diversification is no longer possible. In effect, the result is as depicted in the right part of Figure 11.82. Some of the dedicated assets will be lost! Hence, whether one can benefit from the diversification effect depends on how good the estimates of the covariances are. It is wise to require more safety for the dedicated assets than for the free assets, which is a rational reason for the asset split.

### 11.4.3   Risk Awareness

It is the duty of the financial advisor to explain to the client which investment bears which risk. Behavioral finance is particularly well known for good research on the optimal way of communicating risk. The current state of the literature is that experience sampling is the best method for making the client understand what risk does mean (Kaufmann, Weber, & Haisley, 2013 and Bradbury, Hens & Zeisberger 2015).

Figure 11.83 shows how the concept of experience sampling can be used to sharpen the client's risk awareness. The volatile lines show single sample paths while the least volatile line in the middle shows the expected

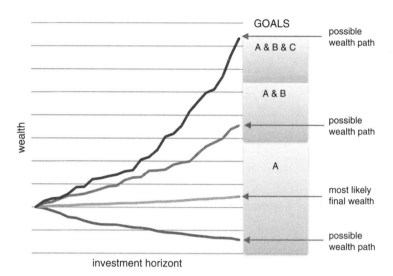

**FIGURE 11.83**    Experience sampling combined with a stack of goals

evolution of wealth, i.e. the average over many sample paths. Starting with the initial wealth, the client can draw sample paths of the future development of the invested wealth. The sample paths can be drawn to represent the expected development of client's wealth in most cases (e.g., in 95% of the expected cases). For simplicity, Figure 11.83 includes only four possible paths, which include the best and the worst case. The client can see that some paths may turn out extremely nice (like the top one), since if this happens the client can achieve all goals over the investment horizon. Other paths may turn out less well, so that only one of the goals can be ensured. There are also other paths (like the bottom one), where none of the goals can be reached because the client might end up losing money. By choosing higher levels of risk, the best- and the worst-case scenario become more extreme. Then it might become possible that all goals are reached with a middle good scenario (the path marked A & B), but the higher risk can also increase the possibility that with a middle bad scenario, none of the goals are reached. This way, the client understands what risk taking means: The higher the risk level, the easier it is to reach more goals but it is also more likely that none of the goals are reached.

The experience sampling methodology is a quick way to sharpen the investor's risk awareness. A more detailed analysis can be done with training modules with the following features:

■ Explaining commitment to the investment strategy based on roller coaster

**FIGURE 11.84** Loss due to discontinuation of investment strategy
*Source*: BhFS Behavioral Finance Solutions

- Explaining trade-offs of strategies based on roller coaster
- Educating the client about the historical performance of stocks
- Explaining the importance of the commitment to a strategy based on the historical performance of stocks
- Explaining the risk–reward trade-off

Figure 11.84 visualizes that discontinuing the investment along the roller coaster results in a severe underperformance. This highlights the importance of a strategy commitment.

The next step explains that more aggressive risk profiles lead to higher temporary drawdowns while finally, their return is higher, as Figure 11.85 illustrates:

The next aspect concerns the pros and cons of various asset classes.

Figure 11.86 shows how stocks and bonds have performed historically in various time periods.

The commitment to strategy, which is the key to financial success, is then explained also in historic perspective. Figure 11.87 illustrates the performance when the investor steps out of the market for some chosen period. One learns that only when one is lucky enough to choose the right period can one outperform a buy-and-hold strategy.

Finally, as illustrated in Figure 11.88, the pros and cons of various investment classes and asset allocations are explained by using their reward–risk trade-off.

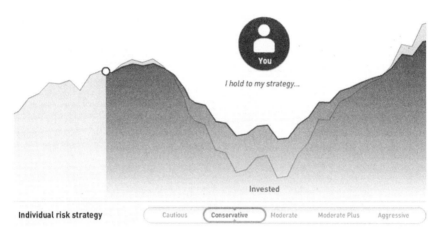

**FIGURE 11.85** Illustrating the pros and cons of various risk profiles on the roller coaster.
*Source*: BhFS Behavioral Finance Solutions

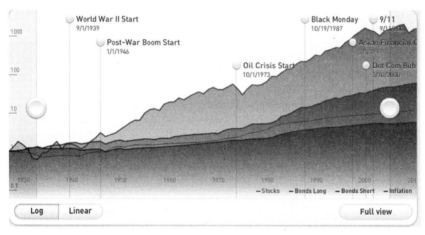

**FIGURE 11.86** Historic performance of stocks and bonds in various periods
*Source*: BhFS Behavioral Finance Solutions

## 11.4.4 Risk Tolerance

Using insights from prospect theory, wealth managers can estimate the risk preferences of the client. The risk preferences address the willingness of the client to take risks and to bear possible losses. In the previous chapter we explained the different aspect of tolerance and mentioned how to assess them.

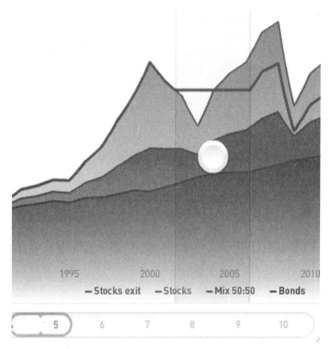

**FIGURE 11.87** Commitment to strategy illustrated by exit periods
*Source*: BhFS Behavioral Finance Solutions

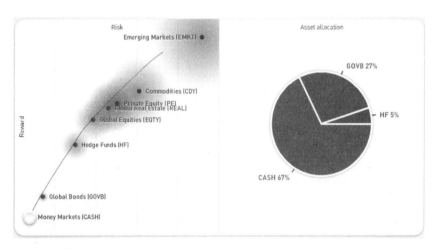

**FIGURE 11.88** Explaining the reward–risk trade-off of various asset classes and investment strategies
*Source*: BhFS Behavioral Finance Solutions

### 11.4.5 Portfolio Construction

The optimal investment strategy is determined on the one hand by the risks and opportunities offered on the market and on the other hand by the preferences and restrictions of the client. Questionnaires are helpful to elicit the latter. Previous return realizations of the assets included in the asset allocation provide information on the risks and the opportunities on the market. By combining both sources of information, one gets the optimal asset allocation of the client, as Figure 11.89 shows. How the optimal asset allocation is determined for behavioral asset allocation problems was explained in detail in Section 6.7.

### 11.4.6 Investment Style

A typical advisory process will determine the client's optimal asset allocation, which is then implemented by the relationship manager choosing different assets. For some clients, the process of assets selection is particularly valuable. Other clients prefer a passive approach and choose cost-efficient index solutions like ETFs.

The preference for an active or for a passive investment approach is one aspect of the client's investment style. Clients who prefer an active investment style need to decide how the best assets should be chosen. There are many different approaches to choose assets. We will call them *investment styles*. One way to categorize the investment styles and simplify the choice is to ask *what types of risks* each of these strategies takes to receive a premium for doing this.

Investment strategies have various risk premiums. For example, there is a premium for holding unfashionable assets (i.e., the value premium), a

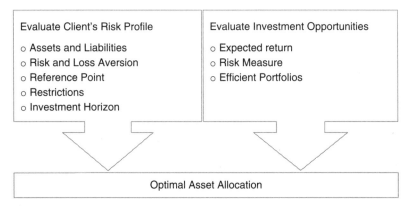

**FIGURE 11.89** Constructing the optimal asset allocation

risk premium for holding illiquid assets, a premium for investing in small companies, a premium for investing in companies with an uncertain growth potential, an inflation premium, and several others. Investment strategies differ also with respect to their exposure to the different types of risks over time. Some strategies shift assets to keep the exposure to a certain type of risk constant; others change the risk exposure over time.

The investment according to risk premiums (also called risk factors) is elegant but too abstract for clients. For the achievement of long-term goals, it is essential that client's understanding and preference for certain types of risks match with the risks taken by the recommended investment strategy. If there is a mismatch, the risk for abandoning the investment advice increases. This is particularly true after losses.

A more intuitive approach is based on the link between risk premiums and lifestyles. For example, the value premium is appropriate for someone who is not afraid of being out of fashion and who buys bargains. The growth premium, on the other hand, is more appropriate for people who are early adopters of new technology (smartphones, google glasses, smart bots, etc.) The assessment of the preferred investment style is important because the previous steps of assessing the risk awareness and risk tolerance deal only with the *amount of risks* that the client should take. The additional assessment of the risk types that the client is willing to take should support a client's confidence in the quality of the investment decision and help the client to go through difficult times of losing money in the short term.

We suggest the use of at least the following investment styles:

- Buy-and-hold
- Rebalancing
- Momentum
- Carry
- Value
- Growth

The profile of the clients following these styles could be described as in Table 16.

### 11.4.7 Documentation and Reporting

In the background of each step of the process, specific information needs to be stored. This is important for at least three reasons. First, storing information used to take an investment decision is necessary for performing double-checks, but is also significant in the case of opinion revisions.

**TABLE 16** Investment styles

| Investment Style | Description |
| --- | --- |
| Buy-and-hold: "Wait and see." | For you, market price movements are unpredictable. Moreover, you do not think that you can profit by news, as the market is faster than you are in interpreting this news. You prefer to save transaction costs and wait instead of making trading decisions that you might regret. |
| Rebalancing: "The right balance is the most important thing." | For you, the best way to invest is splitting your wealth between different asset classes (e.g., equities, bonds, cash etc.). Once you find this allocation, you stick to it by selling when the market price of your investment increases and buying when the market price of your investments decreases. |
| Momentum: "The trend is your friend." | For you, the most important criterium for a successful investment is to participate in market price trends. You do not consider the assessment of company reports as particularly helpful because all information that can be found in the reports is already priced in the market. Risk management is not worth the money since the participation in trends allows generating gains that can compensate for eventual losses. |
| Carry: "Cash is king." | For you, the most important criteria for a successful investment are the cash payments such as interest payments from bond investments and dividend payments from equity investments. The volatility of market prices is not a reason to trade, as ups and downs on the market neutralize each other over time. |
| Value: "Everything has a price but only a few things have a value." | For you, there is a difference between the market price and the value of investment opportunities. If the market price is below (above) the value that you consider as fair, you buy (sell) until this gap closes. To determine the value of an investment, you read company reports and compare measures like book value with the market price of the company. Falling market prices are signals to buy rather than warning signals. Increasing market prices that show the emergence of trends are less important for you, as you do not mind if you miss some of them. |

*(continues)*

**TABLE 16**   (*Continued*)

| Investment Style | Description |
| --- | --- |
| Growth:"Every journey starts with the first step" | For you enterprises have a life-cycle starting with a great idea. A seed investment helps to develop the first product, venture capital helps to scale the enterprise up so that it can compete with other firms, private equity makes it more professional so that finally it can be financed by an initial public offering on the stock market. Now the enterprise takes off – but eventually it will be replaced by a competitor having had an even better idea. You belief that one can identified the best enterprises of the future and invest in those. This fits to your life-style since you are an early adopter of technology. You bought one of the first smart phones and participate in many social media platforms. You understand that not all new enterprises will make it – but by the merits of portfolio diversification you can tame that risk. |

Second, storing the information, which was relevant at the time the decisions have been taken, helps to avoid regret (see Section 2.2.16). Moreover, it prevents hindsight bias (see Section 2.3.1). Third, in certain cases, stored information might be useful as a protection against legal claims.

### 11.4.8   Monitoring

Once a suitable investment strategy has been found, one needs to monitor it over time. The risks and rewards of asset classes might change due to market events and occasionally the situation of the client might change, perhaps due to family events.

A good way of communicating the new situation to the client is to refer to the experience-sampling diagram as Figure 11.90 illustrates. One can show which scenario has already occurred (the line before the paths split) and which paths are most likely if one changes the strategy as a response to changes in the goals or the priorities. A comparison between the previous most likely wealth and the most likely final wealth after changing the strategy in context of the goals provides additional decision support.

### 11.4.9   Goal-Based Investing

In this section, we analyze the case that clients have several investment goals with different risk tolerances attached to them. This approach was initially

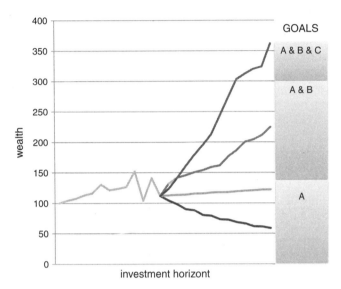

**FIGURE 11.90** The monitoring process

suggested by Shefrin & Statman (2000) in their behavioral portfolio theory with multiple mental accounts, which is built on the SP/A decision theory of Lopes (1987).[4] In the mean-variance framework, a goal-based model has been proposed by Das, Markowitz, Scheid, & Statman (2010), who use goals and the probability to achieve them set by the investors to determine goals' specific risk tolerances (see Example 14). Finally, in a framework with preferences according to prospect theory, a goal-based model was developed by De Giorgi (2012), who additionally suggested a way to optimally choose the amounts to be invested into the different goals—that is, how the investor should optimally split investment amounts among the different goals.

Goal-based approaches for asset allocation also became popular in the wealth management industry (see Chhabra, 2005). Brunel (2015), for example, proposed a multistrategy framework in which each strategy matches to a different investment goal. These goals can be defined as: liquidity, income, capital preservation, and growth. The individual needs

---

[4]The SP/A decision theory assumes that decision makers aim for security (S) against losses, hope for upside potential (P), and need to succeed by reaching their aspirations or goals (A). These three aspects are integrated into a decision model that describes the trade-off between security and potential and add on the top of this the constraint that the probability to achieve decision makers' aspirations is high enough.

are then a combination of the four fundamental goals. Nevins (2004) takes these recommendations further into risk profiling. He suggests separating clients' risk tolerance for several goals rather than estimating an overall risk tolerance for each client. Investment strategies to specific investment goals should increase clients' confidence in the strategies. As strategies are aligned with client's own objectives, clients would not feel as being boxed into a long-term asset allocation, which they have difficulties associating with. Moreover, following this goal-based investment approach, clients would be better prepared for bear markets and more likely to keep perspective and remain disciplined. Finally, when strategies are evaluated based on the progress toward a specific goal, the performance measurement becomes more meaningful.

A potential drawback of the approach is that mapping separate risk profiles into one investment strategy that serves different goals may lead to an overall risk exposure, which may exceed the risk tolerance or even the risk ability of the client (see Example 11.2). It could also happen that the overall risk aversion of the client would allow for more risk taking than what focusing on single goals implies.

To take account of these issues, we argue that clients should form goal-specific portfolios that need to be coordinated from a general perspective. The goal-specific portfolios can be formed as outlined before. For each goal, a portfolio risk profiler determines the risk preferences of the client and a decision support tool suggests the optimal asset allocation. The various portfolio risk profilers then need to be coordinated based on the client's risk ability and the weighting of the client's various goals (see De Giorgi, 2012). The latter is a very difficult but important step to get overall consistency, which can be achieved by a client risk profiler. If a coordination of separate decisions is missing, the resulting decision might become irrational.

The goal-based wealth management process can be implemented as illustrated in Figure 11.91. In the first step, advisors evaluate whether the client has specific investment goals. This is important, as the client's investment goals represent reference points upon which loss-averse clients judge investment performance. As it is possible that the investor exhibits different aversion toward uncertainty and different loss aversion in dependence on the goal in question, it is advantageous to separate the goals in different mental accounts and specify a risk profile for each of them. On this basis, the advisors can define optimal sub-portfolios serving the predefined investment goals. The optimal asset allocation of the client is derived by combining the sub-portfolios into a whole. The weights can be determined in dependence on the relative importance of the goals for

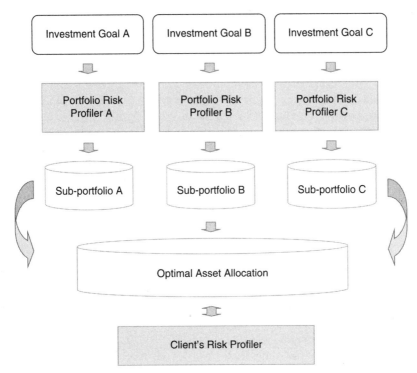

**FIGURE 11.91**   Integrated goal-based wealth management process

the client. Finally, to make sure that the overall risk exposure of the client is in line with the client's risk profile, the asset allocation is fine-tuned according to the overall risk preferences and risk ability of the client. Overall, the portfolio risk profiler makes use of the positive aspects of mental accounting while the client risk profiler avoids the negative aspects. Whether splitting portfolios according to goals or—as we recommended before—ranking them into a stack of goals is better depends on the stability of the goals. If goals are not stable and might change often, then it is preferable to keep them in a stack of goals with one portfolio instead of splitting the wealth into several portfolios. Also, spitting up the wealth according to goals only makes sense if the wealth is sufficiently large so that transaction costs do not eat up the benefits from the goal-based approach.

Example 11.2 illustrates the goal-based investment approach and one of its potential pitfalls.

### EXAMPLE 11.2: Goal-Based Investing

Lucy and John have married and are now planning their life together. Their parents are supporting them with $150,000 and Lucy and John plan to use this money for three goals in one year. First, they would like to buy a house, of which 80% will be financed through mortgage and 20% with their capital. The 20% means $120,000. Second, because they would like to immediately enlarge the family, they also want to buy a new car, which costs around $24,000. Finally, because they didn't manage to do so yet, they plan to go on their honeymoon in one year. They found a deal online for 7 days in a nice resort on the ocean for $10,400.

Their friend, Carl, is a financial advisor, and he helps them select the right investment strategy. Carl only considers investing into two different products: a risky product with an annual expected return $\mu = 18\%$ and standard deviation $\sigma = 30\%$ and a risk-free product with annual return $R_f = 2\%$. Moreover, Carl assumes mean-variance preferences to select the appropriate investment strategy and follows a goal-based approach where the appropriate strategy for each goal is separately determined.

To start with, Carl assesses the overall risk tolerance by asking the following question:

> "An investment offers a 50% chance to increase the initial wealth by 10%. Which negative return are you ready to accept if the investment declines?"

Lucy and John agree that the answer is 1% because they are generally very averse to losses. The answer to the question implies that the investment has mean 4.5% and variance 0.3025% and, because of mean-variance preferences $u(x) = \mu - \alpha\sigma^2$, a utility of $u(x) = 0.045 - \alpha \times 0.003025$. Setting this equal to the utility of not investing $u(0) = 0$, we obtain the risk aversion parameter $\alpha = 14.9$.

In a second step, the investment amount is split among the three goals: $118,000 for the house, $23,000 for the car, and $9,000 for the honeymoon, implying goals' specific target returns of 1.69%, 4.35%, and 15.56%, respectively. The way the split is done is by accounting for the goals' priorities. According to mean-variance preferences (see Section 6.7), the optimal allocation to the risky product is

$$\lambda = \frac{(\mu - R_f)}{\alpha\sigma^2} \approx \frac{1.78}{\alpha},$$

where $\alpha$ denotes the risk tolerance. Instead of asking questions to determine $\alpha$ directly, as was done for the overall assessment of the risk tolerance, Carl asks their friends with which probabilities they could *miss* their goals and obtains this way the corresponding goal-specific risk tolerances.[5] The advantage of assessing risk tolerance through the probability of missing the goal is that it clearly refers to the goal, which is the tangible and concrete objective that Lucy and John intend to achieve. For the three goals, the probabilities indicated by Lucy and John are 1% (one out of hundred), 33% (one out of three) and slightly less than 50%, respectively, implying risk aversion parameters of 313.4, 2.1, and 1.8. Consequently, the optimal allocations to the risky product are 0%, 84%, and 99% for goal 1 (house), goal 2 (car), and goal 3 (honeymoon), respectively, and thus, the overall allocation to the risky product is 19.21%. Solving the formula above with $\lambda = 0.19$, this implies an overall risk aversion of 9.25, lower than the overall risk aversion of 14.9 obtained from the overall assessment of the risk tolerance. Briefly, the goal-based approach in this case has a pitfall, because focusing on single goals generates excessive risk taking.

Instead of focusing on single goals, Carl could have used the overall risk aversion of 14.9 to compute the corresponding investment into the risky product, i.e., 11.95%. With this strategy, however, the probabilities to miss goal 1 (house), goal 2 (car), and goal 3 (honeymoon) are 27%, 55%, and 100%, respectively. Therefore, a goal-based assessment of risk aversion and an overall assessment of risk aversion are generally different, and one needs to ensure consistency. This can be achieved, for example, with an appropriated modeling framework.

---

[5]Under the assumption of normally distributed returns, the probability *not* to reach a target $H$ is equal to $q$, i.e., $P[R_p \leq H] = q$, when $H = \mu_p + \Phi^{-1}(q) * \sigma_p$, where $\mu_p$ and $\sigma_p$ are the portfolio expected return and standard deviation, respectively. Because the optimal portfolio only depends on risk aversion, the equation $H = \mu_p + \Phi^{-1}(q) * \sigma_p$ immediately implies the corresponding level of risk aversion (see Das, Markowitz, Scheid, & Statman, 2010). We have: $\alpha = \frac{\mu - R_f}{\sigma(H - R_f)} * \left( \frac{\mu - R_f}{\sigma} + \Phi^{-1}(q) \right)$.

## 11.5   RELEVANCE OF DIFFERENT THEORIES

The wealth management process can be designed in different ways, depending on the theoretical foundation that one uses. This section discusses how different theories can shape the wealth management process.

In the standard finance framework, the *need analysis* defines the client's goals in financial terms. The behavioral finance perspective evaluates possible misperceptions in the perceived importance of the goals as well as misperceptions in the measures needed to achieve the goals. Moreover, it offers advisors ideas of how to manage such misperceptions.

In the assessment of the risk ability, the traditional approach suggests the implementation of a personal asset and liability management, ensuring with a high probability[6] that the client has enough financial resources to achieve the goal. When the markets turn south so that the client loses substantial wealth, then the client might start worrying about losing everything. From a behavioral finance point of view, an asset split is better at making sure that hard liabilities are met in any case. Then there is no worry related to probabilities but certainty that the liabilities can always be ensured.

An assessment of the risk awareness in the traditional framework is not necessary because clients can learn by experience or because they can delegate the investment decisions to a competent advisor. The behavioral finance perspective suggests an assessment of the factors that lead to a biased perception of the risk and rewards on the financial markets. This is necessary because investors do not necessarily learn from their mistakes (Koestner, Meyer, & Hackethal, 2012) and because those who are less prepared to invest autonomously are least likely to delegate investment decisions to an advisor (Bachmann & Hens, 2015).

The two theoretical perspectives motivate different ways for the assessment of the client's risk tolerance. While traditional finance suggests using the risk aversion, i.e., the tolerance toward deviations from the average payoff, behavioral finance suggests also considering the loss aversion of the client. The financial goals of the client can be used as reference points.

When deciding about the investment style, the traditional approach suggests using a factor analysis to decide which types of risks (market risk, risk of investing in small companies, etc.) the client is willing to hold to achieve the desired investment goals. The behavioral finance perspective suggests a matching between client's personality and the different investment styles.

---

[6]For example, traditional finance uses the concept of value at risk (VaR) so that the client can ensure hard liabilities except for 5% of the possible cases.

## 11.6 COMPLYING WITH THE REGULATORY REQUIREMENTS

Finally, we once more come back to the regulatory requirements. Table 17 compares what a good advisory process based on behavioral finance suggests and what the regulators require (Hens & Sethe, 2017). The regulators demand that advisors assess clients' investment goals, financial situation, knowledge, and experience. These requirements are fulfilling with a needs analysis and an assessment of the risk ability and the risk awareness of the client, respectively.

Further, MiFID requires that advisors assess the risk tolerance of their clients as part of the client's goals. FIDLEG requires an assessment of the risk tolerance only in the commentary that is issued in addition to the law act. The requirement to assess clients' risk tolerance as part of their goals is logically inconsistent with the notion that risk tolerance is not a goal but a restriction for achieving investment goals. Therefore, it is sensible to separate the assessment of the risk tolerance from the evaluation of the client's goals.

The regulators do not require an assessment of a client's investment style. Monitoring is demanded only in discretionary mandates.

## 11.7 INFORMATION TECHNOLOGY IN CLIENT ADVISORY SERVICES

So far, we have described behavioral finance concepts and discussed how to use them to improve the advisory services. Information technology (IT) tools have been presented as illustrations. The question of whether an IT tool is most appropriate in the advisory process needs to be considered on a case-by-case basis.

There are different ways to use IT tools in the advisory process. They can be used before, while, and after advisors talk with their clients. Our

**TABLE 17** The structured wealth management process and the regulatory requirements for private clients

| Structured Wealth Management Process | MiFID/FIDLEG |
| --- | --- |
| Needs analysis | Investment goal |
| Risk ability | Financial situation |
| Risk awareness | Knowledge and experience |
| Risk tolerance | As part of the goals |
| Investment style | Not mentioned |
| Monitoring | Only in discretionary mandates |

recommendation is that risk profiling, which is required by law, should be done when the advisor faces the client, while the training and the diagnostic tool assessing the client's financial personality can be done independent from the advisor.

Figure 11.92 illustrates how advisors can integrate the information technology in their work. At the beginning, client and advisor could engage

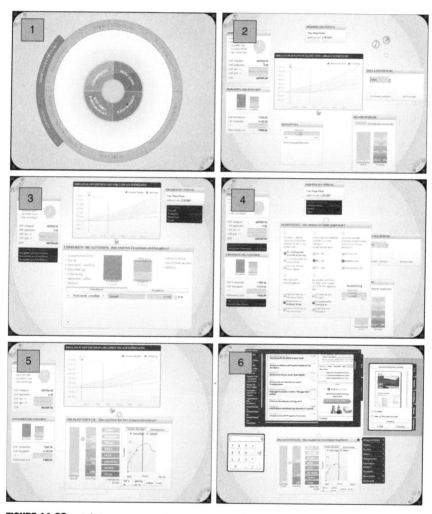

**FIGURE 11.92**   Advisory process in a digital world
*Source*: Nussbaumer (2012): "Essays on transparent IT support for asymmetric client-advisor encounters," University of Zurich.

in small talk, and the advisor will write down important information on his notepad. After this initial phase, the advisor could activate the system and present the general process overview to the client (see part 1 of Figure 11.92). Having discussed the general frame of the advisory session, the advisor may switch to the main overview (see part 2 of Figure 11.92). In this overview, the advisor will briefly explain the visualized information, starting with client information (personal information, cash flow, assets), progressing with risk profile and investment strategy as well as explaining the role of the needs visualization and the projection of growth. Detailed view of some information blocks can be accessed (see part 3 of Figure 11.92) to verify that all relevant data are entered and to see the impact of the entered data. After the discussion of the client's risk profile and the client's goals in part 4 of Figure 11.92, the investment strategy can be defined (see part 5 of Figure 11.92). All relevant information remains accessible so that changes in this information can be immediately assessed. Additional tools can be implemented as well (see part 6 of Figure 11.92).

# CHAPTER 12

# Fintech

**W**e have already seen in chapters 10 and 11 that IT-solutions can help to facilitate the advisory process. In this section, we give a general overview of an important transformation through which the financial advisory industry is currently going.[1] This transformation, called *fintech,* has a huge impact on the way financial advisors structure their wealth management processes. Fintech is an acronym for financial technology. For a long time, financial technology has facilitated asset management.

## 12.1 HISTORY OF FINTECH

Optimization problems like the mean-variance optimization, for example, were defined such that they could be solved with the computers of the time. Note that solving the mean-variance problem means to solve a linear system of equations, which was—based on the algorithm that Friedrich Gauss suggested in the eighteenth century—solved quickly given the technology of the 1950s. One might speculate what decision criterion Markowitz would have suggested if the computers at his time were more powerful! Also, the derivatives revolution of the 1970s would not have been possible without advances in financial technology. At that time, pocket calculators became available, which could evaluate the Black-Scholes formula for option pricing. The main difference these days is that computers are regularly used not only by asset managers but also by clients. Smart phones and the internet have become commonplace. This latest stage of the fintech revolution thus changes the advisor–client relationship.

## 12.2 CURRENT STATE OF FINTECH

Already the very first step of this relationship, the onboarding, can now be done with computers. There is no need to check passports and

---

[1]For a thorough overview, see Sironi (2016).

other documents to open a bank account since passports have become electronically readable and the computer can recognize clients by their face, voice, fingerprint, or iris. As we showed in the previous chapter, financial planning (identification, valuation, and ranking of the client's goals) can be facilitated by computer programs, risk profiling can be supported by experience sampling, etc., and risk awareness can be raised by computer games (gamification). Finally, investment styles can be programmed so that neither the client nor the advisor needs to take discretionary actions.

And indeed, so-called robot advisors (i.e., financial advisors that do not use humans anymore), have been made available to clients. Their sophistication varies. Some use simple questionnaires based on which they suggest investing in ETFs. Others use some variations of experience sampling and then sell active asset management. Consistent with the gap in the regulatory requirement outlined before, so far none of the robot advisors can assess the investment style the clients prefer

## 12.3   ASSESSMENT OF FINTECH SOLUTIONS

Robot advisors are certainly cheaper than human advisors. Whether they are superior to human advisors remains to be seen. So far, they were all made available after the financial crisis of 2007–2008. Some more traditional advisors claim that human advice is superior in times of crisis, as giving financial advice is a hand-holding business like babysitting (Hackethal, Haliassos, & Jappelli, 2012). The race between humans and robots is still open. The point of this book is that both can benefit from the insights of behavioral finance. Knowing typical behavioral biases and the best way to moderate them, knowing that decision theories can give a sound foundation of the advisory process, and knowing how to structure the advisory process based on these insights is essential in wealth management.

# CHAPTER 13

# Case Studies

To wrap-up the insights from this book, we now consider three case studies. The first is a case study taken from the "Bilanz Private Banking Rating." The second is taken from our research project "Behavioral Finance for Retail Banking," which was financed by the Swiss National Science Foundation. The third case study illustrates a goal-based investing approach.

Concerning the "Bilanz Private Banking Rating," its purpose is to check the quality of private banking in Switzerland and to give annual feedback to Swiss banks regarding how they can further improve. The results are published in the magazine *Bilanz* (http://www.bilanz.ch/), which has a large readership and a high reputation in Switzerland.

The "Bilanz Private Banking Rating" includes the following stages:

1. A real client is selected by the jury president with the help of a journalist from *Bilanz*. In this first stage, the client's case is written.
2. Request for proposals: A letter presenting the case and asking for written advice is sent to approximately 80 banks in Switzerland.
3. The jury makes a first screening of the proposals that were sent in and preselects the best 15 or so. These are sent to IVA[1] for a quantitative analysis.
4. The jury makes an in-depth analysis of the quantitative results and complements them with its own qualitative judgment.
5. Three banks are invited to present to the client in front of the jury.
6. Advised by the jury, the client selects the favorite bank.
7. *Bilanz* publishes its reporter's story and awards "Best Private Bank" medals to the winners.
8. In the aftermath, the jury president is invited by some banks to explain their performance and give hints on how they could improve their services in the future.

---

[1]The IVA is domiciled in Munich: https://www.institut-va.de/en/. The name stands for "Institut für Vermögensaufbau," which can be translated as Institute for Wealth Creation.

The Bilanz Private Banking Rating has now run for 10 years. It has become highly recognized by banks in Switzerland. During those 10 years, the quality of advice has improved and moreover, its costs have decreased. To protect the privacy of the clients, the names presented here are fictitious.

## 13.1  CASE STUDY 1: STRUCTURED WEALTH MANAGEMENT

Daniel Handsome is a 25-year-old student of Swiss nationality studying art history who inherited 1.7 Mio Swiss francs (CHF) from his grandfather. He does not need the money to support his living expenses and can invest it for the long term. Since he has no experience with finance but is young, he wants to learn how to invest so that he can eventually manage his portfolio himself. Moreover, he wants to be able to communicate with his bank any time because he plans to study abroad. He looked at the stocks his grandfather left to him but cannot see himself picking stocks based on fundamentals as his grandfather did. He beliefs that prices reveal valuable information for future returns that are not fully explored in the asset management industry.

To analyze this case, we follow the structured wealth management process suggested in Chapter 11. In the needs analysis, the financial advisor should spot that the case description is incomplete. Neither hard liabilities like pension plans or real estate are mentioned, nor does the case description reveal some plans or wishes such as setting up a family. Thus, the financial advisor must ask for those liabilities in his reply to the letter. Daniel replies that now he feels too young for pension planning, but starting a family is a realistic goal, and with that in mind, he considers buying some real estate, worth approximately CHF 1,000,000. Knowing the Swiss tax system, the financial advisor understands that it would not make sense to buy the house from Daniel's wealth but to reserve CHF 200,000 for the down payment. This, together with the long investment horizon, leads to the assessment that Daniel has a high-risk ability. However, his risk awareness is low since he studies art history and has no investment experience. To determine the risk tolerance, the financial advisor must come back to Daniel once more and ask three more questions: How does Daniel trade off losses against gains, how much does he prefer certain payoffs to uncertain ones, and how quickly would he sell once he incurs severe losses? Figure 13.93 shows the answers given by Daniel.

Daniel is categorized as a moderate plus investor as described in Figure 13.94 and Figure 13.95a and b. The suggested asset allocation is shown in Figure 13.96. The key figures associated with the suggested asset allocation are in Figure 13.97. Figure 13.98 shows their description. Finally, Figure 13.99 shows the results of a scenario analysis.

| Aspects | | Your Answers | |
|---|---|---|---|
| Investment | Goal(s) | None defined. | |
| | Amount | USD 1,700,000 | |
| | Liabilities | USD 200,000 | |
| | Time Horizon | 40 Years | |
| Expectations | Expected Return p.a. | 5.0 % | |
| | Reference Point[*] | 0.0 % | |
| Experience | Global Bonds | None | |
| | Global Equities | None | |
| | Hedge Funds | None | Excluded |
| | Global Real Estate | None | Excluded |
| | Commodities | None | |
| | Private Equity | None | |
| Risk Preferences | Attitude to Losses | 0.00 % equal (−3.00 % / 5.00 %) | |
| | Attitude to Uncertainty | 5.00 % equal (0.00 % / 10.00 %) | |
| | Investment Temperament | A loss of 10% leads you to decide on "*No change*". | |

**FIGURE 13.93** Daniel's answers to the risk-profiling questions

## Your Risk Preference Factors

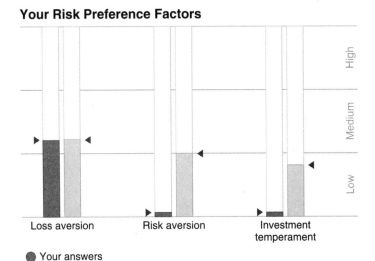

● Your answers

◍ Impact on your profile

**FIGURE 13.94** Daniel's risk profile

Your Risk Preference Profile: Moderate Plus

| Cautious | Conservative | Moderate | Moderate Plus | Aggressive |

Your answers show that you can take greater risks with your investment.

You show a high tolerance for uncertainty with respect to the final performace of your investment and you show no sensitivity to large temporary drawdowns in your performance. However, your moderate tolerance for losses restricts your ability to take more risk.

Your responses indicate that your risk profile is influenced by your attitude to losses. Nonetheless, the other two risk dimensions of attitude to losses and investment uncertainties play a minor role.

**FIGURE 13.95a** Description of Daniel's risk profile – part I

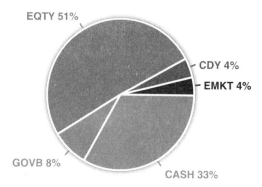

**FIGURE 13.95b** Description of Daniel's risk profile – part II

**Proposed Portfolio**

| | | | |
|---|---|---|---|
| ● | CASH | Money Markets | 33% |
| ● | GOVB | Global Bonds | 8% |
| ● | EQTY | Global Equities | 51% |
| ● | CDY | Commodities | 4% |
| ● | EMKT | Emerging Markets | 4% |

**FIGURE 13.96** Suggested asset allocation

| Key Figures | Proposed Portfolio |
|---|---|
| Expected Return p.a. | 5.21% |
| Expected Volatility p.a. | 9.59% |
| Probability of Loss p.a. | 29.72% |
| Expected Gain p.a. | 10.19% |
| Expected Loss p.a. | 6.26% |
| Maximum Drawdown | 27.04% |

**FIGURE 13.97**   Key figures of the suggested asset allocation

**Expected Return p.a.**
The table presents the statistical figures of your overruled asset allocation and compares it to the original proposed portfolio. These figures are conditional on you following through with our recommendations.

**Expected Volatility p.a.**
Standard deviation is a widely used measurement of variability or diversity. It shows how much variation or "dispersion" it is expected from the expected return over the next year. Standard deviation does not differ variation in the gain respectively in the losses.

**Probability of Loss p.a.**
The degree of likelihood that the portfolio will suffer a loss next year. It is called a loss when the portfolio's return below zero.

**Expected Gain and Losses p.a.**
EN:Die Belohnung einer Anlage ist nicht die erwartete Rendite sondern der erwartete Gewinn. Genauso achtet er weniger auf die Volatilität, wenn es darum geht, das Risiko seiner Anlage zu beurteilen. Risiko bedeutet also vielmehr, welchen Verlust der Anleger erleiden könnte.

**Maximum Drawdown**
The maximum loss from a market peak to a market nadir, and measures how sustained one's losses can be.

**FIGURE 13.98**   Description of the key figures

Comparing this ideal advice with that given in the Bilanz Private Banking Rating study, we first notice that only half of the banks ask for further information. The other half tries to a "shot in the dark." Figure 13.100 shows the average asset allocation recommended by the banks. We see that on average, the banks recommend more than 50% stocks, which is in line with the strong risk ability of Daniel.

The case study will be finalized with an analysis of the investment style that Daniel finds most appropriate. As one can infer from the description of the case, he believes in a price-based strategy. Academic literature shows that this style is profitable (e.g., when one does momentum investing). Thus, the financial advisor shall suggest the moment style we explained in section 11.4.6. Indeed, one of the three banks presenting to Daniel suggested this style. Nevertheless, he chooses one of the other two banks. The reason for this is the offered training program and the features of the online-banking tools.

Normal trend (2004-2007)

Historical performance after investment period

| | |
|---|---|
| Cash | 2.7% |
| Global Equities | 45.7% |
| Proposed Portfolio | 29.1% |

Upward trend (1997-2000)

Historical performance after investment period

| | |
|---|---|
| Cash | 4.7% |
| Global Equities | 100.0% |
| Proposed Portfolio | 51.5% |

Downward trend (2008-2009, financial crisis)

Historical performance after investment period

| | |
|---|---|
| Cash | 7.8% |
| Global Equities | –34.1% |
| Proposed Portfolio | –14.1% |

**FIGURE 13.99** Scenario analysis

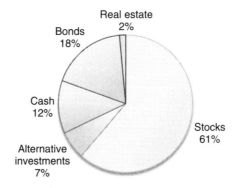

**FIGURE 13.100** Average recommendations

## 13.2   CASE STUDY 2: EXPERIENCE SAMPLING

Mrs. and Mr. Fisher are in their mid-thirties, married, and have two children, Amelie, 7 years old, and Ben, 5 years old. The family income is CHF 100,000. They live in a house worth CHF 1 million, from which CHF 200,000 has been paid and CHF 800,000 remains on the mortgage. The yearly living expenses are CHF 80,000. Besides paying back the mortgage, the family wants to finance a university education for their children (Oxford, Stanford or ETH) and increase the pension they will eventually get when they retire. Given the age of the kids, the college funds are needed in about 10 years. The family sets the following priorities: (1) house; (2) education; (3) retirement. They can currently lock in an interest rate of 1% for a 10-year mortgage, and education (including living expenses) costs will be between CHF 20,000 and CHF 50,000 a year for three years, unless their children receive significant scholarships—and for sake of our example, we will assume they are cuter than they are brilliant. The family wants to plan for 10 years. The residual income of CHF 20,000 a year can be spent on the mortgage, an investment plan for the education of their children and a retirement plan. Since the Smiths live in Switzerland for tax reasons, it does not make sense to reduce the mortgage by repayments other than the interest payments.

Applying the asset split, CHF 8,000 a year are fixed for the mortgage. But how much risk shall the family take to finance the education and the retirement top-up? Our research shows that this question is best assessed by a combination of experience sampling and loss tolerance. The idea of experience sampling is comparable to flight simulators for aircraft pilots. Potential financial outcomes such as investment returns are randomly drawn (simulated) interactively by the investor, and the distribution of possible outcomes builds up step-by-step on the screen, as Figure 13.9 shows. Investors can increase or reduce their risk, observe the changes in the distribution of results, and interactively adjust the risk to achieve a distribution that they feel comfortable with.

Experience sampling is the best method to increase the risk awareness. It should be combined with a method to assess the risk tolerance, which is best achieved with the gain-loss method, as explained in Chapter 10. It fixes a potential gain and asks for the maximal loss the investor is willing to accept for that gain. The latter should be done iteratively—starting from a loss that is as high as the gain, which is then reduced step-by-step. In each step, the investor is asked whether the investment is now acceptable and the iteration stops once it is. Combining the two methods one can assess the risk awareness and the risk tolerance—and to be safe, one should base the advice on the aspect of risk in which the investor is more conservative.

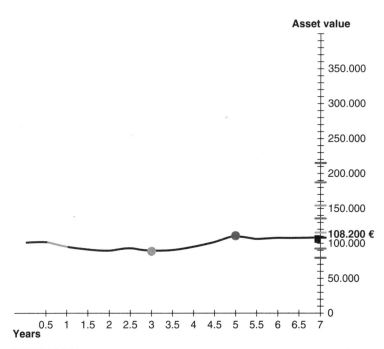

**FIGURE 13.101**   Experience sampling

Having completed these risk assessments, the Fisher family decides to invest the remaining CHF 12,000 a year into two savings contracts: one for the education of the children and one for retirement. The former requires CHF 8,000 a year and targets at a total wealth of $100,000 (Oxford), which could, however, also end up as CHF 60,000 (ETH) or at CHF 125,000 (Stanford). In the latter, they invest the remaining CHF 4,000, which after 10 years would accumulate to CHF 60,000 or CHF 20,000. Thus, this investment is considerably riskier—but since the retirement is in only 30 years, appropriate adjustments can be made after 10 years.

## 13.3   CASE STUDY 3: GOAL-BASED APPROACH

In this section, we propose a case study that illustrates a goal-based approach to select the appropriate investment strategy. We apply a modeling framework based on prospect theory, where the allocation of wealth among the goals is optimized to achieve consistency between the goal-based assessment of risk tolerance and an overall assessment of risk aversion.

Mike and Julie McGeorge live in Florida with their 10-year-old daughter, Emily. Five years ago, Mike and Julie invested their savings into a small business. With the revenue from the company, they can now cover their living expenses and repay a loan they initiated 5 years ago to finance their start-up. However, during the last five years, they didn't save any money. Last week, they inherited $250,000 from Julie's parents. They decided that $50,000 will be set aside as a reserve for future unexpected expenses, while $200,000 will be invested to reach three goals they have always dreamed of.

The first goal is to allow Emily to attend a top university, because so far, she achieved very good results at school, she is extremely dedicated, and she would like to become a medical doctor. The cost is estimated at $100,000 in about 8 years, when Emily will complete college. The second goal is to buy a house in 5 years. Their rented house is small but nevertheless quite expensive. However, because they are currently very focused on further developing their business, they prefer to postpone buying a home for 5 years because they would prefer to build, which would also require time and effort to personalize the home as they would love to. Their dream house is worth $900,000 and they could finance 80% of this amount with a mortgage, so the remaining cost is estimated at $180,000. Finally, given that the last 5 years have been extremely intensive for the family, they would like to enjoy a long vacation in a couple of years. They have never visited Canada or Mexico, and they would love to combine both destinations in a long trip. Emily will also be very enthusiastic about this, because she really loves discovering new places.

They ask their financial advisor for a recommendation. He suggests a goal-based investment approach, where each goal is considered independently from the others and a specific asset allocation for each goal is determined (see Section 11.5). Mike and Julie find this approach very intuitive and understandable. Because focusing on single goals might lead to the situation where the overall asset allocation is too risky, the bank adopts a goal-based methodology that ensures that the overall asset allocation is in line with an overall risk profile, which is assessed at the beginning of the advisory process.

For Mike and Julie, the education of Emily has high priority, and $70,000 is allocated to this goal. However, they want to ensure that at least $50,000 is not at risk, as they will be disappointed if in 8 years less than $85,000 will be available for Emily. The house is the next most important goal, and they allocate $120,000 to it. Mike and Julie are less risk averse with respect to this goal, but having less than $140,000 will be quite disappointing, as in this case they need an additional $40,000 for their 20% contribution to the house, and their current savings are just slightly higher, at $50,000. Finally, the remaining $10,000 is for the vacation, which is a

wish, but not really a must. In any case, if feasible, they plan to spend a
month between Canada and Mexico, and this could cost up to $15,000.
However, if not feasible, they will maybe only spend a couple weeks in
Canada. Thus, they would be quite disappointed if they lost money from
their initial budget of $10,000. Table 18 summarizes Mike and Julie's
goals.

The inputs in the risk-profiling tool are shown in Table 19 Specifically,
we observe that for the education of Emily, Mike and Julie set a reserve of
$50,000, while for the other two goals, there is not a reserve.

Next, because the financial advisor suggested that they follow a
goal-based approach, for each goal he determines Mike and Julie's risk tolerance and ability, and the corresponding optimal asset allocation. Therefore,
Mike and Julie go through a risk profiler for each of their goals, and the
optimal asset allocations corresponding to the goals are then determined.
The answers concerning loss aversion are reported in Table 20.

The three optimal strategies significantly differ, because Mike and
Julie's risk tolerance strongly depends on the specific goal they have in
mind (Table 21). For example, for goal 1, the education of Emily, they set a
reserve that is around 70% of the investment amount. Therefore, following
an asset split for goal 1, at least 70% of the investment for goal goes into
cash. Moreover, Mike and Julie are quite loss averse when it comes to
Emily's education, but nevertheless, some investment into equity is needed
because the expected annual return to achieve the goal is above 4%. The
loss aversion for goal 2 (the house) is lower and the expected return on goal
2 is much higher. Therefore, the corresponding asset allocation only has
20% into cash and 12% into bonds. The rest goes into equity and a hedge
fund. Finally, for goal 3, the long vacation, Mike and Julie are willing to
take more risk, and thus 100% goes into equities. Indeed, the investment
for the vacation is only 5% of the total amount, and, moreover, their

**TABLE 18** Summary of Mike and Julie's goals

| Goal | Investment | Reserve | Horizon | Expectation (Annual Return) | Reference Point | Loss Aversion |
|------|-----------|---------|---------|-----------------------------|-----------------|---------------|
| Education Emily | $70,000 | $50,000 | 8 years | $100,000 (4.6%) | $85,000 (2.5%) | High |
| House | $120,000 | $0 | 5 years | $180,000 (8.5%) | $140,000 (3.1%) | Medium |
| Vacation | $10,000 | $0 | 2 years | $15,000 (23%) | $10,000 (0%) | Low |

**TABLE 19** Input risk profiler for investment amount, reserve, and investment horizon

| Goal | Input Investment Amount / Reserve / Time Horizon |
|------|--------------------------------------------------|
| Education Emily | How much are you looking to invest and of this amount how much do you require as reserve? — How many years do you wish to invest? — Investment amount [USD] 70'000 — Reserve [USD] 50'000 — Time horizon [Years] 8 |
| House | How much are you looking to invest and of this amount how much do you require as reserve? — How many years do you wish to invest? — Investment amount [USD] 120'000 — Reserve [USD] 0 — Time horizon [Years] 5 |
| Vacation | How much are you looking to invest and of this amount how much do you require as reserve? — How many years do you wish to invest? — Investment amount [USD] 10'000 — Reserve [USD] 0 — Time horizon [Years] 2 |

expectation and thus also their loss tolerance with respect to this goal are very high. Indeed, in their view, either they will do a memorable vacation or they will postpone it to a later point in time and this time just spend a couple weeks in Canada.

We compute the overall asset allocation as a weighted sum of goals' based asset allocations. We see in Figure 13.102 that cash and equity account for almost 80% of the overall strategy. As previously discusses, cash mainly comes from the first goal, the education of Emily, for which Mike and Julie set a reserve and are very loss averse, while equity mainly comes from the second and third goals. The overall strategy has an expected return of 5.6%

**TABLE 20**    Input risk profiler for loss aversion

| Goal | Input Loss Aversion |
|------|---------------------|
| Education Emily | |
| House | |
| Vacation | |

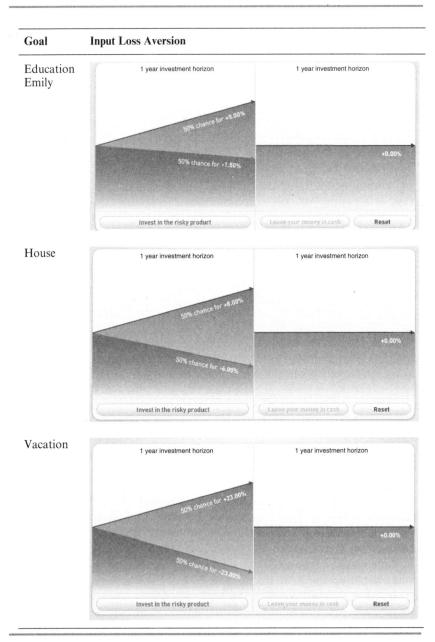

**TABLE 21** Optimal asset allocation for each goal

| Goal | Optimal Asset Allocation for Each Goal |
|------|----------------------------------------|

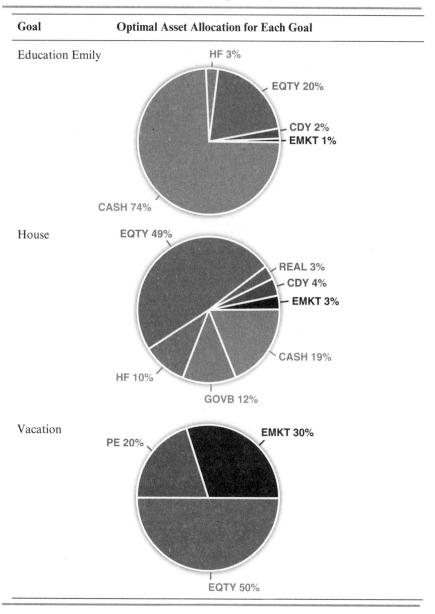

Education Emily

HF 3%
EQTY 20%
CDY 2%
EMKT 1%
CASH 74%

House

EQTY 49%
REAL 3%
CDY 4%
EMKT 3%
CASH 19%
GOVB 12%
HF 10%

Vacation

PE 20%
EMKT 30%
EQTY 50%

Overall Asset Allocation

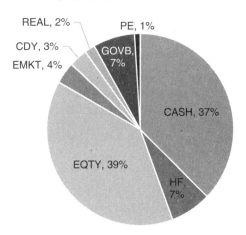

**FIGURE 13.102** Overall asset allocation of Mike and Julie McGeorge

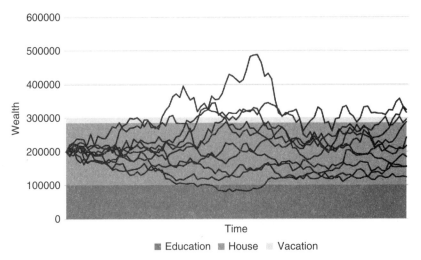

**FIGURE 13.103** Simulation of the portfolio distribution

and a volatility of 12.2%. We point out that if goals are not appropriately weighted in the overall assessment (e.g., too much capital is allocated to goals where the risk tolerance is higher, the overall exposure to risk implied by a goal-based approach might be higher than allowed by an overall assessment of risk tolerance).

After the goal-based risk profiles are determined and the corresponding optimal asset allocations are computed, the financial advisor performs a simulation exercise (experience sampling) to improve risk awareness (see Subsection 11.4.3)—that is, to illustrate how often the proposed asset allocation will allow the family to achieve their investment goals. Ten future scenarios are generated to allow Mike and Julie to examine the likelihood that goal will be reached. This is illustrated in Figure 13.103. Very likely, Mike and Julie must give up on their long vacation between Mexico and Canada (only 2 scenarios out of 10 reach this goal), but quite likely, their dream house will become reality in 5 years. However, it might require some extra cash from the reserves (7 scenarios out of 10). Finally, it is quite likely that Emily will be able to attend a top university, show her great potential there, and become a medical doctor (10 scenarios out of 10). This result is fully in line with Mike and Julie's priorities!

# CHAPTER 14

# Conclusions

**O**ver the last 30 years, behavioral finance has successfully integrated insights from psychology into finance to understand the behavior of investors and financial markets. Nowadays, behavioral finance is a well-established and growing research area that also attracted the attention of practitioners, because it convincingly applied its scientific developments to their practical needs.

In this book, we argued that private banking can strongly profit from behavioral finance research to structure the wealth management process. The constant pressure on product margins and the advent of fintech initiatives is shifting the focus from products to services and personalization. Therefore, the wealth management process will face important transformations, from product centric to client centric. In this context, behavioral finance delivers the necessary scientific foundation to understand clients' needs as well as their decision-making process, taking also into account the cultural dimension.

We discussed that behavioral finance differs from traditional finance on two important aspects. First, while traditional finance imposes rationality, behavioral finance recognizes that investors often behave irrationally. We described the most important behavioral biases, how they affect the behavior of investors, and how they can be mitigated. Second, traditional finance theory is normative (i.e., built on specific principles of rationality), while behavioral finance theory is descriptive (i.e., built on experimental and empirical data on investors' behaviors). We discussed traditional decision theories (expected utility theory and mean-variance) as well as the behavioral decision theory (prospect theory). Finally, we studied the implications of the different theories for static and dynamic asset allocation, for product design, as well for life-cycle planning.

To convince the reader of the importance of behavioral finance research for private banking, we also presented practical applications of the theoretical developments in behavioral finance to the wealth management process. Specifically, we provided a diagnostic test to determine the investment personality and a risk profiler founded on prospect theory to assess risk tolerance and risk ability. These instruments allow advisors to structure the wealth management process and to gain important information about clients—a central and necessary step for being well-equipped to face the important transformations of the banking industry in the next decades

Nobel Prize winner Richard Thaler wrote: "I predict that in the not-too-distant future, the term 'behavioral finance' will be correctly viewed as a redundant phrase. What other kind of finance is there? In their enlightenment, economists will routinely incorporate as much 'behavior' into their models as they observe in the real world. After all, to do otherwise would be irrational" (Thaler, 1999). We also believe that ignoring the behavior of clients would be irrational, because in the long-run it will affect the quality of the services and thus clients' satisfaction. Moreover, in the era of digitalization, there will be a massive increase in the amount of data collected and stored. These data will be extremely precious to further improve the understanding of clients and the quality of services. However, to make sense out of data, one needs to be able to analyze and interpret it, and this calls for a solid scientific foundation of the advisory process so that finally, financial advice becomes a science more than an art.

# CHAPTER 15

# Appendix: Mathematical Arguments

## 15.1 PROOF THAT EXPECTED UTILITY SATISFIES THE AXIOMS OF RATIONAL CHOICE

Transitivity:

Suppose $Eu(A) > Eu(B)$ so that lottery A is chosen over lottery B, $Eu(B) > Eu(C)$ so that lottery B is chosen over lottery C. Since $Eu(A)$, $Eu(B)$ and $Eu(C)$ are real numbers these numbers can be ordered from high to low so that from $Eu(A) > Eu(B)$ *and* $Eu(B) > Eu(C)$ it follows that $Eu(A) > Eu(C)$. That is, lottery A is chosen over lottery C.

Independence Axiom:

To prove that expected utility satisfies the independence axiom, we need to be a bit more formal. A lottery is given by a collection of payoffs $x_1, \ldots, x_n$ and their probabilities $p_1, \ldots, p_n$. Without loss of generality, we can assume that all lotteries have the same payoffs but might differ in the probabilities.[1] Thus, given the possible outcomes the lotteries are determined by the probabilities of these outcomes. To distinguish the lotteries we will then index the probabilities with the lottery, i.e., $p_1^X, \ldots, p_n^X$ denotes the probabilities of lottery X and $p_1^Y, \ldots, p_n^Y$ are the probabilities of lottery Y. Having said this, the statement of the independence axiom is:

If X is preferred to Y, then $pX + (1 - p)Z$ is preferred to $pY + (1 - p)Z$.[2] The expected utility of the first lottery is computed as $p \sum_{i=1}^{n} p_i^X u(x_i) + (1 - p) \sum_{i=1}^{n} p_i^Z u(x_i)$ while the expected utility of the second lottery is computed as $p \sum_{i=1}^{n} p_i^Y u(x_i) + (1 - p) \sum_{i=1}^{n} p_i^Z u(x_i)$. Thus, both expressions of expected utility have the second term in common and

---

[1] Suppose the lottery X has the payoffs 2 and 4 occurring with the probabilities 0.5 and 0.5 while the lottery Y has the payoffs 4 and –1 occurring with the probabilities 0.9 and 0.1. Then we can as well say the lottery X and Y have the same payoffs –1, 2 and 4. While these common payoffs occur in the lottery X with the probabilities 0, 0.5, and 0.5, they occur in the lottery Y with the probabilities 0.1, 0, 0.9.

[2] Note that if X and Z are probabilities, so is $pX + (1 - p)Z$.

the first lottery has a higher expected utility than the second if the expected utility of $X$ is higher than the expected utility of $Y$.

Monotonicity is satisfied as long as the utility function $u$ is increasing. For $u(x) = \frac{x^\alpha}{\alpha}$ this is true for all values of $\alpha$. This was the reason why we divided $x^\alpha$ by $\alpha$. Otherwise, for negative $\alpha$ the utility function would be decreasing[3].

## 15.2 DERIVATION OF THE FOURFOLD PATTERN OF RISK TAKING

To derive the fourfold pattern of risk taking, consider a lottery with just two outcomes, e.g., $x_1$ and $x_2$. Recall also that a risk-loving decision maker prefers the lottery to the guaranteed payoff equal to the expected value of the lottery:

$$v(px_1 + (1-p)x_2) < w(p)v(x_1) + w(1-p)v(x_2).$$

Supposing, furthermore, that $x_2 = 0$, we get risk taking as a combination of $x_1$ being negative or positive and the size of the probabilities. Rewriting the definition just given for this case leads to $v(px_1) < w(p)v(x_1)$. If we replace the utility function with the piece-wise power function of Kahneman and Tversky, then we get $v(p)v(x_1) < w(p)v(x_1)$, which is equivalent to $p^\alpha v(x_1) < w(p)v(x_1)$ or $p^\alpha < w(p)$ for gains and $p^\alpha > w(p)$ for losses. These conditions are illustrated graphically in Figure 15.104, for example, for $\alpha = 0.88$ and $\gamma = 0.65$.

Hence, if the investor must decide whether to play a lottery paying 0 or more, the investor will prefer to gamble instead of receiving the average lottery payoff as a guaranteed payment if the chances to get the large payoff with the lottery are small. This is because the investor overweighs the probability of reaching the utility level associated with the gain. For the same reason of probability overweighting, investors facing losses would buy insurance, i.e., pay a premium to an insurance company (a sure loss) for avoiding the risk for losses when playing a lottery.

## 15.3 MEAN-VARIANCE AS A SPECIAL CASE OF PROSPECT THEORY

We show that for a piecewise quadratic value function prospect theory without probability weighting (and thus also expected utility) coincides with

---

[3]Suppose for example $\alpha = -1$ then $x^\alpha = 1/x$, which is decreasing while $-1/x$ is increasing.

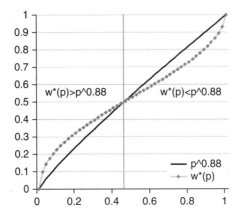

**FIGURE 15.104**   Risk taking in dependence on the probability for gains and losses

mean-variance analysis whatever the return distribution. For this purpose, consider the following value function:

$$
v(\Delta x) =
\begin{cases}
\Delta x - \dfrac{\alpha^{+}}{2}(\Delta x)^2 & \text{if } \Delta x \geq 0 \\[2ex]
\beta\left(\Delta x - \dfrac{\alpha^{-}}{2}(\Delta x)^2\right) & \text{if } \Delta x < 0
\end{cases}
$$

where $\Delta x$ is defined as the portfolio return relative to the investor's reference point. Note that for $\alpha^{+} > 0$ and $\alpha^{-} < 0$, the function is s-shaped—i.e., concave for gains and convex for losses as the piecewise power function of Kahneman and Tversky. Moreover, the parameter $\beta > 1$ indicates again the degree of loss aversion.

An important property of the piecewise quadratic value function is that for $\beta = 1$ and $\alpha^{+} = \alpha^{-}$, the prospect utility of an investor is

$$
\sum_{i=1}^{n} p_i(x_i - RP) - \frac{\alpha}{2}\left[\sum_{i=1}^{n} p_i(x_i - RP)^2\right] = \mu(x - RP) - \frac{\alpha}{2}(x - RP)^2
$$

Note that

$$
\mu(x - RP) - \frac{\alpha}{2}(x - RP)^2 = \mu(x - RP) - \frac{\alpha}{2}(\mu(x^2) - 2\mu(x)RP - RP^2)
$$

And since $\mu(x^2) = \sigma^2(x) + \mu^2(x)$, we see that the objective function depends on $x$ only via the mean and variance of $x$. Thus, it is a mean-variance objective function.

For example, if the reference point is the expected return of the investor's portfolio, $RP = \mu$, we get $PT(R) + RP = \mu - \frac{\alpha}{2}\sigma^2$, which is the simple mean-variance objective function that we used before.

## 15.4   PROSPECT THEORY OPTIMAL ASSET ALLOCATION

We first introduce a value function that delivers robust asset allocations—that is, asset allocations that do not change drastically on small changes of the exogenous parameters (the probabilities of the returns, the degree of loss and of risk aversion). One utility function that satisfies the conditions above is the piecewise quadratic value function with the following form:

$$
v(\Delta x) = \begin{cases} \Delta x - \dfrac{\alpha^+}{2}(\Delta x)^2 \text{ if } \dfrac{1}{\alpha^+} > \Delta x \geq 0 \\[3mm] \beta\left(\Delta x - \dfrac{\alpha^-}{2}(\Delta x)^2\right) \text{ if } \dfrac{1}{\alpha^-} < \Delta x < 0 \end{cases}
$$

where $\Delta x$ is defined as the portfolio return relative to the investor's reference point. The restrictions are technical requirements that prevent the utility from falling (increasing) after the gain (loss) reaches the level $\frac{1}{\alpha^+}$ and $\frac{1}{\alpha^-}$, respectively. Beyond this gain (loss), we assume a constant utility.

Hence, the piecewise quadratic value function takes the form:

$$
v(\Delta x) = \begin{cases} \dfrac{1}{2\alpha^+} \text{ if } \Delta x \geq \dfrac{1}{\alpha^+} \\[3mm] \Delta x - \dfrac{\alpha^+}{2}(\Delta x)^2 \text{ if } \dfrac{1}{\alpha^+} > \Delta x \geq 0 \\[3mm] \beta\left(\Delta x - \dfrac{\alpha^-}{2}(\Delta x)^2\right) \text{ if } \dfrac{1}{\alpha^-} < \Delta x < 0 \\[3mm] \dfrac{1}{2\alpha^-} \text{ if } \Delta x \leq \dfrac{1}{\alpha^-} \end{cases}
$$

What is the optimal asset allocation of this investor? Consider the simple case with one risky and one riskless asset.[4] The return of the riskless asset is $R_f$. The risky asset has two possible returns $R_u$ and $R_d$. The probability that $R_u$ realizes is $p$. Let now $\lambda$ be the percentage of wealth invested in the risky

---

[4]The general case of multiple assets is demonstrated in math box 2.5 of Hens and Bachmann (2008): *Behavioral Finance for Private Banking*, Wiley Finance.

asset. Thus, the portfolio return can be either $R_f + (R_u - R_f)\lambda$ or $R_f + (R_d - R_f)\lambda$. Suppose also that there is an investor with a piecewise quadratic value function as already suggested:

$$
v(R_i) = \begin{cases} R_i - RP - \dfrac{\alpha^+}{2}(R_i - RP)^2 \text{ if } R_i \geq RP \\ \beta\left(R_i - RP - \dfrac{\alpha^-}{2}(R_i - RP)^2\right) \text{ if } R_i < RP \end{cases}
$$

where $R_i$ is the return of the portfolio with risky assets (excess return).

Thus, under the assumption that $\frac{1}{\alpha^-} \leq R_S \leq \frac{1}{\alpha^+}$, the optimal percentage of wealth that should be invested in the risky asset given that the reference point is equal to the return of the riskless asset:

$$
\lambda = \frac{w(p)(R_u - R_f) + \beta(1 - w(p))(R_d - R_f)}{\alpha^+ w(p)(R_u - R_f)^2 + \beta\alpha^-(1 - w(p))(R_d - R_f)^2}
$$

which is robust to small changes of the parameters if the numerator stays positive.

Note that the percentage of wealth invested in the risky asset increases with the expected return of the risky asset, i.e., $\mu = pR_u + (1 - p)R_d$, and decreases with the investor's loss aversion but also with the investor's risk aversion for gains and losses if the latter is not too negative. Thus, also intuitively, the solution makes sense.

## 15.5 NO TIME DIVERSIFICATION THEOREM

The "no time diversification" theorem can be easily proved by considering a two-period economy with four possible states, denoted by $\{R^+R^+\}$, $\{R^+R^-\}$, $\{R^-R^+\}$, and $\{R^-R^-\}$ where $R^+$ is a return after one good period and $R^-$ is the return after one bad period[5]. Let $\lambda_0$ be the percentage of wealth invested in risky assets at the beginning of the investment, $\lambda^+$ be the percentage of wealth invested in risky assets after a good period, and $\lambda^-$ be the percentage of wealth invested in risky assets after a bad period. Then, the final

---

[5]To be more precise, R is a vector of gross returns of various assets and $\lambda$ is a vector of asset allocations. Thus $R^+\lambda_0$, for example, is the scalar product yielding the return the portfolio formed in period 0 attains in the state +.

wealth of the investors in the four final states is: $(R^+\lambda^+)(R^+\lambda_0)w_0$, respectively $(R^-\lambda^+)(R^+\lambda_0)w_0$, $(R^+\lambda^-)(R^-\lambda_0)w_0$, and $(R^-\lambda^-)(R^-\lambda_0)w_0$.

$$
\max_{\lambda_0\lambda^+\lambda^-} p^2\frac{\left[(R^+\lambda^+)(R^+\lambda_0)w_0\right]^\alpha}{\alpha} + p(1-p)\frac{\left[(R^-\lambda^+)(R^+\lambda_0)w_0\right]^\alpha}{\alpha}
$$

$$
+(1-p)p\frac{\left[(R^+\lambda^-)(R^-\lambda_0)w_0\right]^\alpha}{\alpha} + (1-p)^2\frac{\left[(R^-\lambda^-)(R^-\lambda_0)w_0\right]^\alpha}{\alpha}
$$

An investor with a CRRA solves the following optimization problem:

$$
\max_{\lambda_0\lambda^+\lambda^-} p^2\frac{\left[(R^+\lambda^+)(R^+\lambda_0)w_0\right]^\alpha}{\alpha} + p(1-p)\frac{\left[(R^-\lambda^+)(R^+\lambda_0)w_0\right]^\alpha}{\alpha}
$$

$$
+(1-p)p\frac{\left[(R^+\lambda^-)(R^-\lambda_0)w_0\right]^\alpha}{\alpha} + (1-p)^2\frac{\left[(R^-\lambda^-)(R^-\lambda_0)w_0\right]^\alpha}{\alpha}
$$

where $p$ is the probability for achieving $R^+$.

For this problem, $\lambda^+ = \lambda^-$ because $p\frac{(R^+\lambda_0w_0)^\alpha}{\alpha}$ is a common factor in the first two terms and $(1-p)\frac{(R^-\lambda_0w_0)^\alpha}{\alpha}$ is a common factor in the third and fourth term, and what remain is just the same problem. Further, $\lambda_0 = \lambda^+ = \lambda^-$ because adding the first two terms of the problem we get: $\left(p\frac{(R^+\lambda^+)^\alpha}{\alpha} + (1-p)\frac{(R^-\lambda^-)^\alpha}{\alpha}\right)p\frac{(R^+\lambda_0w_0)^\alpha}{\alpha}$ and adding the third and the fourth term of the optimization problem we get: $\left(p\frac{(R^+\lambda^+)^\alpha}{\alpha} + (1-p)\frac{(R^-\lambda^-)^\alpha}{\alpha}\right)p\frac{(R^-\lambda_0w_0)^\alpha}{\alpha}$. Hence, cancelling the common factor in the brackets, we have the same optimization problem again.

To see whether for a mean-variance investor, in the case of a random walk, there is no time diversification as well, consider the objective function $\mu(R) - \alpha\sigma^2(R)$, where R is the portfolio return and $\alpha$ is the degree of risk aversion. Denote the one-period rate of return $R_1$ and the T-period return $R_T$, where $1 + R_T = (1 + R_1)^T$. Hence, the expected return over T-periods is $\mu^T = \mu_1^T$ where $\mu_1$ is the expected return over one period. The variance of the returns over $T$ periods is $\sigma_T^2 = (\sigma_1^2 + \mu_1^2)^T - \mu_1^{2T}$ where $\sigma_1^2$ is the variance of the one-period returns (Haim Levy, 1972). Hence, the variance of the returns increases more than the expected return and the investors would decrease his asset allocation with a longer investment horizon. Hence, there is no time diversification.

Moreover, there is one more reasonable case in which the no-time diversification property also holds. For example, if one uses logarithmic returns so that the returns can be simply added over time, then the mean and variance over $T$ years will be $T$ times the mean and variance over one year. In this case, the time horizon does not matter for the asset allocation and there will be no time diversification as well.

# References

Acker, D., & Duck, N. W. (2008). Cross-cultural overconfidence and biased self-attribution. *The Journal of Socio-Economics*, *37*, 1815–1824.

Ackert, L. F., Church, B. K., Tompkins, J., & Zhang, P. (2005). What's in a name? An experimental examination of investment behavior. *Review of Finance*, *9*(2), 281–304.

Aggarwal, R. K., & Boyson, N. M. (2016). The Performance of Female Hedge Fund Managers. *Review of Financial Economics*, *29*, 23–36.

Argote, L., Devadas, R., & Melone, N. (1990). The base-rate fallacy: Contrasting processes and outcomes of group and individual judgment. *Organizational Behavior and Human Decision Processes*, *46*(2), 296–310.

Arkes, H., Hirshleifer, D., Jiang, D., & Lim, S. (2008). Reference point adaptation: Tests in the domain of security trading. *Organizational Behavior and Human Decision Processes*, *105*(1), 67–81.

Arkes, H. R., Hirshleifer, D., Jiang, D., & Lim, S. S. (2010). A cross-cultural study of reference point adaptation: Evidence from China, Korea, and the US. *Organizational Behavior and Human Decision Processes*, *112*(2), 99–111. https://doi.org/10.1016/j.obhdp.2010.02.002

Ayton, P., & Fischer, I. (2004). The hot hand fallacy and the gambler's fallacy: two faces of subjective randomness? *Memory & Cognition*, *32*(8), 1369–1378.

Bachmann, K. (2017). Can a competent advice eliminate the outcome bias in investment decision making? *SSRN Working Paper 3009058*.

Bachmann, K., & Hens, T. (2015). Investment competence and advice seeking. *Journal of Behavioral and Experimental Finance*, *6*, 27–41.

Bachmann, K., & Hens, T. (2016). Is there Swissness in investment decision behavior and investment competence? *Financial Markets and Portfolio Management*, *30*(3), 233–275.

Bachmann, K., Hens, T., & Stoessel, R. (2017). Which measures predict risk taking in a multi-stage controlled decision process? *SSRN Working Paper 2535859*.

Bär, M., Niessen, A., & Ruenzi, S. (2007). The impact of work group diversity on performance: Large sample evidence from the mutual fund industry. *Econstore Working Paper*.

Barber, B. M., & Odean, T. (2000). Trading is hazardous to your wealth: the common stock investment performance of individual investors. *The Journal of Finance*, *55*(2), 773–806.

Barber, B. M., & Odean, T. (2001). Boys will be boys: gender, overconfidence, and common stock investment. *The Quarterly Journal of Economics*, (February), 261–293.

Barber, B. M., & Odean, T. (2008). All that glitters: the effect of attention and news on the buying behavior of individual and institutional investors. *Review of Financial Studies, 21*, 785–818.

Barberis, N., & Huang, M. (2009). Preferences with frames: a new utility specification that allows for framing of risks. *Journal of Economic Dynamics and Control, 33*(8), 1555–1576.

Barberis, N., & Xiong, W. (2012). Realization utility. *Journal of Financial Economics, 104*(2), 251–271.

Baron, J., & Hershey, J. C. (1988). Outcome bias in decision evaluation. *Journal of Personality and Social Psychology, 54*(4), 569–579.

Baucells, M., Weber, M., & Welfens, F. (2011). Reference-point formation and updating. *Management Science, 57*(3), 506–519. https://doi.org/10.1287/mnsc.1100.1286

Beike, D. R., Markman, K. D., & Karadogan, F. (2009). What we regret most are lost opportunities: a theory of regret intensity. *Personality and Social Psychology Bulletin, 35*(3), 385–397.

Benartzi, S., & Thaler, R. H. (1995). Myopic loss aversion and the equity premium puzzle. *Quarterly Journal of Economics, 110*, 73–92.

Benartzi, S., & Thaler, R. H. (2001). Naive diversification strategies in defined contribution saving plans. *American Economic Review, 91*(1), 79–98.

Bernard, V. L., & Thomas, J. K. (1989). Post-earnings-announcement drift: delayed price response or risk premium? *Journal of Accounting Research, 27*, 1–36.

Bernoulli, D. (1738). Specimen theoriae novae de mensura sortis. *Commentarii Academiae Scientiarum Imperialis Petropolitanae, 5*(1731), 175–192.

Blais, A.-R., & Weber, E. U. (2006). A domain-specific risk-taking (DOSPERT) scale for adult populations. *Judgment and Decision Making, 1*(1), 33–47.

Bogan, V. L., Just, D. R., & Dev, C. S. (2013). Team gender diversity and investment decision-making behavior. *Review of Behavioral Finance, 5*(2), 134–152.

Bradbury, M. A. S., Hens, T., & Zeisberger, S. (2014). Improving investment decisions with simulated experience. *Review of Finance, 19*, 1–34.

Brinson, G. P., Hood, L. R., & Beebower, G. L. (1995). Determinants of portfolio performance. *Financial Analysts Journal, 51*(1), 133–138.

Brinson, G. P., Singer, B. D., & Beebower, G. L. (1991). Determinants of portfolio performance II: An Update. *Financial Analysts Journal, 47*(3), 40–48.

Brunel, J. L. P. (2015). *Goals-Based Wealth Management: An Integrated and Practical Approach to Changing the Structure of Wealth Advisory Practices.* Hoboken, NJ: John Wiley & Sons.

Bruner, J. S., & Postman, L. (1949). On the perception of incongruity: a paradigm. *Journal of Personality, 18*(2), 206–223.

Canner, N., Mankiw, N. G., & Weil, D. N. (1997). An asset allocation puzzle. *American Economic Review, 87*(1), 181–191.

Chapman, G. B., & Johnson, E. J. (1999). Anchoring, activation, and the construction of values. *Organizational Behavior and Human Decision Processes, 79*(2), 115–153.

Cheng, F. F., & Wu, C. S. (2010). Debiasing the framing effect: The effect of warning and involvement. *Decision Support Systems, 49*(3), 328–334.

Chhabra, A. B. (2005). Beyond Markowitz: a comprehensive wealth allocation framework for individuals. *Journal of Wealth Management, 7*(4), 8–34.

Chui, A. C. W., Titman, S., & Wei, K. C. J. (2010). Individualism and momentum around the world. *Journal of Finance, 65*(1), 361–392.

Cillo, A., & De Giorgi, E. (2017). The willingness to pay for editing. Working Paper, *University of St.Gallen.*

Combs, B., & Slovic, P. (1979). Newspaper coverage of causes of death. *Journalism & Mass Communication Quarterly, 56*, 837–849.

Dalbar Inc. (2016). *DALBAR's 22nd Annual Quantitative Analysis of Investor Behavior.*

Das, S. R., Markowitz, H., Scheid, J., & Statman, M. (2010). Portfolio optimization with mental accounts. *Journal of Financial and Quantitative Anaylsis, 45*(2), 311–334.

De Bondt, A., & Thaler, R. (1985). Does the stock market overreact? *Journal of Finance, 40*(3), 793–805.

De Giorgi, E. G. (2012). *Loss aversion with multiple investment goals. Mathematics and Financial Economics.*

De Giorgi, E. G., & Legg, S. (2012). Dynamic portfolio choice and asset pricing with narrow framing and probability weighting. *Journal of Economic Dynamics and Control, 36*(7), 951–972.

De Giorgi, E., & Hens, T. (2009). Prospect theory and mean-variance analysis: does it make a difference in wealth management? *Investment Management and Financial Innovations, 6*(3), 122–129.

De Giorgi, E., Hens, T., & Mayer, J. (2011). A note on reward-risk portfolio selection and two-fund separation. *Finance Research Letters, 8*(2), 52–58.

De Giorgi, E., & Mahmoud, O. (2016). Naive diversification preferences and their representation. Working Paper, *University of St.Gallen.*

De Giorgi, E., & Mahmoud, O. (2017). How elementary is diversification? A study of children's portfolio choice. *Working Paper, University of St.Gallen.*

DeMiguel, V., Garlappi, L., & Uppal, R. (2009). Optimal versus naive diversification: How inefficient is the 1/N portfolio strategy? *Review of Financial Studies, 22*(5), 1915–1953.

Dierkes, M., Erner, C., & Zeisberger, S. (2010). Investment horizon and the attractiveness of investment strategies: A behavioral approach. *Journal of Banking & Finance, 34*(5), 1032–1046.

Dorn, D., & Huberman, G. (2005). Talk and action: What individual investors say and what they do. *Review of Finance, 9*(4), 437–481.

Edwards, W. (1968). Conservatism in human information processing. *Conservatism in Human Information Processing*, 17–52.

Gilovich, T., Vallone, R., & Tversky, A. (1985). The hot hand in basketball: on the misrepresentation of random sequences. *Cognitive Psychology, 17*, 295–314.

Goetzmann, W. N., & Kumar, A. (2008). Equity portfolio diversification*. *Review of Finance*, 433–463. https://doi.org/10.1093/rof/rfn005

Griffin, D., & Tversky, A. (1992). The weighing of evidence and the determinants of confidence. *Cognitive Psychology, 24*(3), 411–435.

Hackethal, A., Haliassos, M., & Jappelli, T. (2012). Financial advisors: a case of babysitters. *Journal of Banking and Finance, 36*, 509–524.

Hariri, A. R., Brown, S. M., Williamson, D. E., Flory, J. D., de Wit, H., & Manuck, S. B. (2006). Preference for immediate over delayed rewards is associated with magnitude of ventral striatal activity. *The Journal of Neuroscience*, *26*(51), 13213–13217.

Heath, C., & Soll, J. B. (1996). Mental accounting and consumer choices. *Journal of Consumer Research*, *23*, 40–52.

Hens, T., & Janos Mayer. (2014). Theory matters for financial advice! *SSRN Working Paper 2417188*.

Hens, T., & Mayer, J. (2017). Decision theory matters for financial advice. *Computational Economics*, 1–32.

Hens, T., & Sethe, R. (2017). Die Bestimmung der Angemessenheit und der Geeignetheit von Finanzdienstleistungen und Finanzinstrumenten. In R. Sethe, R. Weber, W. . Stoffel, & J. L. Chenaux (Eds.), *Aktuelle Herausforderungen des Gesellschafts- und Finanzmarktrechts - Festschrift für Hans Caspar von der Crone zum 60. Geburtstag* (pp. 589–618). Schulthess Juristische Medien AG, Zurich.

Heuer, J., Merkle, C., & Weber, M. (2017). Fooled by randomness: investor perception of fund manager skill. *Review of Finance*, *21*(2), 605–635.

Hofstede, G. (2001). *Culture's Consequences: Comparing Values, Behaviors, Institutions, and Organizations across Nations*, Sage Publications, Thousand Oaks, CA.

Huber, J. (2007). 'J'-shaped returns to timing advantage in access to information— Experimental evidence and a tentative explanation. *Journal of Economic Dynamics and Control*, *31*(8), 2536–2572.

Huisman, R., van der Sar, N. L., & Zwinkels, R. C. J. (2012). A new measurement method of investor overconfidence. *Economics Letters*, *114*(1), 69–71.

Ibbotson, R. G., & Kaplan, P. D. (2000). Does asset allocation policy explain 40, 90, or 100 percent of performance? *Financial Analysts Journal*, *56*(1), 26–33.

Ilmanen, A. (2011). *Expected Returns: An Investor's Guide to Harvesting Market Rewards* (1 edition). Hoboken, NJ: John Wiley & Sons.

Jonas, E., Schulz-Hardt, S., Frey, D., & Thelen, N. (2001). Confirmation bias in sequential information search after preliminary decisions: an expansion of dissonance theoretical research on selective exposure to information. *Journal of Personality and Social Psychology*, *80*(4), 557.

Jones, S. K., Yurak, T. J., & Frisch, D. (1997). The effect of outcome information on the evaluation and recall of individuals' own decisions. *Organizational Behavior and Human Decision Processes*, *71*(1), 95–120.

Kahneman, D., Slovic, P., & Tversky, A. (1974). Judgment under uncertainty. *Science*, *185*(4157), 1124–1131.

Kahneman, D., & Tversky, A. (1973). On the psychology of prediction. *Psychological Review*, *80*, 237–251.

Kahneman, D., & Tversky, A. (1979). Prospect theory: an analysis of decision under risk. *Econometrica*, *47*(2), 263–291.

Kaufmann, C., Weber, M., & Haisley, E. (2013a). The role of experience sampling and graphical displays on one's investment risk appetite. *Management Science*, *59*(2), 323–340.

Kaufmann, C., Weber, M., & Haisley, E. (2013b). The role of experience sampling and graphical displays on one's investment risk appetite. *Management Science*, 59(2), 323–340.

Klayman, J., & Ha, Y. (1987). Confirmation, disconfirmation, and information in hypothesis testing. *Psychological Review*, 94(2), 211–228.

Knox, R. E., & Inkster, J. a. (1968). Postdecision dissonance at post time. *Journal of Personality and Social Psychology*, 8(4), 319–323.

Knutson, B., Taylor, J., Kaufman, M., Peterson, R., & Glover, G. (2005). Distributed neural representation of expected value. *The Journal of Neuroscience*, 25(19), 4806–4812.

Koestner, M., Meyer, S., & Hackethal, A. (2012). *Do individual investors learn from their mistakes?* SSRN Working Paper 2122652.

Koriat, A., Lichtenstein, S., & Fischhoff, B. (1980). Reasons for confidence. *Journal of Experimental Psychology: Human Learning and Memory*, 6(2), 107–118.

Kuhnen, C. M., & Knutson, B. (2005). The neural basis of financial risk taking. *Neuron*, 47(5), 763–770.

Kuhnen, C. M., & Knutson, B. (2011). The influence of affect on beliefs, preferences, and financial decisions. *Journal of Financial and Quantitative Analysis*, 46(3), 605–626.

Lehenkari, M. (2009). The hedonic editing hypothesis: Evidence from the Finnish stock market. *Journal of Behavioral Finance*, 10(1), 9–18.

Levinson, J. D., & Peng, K. (2007). Valuing cultural differences in behavioral economics. *Psychology*, 4(1), 32–47.

Levy, H. (1972). Portfolio performance and the investment horizon. *Management Science*, 18(12), B645–B653.

Levy, H., & Levy, M. (2004). Prospect theory and mean-variance analysis. *The Review of Financial Studies*, 17(4), 1015–1041.

Lopes, L. L. (1987). Between hope and fear: the psychology of risk. *Advances in Experimental Social Psychology*, 20, 255–295.

Makridakis, S., Gaba, A., & Hogarth, R. (2010). *Dance with chance: making luck work for you*. Oneworld Publications.

Mankiw, N. G., & Zeldes, S. P. (1991). The consumption of stockholders and non-stockholders. *Journal of Financial Economics*, 29(1), 97–112.

Markowitz, H. (1959). *Portfolio selection*. New York: John Wiley & Sons.

Markowitz, H. M. (1952). Portfolio selection. *The Journal of Finance*, 7(60), 77–91.

Merton, R. C. (1969). Lifetime portfolio selection under uncertainty: the continuous-time case. *The Review of Economics and Statistics*, 51(3), 247–257.

Mitton, T., & Vorkink, K. (2007). Equilibrium underdiversification and the preference for skewness. *The Review of Financial Studies*, 20(4), 1255–1288.

Mussweiler, T., & Pfeif, T. (1991). Overcoming the inevitable anchoring effect: considering the opposite compensates for selective accessibility. *Personality and Social Psychology Bulletin*, 26(10), 1142–1150.

Nevins, D. (2004). Goals-Based Investing: Integrating traditional and behavioral finance. *The Journal of Wealth Management*, 6(4), 8–23.

Northcraft, G. B., & Neale, M. A. (1987). Expert, amateurs and real estate: an anchoring-and-adjustment perspective on property pricing decisions. *Organizational Behavior and Human Decision Processes*, 39(1), 201–279.

Nussbaumer, P. (2012). Essays on the transparent IT support for asymmetric client-advisor encounters. Ph.D. thesis Department of Informatics, University of Zurich.

Odean, T. (1998). Are investors reluctant to realize their losses? *Journal of Finance*, 53, 1775–1798.

Plous, S. (1995). A comparison of strategies for reducing interval confidence in group judgments.pdf. *Journal of Applied Psychology*, 80(4), 443–454.

Ratner, R. K., & Herbst, K. C. (2005). When good decisions have bad outcomes: the impact of affect on switching behavior. *Organizational Behavior and Human Decision Processes*, 96(1), 23–37. https://doi.org/10.1016/j.obhdp.2004.09.003

Rice, D.F. (2005). Variance in risk tolerance measurement - Toward a uniform solution. Ph.D. thesis Golden Gate University, San Francisco.

Rieger, M. O., & Hens, T. (2012). Explaining the demand for structured financial products: survey and field experiment evidence. *Zeitschrift für Betriebswirtschaft*, 82(5), 491–508.

Rieger, M. O. (2011). Co-monotonicity of optimal investments and the design of structured financial products. *Finance and Stochastics*, 15(1), 27–55.

Samuelson, P. A. (1969). Lifetime portfolio selection by dynamic stochastic programming. *Review of Economics and Statistics*, 51(3), 239.

Schulz-Hardt, S., Frey, D., Lüthgens, C., & Moscovici, S. (2000). Biased information search in group decision making. *Journal of Personality and Social Psychology*, 78(4), 655–669.

Shadwick, W. F., & Keating, C. (2002). A universal performance measure. *Journal of Performance Measurement*, 6(3), 59–84.

Shefrin, H. M., & Thaler, R. H. (1988). The behavioral life-cycle hypothesis. *Economic Inquiry*, 26(4), 609–643.

Shefrin, H., & Statman, M. (2000). Behavioral portfolio theory. *Journal of Financial and Quantitative Analysis*, 35(2), 127–151.

Simons, D. J., & Chabris, C. F. (1999). Gorillas in our midst: Sustained inattentional blindness for dynamic events. *Perception*, 28(9), 1059–1074.

Sironi, P. (2016). *FinTech Innovation: From Robo-Advisors to Goal Based Investing and Gamification*. Hoboken, NJ: John Wiley & Sons.

Spina, R. R., Ji, L. J., Guo, T., Zhang, Z., Ye, L., & Fabrigar, L. (2010). Cultural differences in the representativeness heuristic: expecting a correspondence in magnitude between cause and effect. *Personality and Social Psychology Bulletin*, 36(5), 583–597.

Stoessel, R. & A. Meier (2015). Framing effects and risk perception: Testing graphical representations of risk for KIID. Chapter 4 in Stoessel, R. (2015). Risk assessment and risk communication in theory and practice. Ph.D. dissertation, department of finance, University of Zurich.

Strahilevitz, M. A., Odean, T., & Barber, B. M. (2011). Once burned, twice shy: how naive learning, counterfactuals, and regret affect the repurchase of stocks previously sold. *Journal of Marketing Research*, 48(SPL), 102–120.

Taleb, N. N. (2007). *The black swan: the impact of the highly improbable*. New York: Random House Group.

Thaler, R. (1985). Mental accounting and consumer choice. *Marketing Science, 4*, 199–214.

Thaler, R. H. (1999a). Mental accounting matters. *Journal of Behavioral Decision Making, 12*(3), 183–206.

Thaler, R. H. (1999b). The end of behavioral finance. *Financial Analysts Journal, 55*(6), 12–17.

Thaler, R. H., & Benarzi, S. (2004). Save more tomorrow: Using behavioral economics to increase employee saving. *Journal of Political Economy, 112*(S1), S164–S187.

Thaler, R. H., & Bernarzi, S. (2004). Save more tomorrow: using behavioral economics to increase employee saving. *Journal of Political Economy, 112*, 164–187.

Tobin, J. (1958). Liquidity preference as behavior towards risk. *The Review of Economic Studies, 25*(2), 65-86.

Tom, S. M., Fox, C. R., Trepel, C., & Poldrack, R. A. (2007). The neural basis of loss aversion in decision-making under risk. *Science, 315*(5811), 515–518.

Tversky, A., & Kahneman, D. (1981). The framing of decisions and the psychology of choice. *Science, 211*(4481), 453–458.

Tversky, A., & Kahneman, D. (1992). Advances in prospect theory: cumulative representation of uncertainty. *Journal of Risk and Uncertainty, 5*(4), 297–323.

Von Neumann, J., & Morgenstern, O. (1944). *Theory of Games and Economic Behavior*. Princeton University Press.

Wang, M., Rieger, M. O., & Hens, T. (2016a). How time preferences differ: Evidence from 53 countries. *Journal of Economic Psychology, 52*, 115–135.

Wang, M., Rieger, M. O., & Hens, T. (2016b). The impact of culture on loss aversion. *Journal of Behavioral Decision Making*.

Wakker, Peter P. (2010). *Prospect theory: For risk and ambiguity*. Cambridge University Press: Cambridge, UK.

Wason, P. C. (1960). On the failure to eliminate hypotheses in a conceptual task. *Quarterly Journal of Experimental Psychology, 12*(3), 129–140.

Weber, E., Blais, A., & Betz, N. (2002). A domain-specific risk-attitude scale: measuring risk perceptions and risk behaviors. *Journal of Behavioral Decision Making, 15*(4), 263–290.

# Index